NEWNESS OF LIFE

*A Modern Introduction
to
Catholic Ethics*

JAMES GAFFNEY

PAULIST PRESS
New York/Ramsey/Toronto

NIHIL OBSTAT
Rev. Frank J. McNulty
Censor Librorum

IMPRIMATUR
✠ Peter L. Gerety, D.D.
Archbishop of Newark
December 12, 1978

Library of Congress
Catalog Card Number: 79-84404

ISBN: 0-8091-2202-2

Published by Paulist Press
Editorial Office: 1865 Broadway, New York, N.Y. 10023
Business Office: 545 Island Road, Ramsey, N.J. 07446

Printed and bound in the
United States of America

CONTENTS

How can we who died to sin still live in it?
Do you not know that all of us,
who have been baptized into Christ Jesus
were baptized into his death?
We were buried therefore with him
by baptism into death,
so that
as Christ was raised from the dead
by the glory of the Father,
we too might walk in newness of life.

(Romans 6:4)

PREFACE

The dominant perspective of this book is described at some length in the introductory chapter. This brief preface is mainly for the sake of saying what sort of book it might be thought to be, but definitely is not.

In the first place it is not, in any but a very incidental way, a book of casuistry. It is not a collection of more or less typical moral dilemmas accompanied by what the author considers their best solutions. Works of casuistry are indisputably valuable if they are well done. They cannot be well done unless they are carefully and thoroughly done. And if the moral dilemmas they deal with are not so simple as to make their treatment in a book superfluous, the requisite care and thoroughness can only be achieved by subtle and extended analyses. No book of moderate size can contain more than a few such analyses. Consequently, the works of casuistry that are worth reading treat, for the most part, either miscellaneous samplings of various moral dilemmas, or sets of moral dilemmas belonging to a limited topic. A general work of casuistry can only avoid triviality by assuming encyclopedic dimensions.

In the second place, this book is not a catechism, at least in the traditional sense of being a collection of concise answers to distinct and pointed questions. Ethics, including religious ethics, simply does not lend itself to that sort of treatment. And where that sort of treatment has been applied to ethics, anything of value that is said is always visibly straining against the frustrating confines of an uncongenial format. Catholic tradition itself bears witness to this by its very different way of transmitting doctrinal material and ethical material. Doctrines have from earliest times found their way quite readily into the terse formulations of creeds, dogmas, and received opinions, which can be stated even more tersely in popular resumes. Ethical traditions have not assumed similar forms, and where efforts have been made to convey moral instruction with catechetical compactness, the results have tended to be not ethical explanations but codifications of unofficial law. One result of this has been a widespread confusion among Catholics of two very different activities in the Church and by the Church: the teaching of ethics, and the promulgating of laws.

The only effective way that general ethics can be taught is by discussion. To try to teach it in a book condemns one to the limitations of monologue, but it must at least be discursive monologue. Discourses need not be rambling, but they cannot be telegraphic. The only way that general ethics can be learned is by critical reflection. To try to learn it from a book condemns one to the limitations of an odd sort of dialogue, in which the other party has said his say and perhaps shot his bolt, but in any case cannot respond to cross-examination. Once the book has effectively mummified its author, the life of its discourse can be preserved only by the liveliness of students' and teachers' minds. The best the prospective mummy can hope for is that reasonably significant and interesting contours should be discernible beneath the wrappings and lend themselves to the shaping of living thoughts. Should it prove otherwise, let the tomb be sealed, the book closed, and partial indulgence granted.

To Kay,
newly a Gaffney,
more newly a Catholic,
welcome!

Chapter One

A MODERN INTRODUCTION TO
CATHOLIC ETHICS

My purpose, indicated somewhat cryptically by my subtitle, may need some elucidation. For "a modern introduction to Catholic ethics" is open to a variety of interpretations. Let it be noted, therefore, in the first place, that the adjective "modern" modifies the noun "introduction." No claim of specific modernity is made for the general contents of the book. It is not what is introduced, but the introduction itself that is intended to be modern, in the sense that its characteristic outlook and idiom are, as far as possible, typical of the present age. I have accordingly tried to remain aware of the facts, problems, and possibilities that my contemporaries tend to be habitually aware of, even though persons of other times may have been slightly or not at all aware of them. I have likewise tried to avoid language and illustrations that are more representative of the past than of the present. In this spirit I have even for the most part avoided direct quotations of traditional sources, preferring modern paraphrase of even somewhat classic phrases.

Nevertheless, the book's subject matter is "Catholic ethics," and there is nothing very modern about that. Some might even argue that it is distinctly modern to be complacently altogether ignorant of this subject matter. The term ethics is used here, as explained early in the book, as referring to what one thinks about morality rather than to what one does about it. It refers to principles or convictions determining what one considers right and wrong in moral conduct. It is not, therefore, a description of how well or ill people behave themselves, but of what they understand good and bad behavior to be. The book is not directly concerned with how well or ill Catholics seem to be living up to traditional convictions. It is the convictions themselves with which it is concerned.

The moral convictions treated here are referred to as "Catholic ethics" in a plain and public sense, without intentional subtlety or novelty. Catholic means here, as in most ordinary speech, pertaining to the Roman Catholic Church. At the same time, I do not take it to mean "peculiar" to the Roman Catholic Church. But if certain aspects of ethics do happen to seem peculiar to Roman Catholicism, they belong here no less than other aspects that may be more widely shared. Since Roman Catholic ethics does not, as far as I know, include any principles determining what or how much ethics is proper to Roman Catholicism, no such principles will be proposed or discussed in these pages.

The most difficult matter in an enterprise of this kind is to set reasonable boundaries, determining what to include and what to leave out. Catholic ethics, like Catholic theology, is only roughly definable, and personal judgments about it are sure to differ. In the first place, it cannot be strictly equated with biblical ethics, for there are obviously ethical positions highly typical of Roman Catholicism that are by no means conspicuous in the Bible, even as there are ethical statements in the Bible that have generated few echoes in Roman Catholicism. Neither, however, can Catholic ethics be simply equated with official ethical pronouncements of the Church's hierarchy, for these are few and random, being usually evoked by some widespread public departure from what was already assumed to constitute Christian ethics. Broadly speaking, what I mean by Catholic ethics is a broad stream of ethical tradition that has been part of a religious culture associated with the Roman Catholic Church, and shared only partly by other Christian communities since the great divisions of Christianity took place.

Identifying what really belongs to a tradition is never easy. Since this is a popular introduction rather than a history or a comprehensive treatise, I have tried to concentrate on what seems to belong fairly obviously to Catholic ethical tradition, and I have readily omitted what seemed doubtfully appropriate. Still, traditions that have been around very long offer a further difficulty in that so many things seem to get picked up or dropped off as they go their historical way. For example, there was a time, and a long time, when approval of holy wars, such as the Crusades, must have seemed an obvious part of Catholic ethical tradition. There was also a time when the disapproval of usury, in the sense of lending money at interest, must likewise have seemed part of the tradition. But given subsequent developments, neither the goodness of military Crusades nor the badness of lending at interest seems appropriate for substantial inclusion in "a modern presentation of Catholic ethics." On the whole, I have inclined to "play it safe," in the sense of readily omitting material whose claim to be part of Catholic ethical tradition is highly disputable.

At this point it seems important to assert that I do not consider Catholic ethical tradition to be in any sense perfect. I am strongly persuaded that Catholicism could be improved by incorporating certain ethical developments that have taken place largely outside it, and I believe it is currently being improved precisely in this way. I am likewise not unwilling to concede that what seem to be genuinely traditional elements might in some instances be advantageously modified and supplemented, or even discarded and replaced. Moreover, although I do firmly believe in the permanent validity of certain basic elements in that tradition, I am not prepared to maintain that these genuine fundamentals are in any exclusive sense the property of Catholic tradition.

In the light of such remarks, one may be prompted to ask, then, why bother? If this Catholic tradition is admitted to be imperfect and impermanent, what point can there be in issuing yet another popular summary of it? Part of my answer to that question is a conviction, grown stronger over the years, that most ordinary people need ethical tradition if they are to avoid ethical incoherence. They have neither the time nor the talent to either personally construct or critically adopt a comprehensive moral theology or philosophy. And the question is, if they do need an ethical tradition, where are they going to get one? Presumably, if it is to mean anything to them, from some social group of long standing to which they willingly and heartily belong. And presumably the social group must be one whose range of concern is no more restricted than the range of ethics itself. Such are social groups formed around broad ideologies, or philosophies, or faiths. For a sincerely committed Catholic it is hard to see how any social group should seem better suited to this purpose than his or her Church, which has moreover traditionally claimed to be the primary moral teacher of her members. Indeed, it would seem difficult to reconcile any serious adherence to that Church with an altogether casual disregard of that claim.

Currently, we occupy a peculiar situation. Catholic ethical tradition is increasingly unknown to any but the experts, whereas what the experts chiefly address themselves to in public are actual or anticipated changes in that tradition. As a result, the ordinary laity, especially those too young to remember when things were different, find themselves in a strange position. They tend to be strongly aware, in general and in some particulars, that their tradition is changing, and yet remarkably unaware of what their tradition is. Well acquainted with change, but ill acquainted with what is changing, they are in no position to judge either why or how much it is changing. For all its apparent absurdity, the situation is understandable. Not at all long ago, Catholic ethical tradition was pretty well imparted, in proportion to individual mental capacities, to the average Catholic. By better educated and more reflective Catholics, it was also thought to be unsatisfactory in a number of respects, and to be unwholesomely stagnant and oppressively doctrinaire. Then, with a sudden new atmosphere of freedom in the Church, criticism and reform became the order of the day. The more respectable critics and reformers knew, of course, what they were criticizing and trying to reform. But for a later generation of observers, the criticisms and reform proposals to a great extent eclipsed the tradition itself. A young Catholic nowadays is in more or less the position of one who is constantly offered glimpses of various plans for remodeling an elaborate structure whose original blueprints he has never examined. In such circumstances, while professionals find exhilaration and purpose, others find frustration and boredom, which they may dispose of by cultivating nonchalance. As often before in other contexts, an age of dogmatism closely followed by an age of criticism has engendered an age of scepticism.

Accordingly, what this book seeks to do is display to nonprofessionals, in a very simplified fashion, the main lines of a generally recognized blueprint of Catholic ethics that was gradually sketched out until recent decades. It is, on the other hand, no part of the purpose of this book to suggest that remodelling is not in order, or that it can safely be postponed.

STUDY QUESTIONS

1. In what sense are the contents of the following pages intended to be modern?

2. What is the general meaning here assigned to the term "ethics"?

3. What is the general meaning here assigned to the term "Catholic"?

4. Why cannot Catholic ethics be simply identified with biblical ethics?

5. Why cannot Catholic ethics be simply identified with official Church teachings?

6. What are some apparent instances of notable change in Catholic ethical tradition?

7. Is Catholic ethics here understood to be distinctively or peculiarly Catholic?

8. Is Catholic ethics here assumed to be a substantially perfect system?

9. What practical reason is there for studying Catholic ethical tradition?

10. What is peculiar about current acquaintance with this tradition among ordinary young Catholics?

11. Do you feel more knowledgeable about the changes in the Catholic ethical tradition or the tradition itself? Why?

Chapter Two

RELIGION AND ETHICS

EXPLICIT AND IMPLICIT RELIGION

What most ordinary people of our culture who think of themselves as religious seem to mean by religion is, in the first place, a human response to some god or gods. For such people, being religious implies at the very least that one is not an atheist or agnostic in theory or practice. It implies, therefore, that one is convinced that god or gods exist, knows something about this god or these gods, and does something, presumably appropriate, about the god or gods one believes in.

Most, if not all such people also think of religion as not simply an appropriate response to a god or gods, but as at least including some prearranged pattern of response in which members of some human group, often called a church or sect, characteristically participate.

Nowadays there are frequent discussions, which may seem somewhat paradoxical, about whether certain types or groups of human beings who expressly state that they and their activities are non-religious, or even anti-religious, may not "really" be religious in some subtle, unwitting, but nevertheless significant fashion. Perhaps the most familiar illustration is provided by recurrent debates over whether or not avowedly atheistic Communists are "really" practicing a peculiar sort of religion as well as an economic and political program. Similarly, the phrase "anonymous Christian" has gained currency in recent years, as connoting the idea that there are people who, without in the least considering themselves, or wishing others to consider them as Christians, betray in their behavior a genuinely religious dimension of life that is in essential accord with Christianity.

These ideas are important ones, and discussion of the issues they raise can be very enlightening. They will make some reappearances later, but at this point I mention them precisely in order to set them deliberately aside. For the most part, in alluding to morals or ethics as religious, or more specifically as Christian or Catholic, I shall have in mind the morals or ethics characteristic of people who identify themselves in the plainest and most familiar sense as religious, or Christian, or Catholic people. Exceptions to this policy of usage will be noted where they occur.

VARIOUS RELIGIONS, VARIOUS GODS

If religion is supposed to be an appropriate human response to some god or gods, the kind of religion cultivated by any person or community will be determined to a great extent by how that person or community conceives of or envisages their god or gods. Most people are aware that there have been ruthless religions that worshipped implacable gods, flattering religions that worshipped conceited gods, anxious religions that worshipped impetuous gods, and obscene religions that worshipped lascivious gods. Here, no doubt, we are describing these gods and religions in terms of the moral and psychological preconceptions of our own culture, but that is, in fact, how we normally perceive them, just as we perceive others as tranquil religions dedicated to gentle gods, or affectionate religions devoted to loving gods. We know, too, that there are some extremely vague religions, with correspondingly obscure notions of gods, and some extraordinarily intricate religions whose ideas about god or gods are immensely complicated and may even be kept secret from those who are not thought to possess special mental qualifications for understanding them. At all events, we cannot hope to understand, nor should we presume to criticize, any religion until we have at least a fair idea of the sort of god or gods it presupposes.

MORALITY AND ETHICS AS PART OF RELIGION

If religion means how people respond appropriately, according to their understanding, to a god or gods, then religious morality or ethics refer to the moral or ethical aspects of that response. This presumes, of course, that the sort of god one believes in is neither opposed nor indifferent to morality or ethics. An amoral or anti-ethical god would have, I suppose, to preside over a religion that had no moral or ethical aspects, and if the devotees of such a god had any morality or ethics it would not be religious morality or religious ethics.

MORALITY AND ETHICS DISTINGUISHED

In using the terms morality and ethics, as I have been doing, in combination, I have not wished to imply that they are synonyms or that they are logically altogether inseparable, although they are, of course, closely related in meaning. Terms that are used as popularly as morality and ethics are never used very meticulously, or understood with perfect uniformity. Often enough, one person means by ethics what another means by morality, and vice versa. But even if it involves being somewhat stricter than a good dictionary would require, it can be helpful to make this broad distinction between morality and ethics.

The distinction is basically a distinction between the realm of theory and the realm of practice. Most people would find it perfectly intelligible to say of someone that he or she had an admirable system of ethics and yet lived a frightfully immoral life. In such statements, ethics refers to a set of ideas about what is right and wrong, whereas morality refers to practical behavior as judged according to someone's ideas about right and wrong. Most of us know people whose ideas about right and wrong do not seem very enlightened or impressive, but whose typical behavior, in the light of our own ideas about right and wrong, are impressive indeed. There have been saints whom no one in his or her right mind would choose as ethics professors, and there have been ethics professors whom no one in his or her right mind would nominate for canonization!

RELIGIOUS ETHICS AND RELIGIOUS MORALITY

Understanding ethics as referring to how one thinks about right and wrong, and morality as referring to actual conduct with respect to its rightness or wrongness, one can speak meaningfully about religious ethics and religious morality. For part of religion, that is, part of the way people respond to their god or gods, is usually intellectual. They conceive definite ideas and form definite beliefs about god or gods. They may gather beliefs together into creeds, or organize them in symbolic systems called mythologies or conceptual systems called theologies. And to the extent that these beliefs or systems of belief include or imply notions about what is right and wrong, we have the elements of religious ethics. Religious morality would refer to the actual conformity of people's behavior to standards of right and wrong that seem to be inherent in their religious beliefs.

MORAL GOOD AND NON-MORAL GOOD

I have been using the terms right and wrong to express what morality and ethics are concerned with. The terms good and evil would have served equally well for the same purpose. But neither the terms right and wrong nor the terms good and evil are applied exclusively to moral or ethical matters, and this can be a source of confusion. Sometimes behavior is described as good or right without any intention of referring to ethics or morality. When, for example, we hear that somebody had a good life, we do not feel justified in drawing any conclusions about that life's moral qualities. But if we are told, with a slight change of phrase, that somebody lived a good life, we normally understand that moral praise is being bestowed. Nor is there anything unconventional about referring to the right way of doing something which happens to be morally indifferent or even, perhaps, morally wrong. We do, therefore, distinguish spontaneously between what is said to be morally or ethically good or right, and what is called good or right in some non-moral, non-ethical sense.

Unfortunately, this distinction is easier to apply than it is to explain. Perhaps the only way we could explain would be by stating precisely what is meant by good or right, without reasoning in circles by using terms synonymous with good and right. Despite a long history of attempts, it is by no means clear that this can be done. But the mere fact of being unable to explain something in different terms does not necessarily imply that we do not know what we are talking about. It may imply rather that what we are talking about is something very basic and simple, perfectly recognizable in the concrete, even though quite unanalyzable in the abstract. It seems that in talking about the good we are referring to something obvious enough in itself, but irreducible to anything more fundamental than itself.

Even if we cannot satisfactorily define precisely what is meant by good, and then further define what kind of good is called moral good, we can at least observe that moral goodness seems to be referred to only in certain limited contexts. For one thing, we attribute moral goodness only to persons, individually or collectively, and the behavior, internal or external, of persons. Moreover, in speaking of the moral goodness of behavior, we always suppose that the behavior in question is to some degree free and deliberate, not automatic or unaware. And in speaking of the moral goodness of persons we always seem to imply that their goodness either is or at least might be evidenced in their behavior. By a morally good person what we usually mean is a person who characteristically performs, or is disposed to perform, the kinds of action we think of as morally good.

DIVINE COMMANDS AND MORAL GOODNESS

One of the attempts that have been made to explain the morally good in terms of something supposedly more fundamental has been typical of one kind of religious ethics. This attempt has been made by people whose god or gods are thought to take morality very seriously, and of whose religion, therefore, morality constitutes an essential aspect. The gods envisaged by such religions are understood to commend or enjoin certain patterns of what we should normally think of as moral behavior. And the question is sometimes raised, whether god or the gods enjoin certain kinds of behavior because they are morally right or good, or whether on the contrary, they are morally right or good precisely and exclusively because god or the gods command them. Some who choose the latter answer go on to say that what is really signified by calling something morally good is that it is divinely commanded. To say that, of course, is really to make nonsense of the question whether the gods command certain behavior because it is morally good. If morally good means divinely commanded, that question would be asking whether certain behavior is divinely commanded because it is divinely commanded. Likewise, if morally good simply means divinely commanded, religious ethics is the only real ethics; the principles of morality and the commands of the gods are synonymous phrases, and there would be no difference between knowing that something was morally right and knowing that it was divinely enjoined. Although such a conception of ethics has had its advocates among religious people, it has also been widely rejected. But it has been rejected in quite different ways by quite different religions.

GOOD GODS AND BAD GODS

One kind of religion that refuses to equate what is divinely commanded with what is morally good is a kind of religion that believes in more than one god, among whom some god or gods actually oppose moral goodness while others favor it. Consequently, one god might actually advocate immorality while another advocated morality. It would appear that in such a religion one should have to possess some moral convictions independently of the gods merely in order to tell which was which. To rely ultimately on the gods for basic moral enlightenment would clearly be futile.

KNOWING THE GOOD AND WILLING THE GOOD

But even religions that believe in only one god and in that god's moral goodness, may still deny that morally right and divinely commanded are simply two ways of saying precisely the same thing. They may concede that whatever god commands is morally good without conceding that what makes it good is simply the fact that god commands it. And they may consider it important to say this in order to express the idea that god does not command arbitrarily but wisely, in virtue of his knowledge of what is good.

Closely related to this idea that god commands according to his knowledge of what is good, may be the further idea that human beings can acquire for themselves some genuine knowledge of what is morally good and, on the basis of that knowledge can, so to speak, give appropriate commands to themselves. One may thus distinguish between ethical principles that are directly revealed by a god and those that are discovered in human experience. Some principles might be acquired in both ways. And it should perhaps be noted that to acquire ethical convictions on the basis of human experience, independently of any explicit commandment of a god, does not necessarily mean acquiring them independently of the god. For if the capacity for human experience and the conditions of human experience are themselves created by a god, then what results from human experience cannot be independent of the god.

GENERAL AND PARTICULAR DIVINE COMMANDS

One further distinction may be useful when considering religious ethics as based on divine injunctions. For if we understand the injunctions of god or of the gods as analogous to human injunctions, we can think of them in quite different ways. We may think of them as general and more or less permanent; that is, god may enjoin that some type of behavior is to be constantly refrained from or regularly performed. We may also think of divine injunctions as particular and occasional; that is, god may enjoin some individual person to do or not do some quite specific or even unique action. Divine injunctions of the former kind may be described as divine laws or rules. Some term like orders or commands might be appropriate for the latter kind of divine injunction, but actual usage has tended to apply these terms indiscriminately to any kind of divine requirement.

DIVINE EXAMPLE

To conceive of god or the gods as giving moral injunctions, whether general or specific, is probably the simplest way of construing religious ethics, but it is not the only way. For morality can be based on ways of responding to god or to the gods that are quite different from simply obeying divine imperatives. One very important way of finding a religious basis for morality is by looking to the gods not so much for precept as for example. Thus the character and behavior of the gods may be thought of as representing the ultimate moral ideal, so that human beings are more or less moral according as their character and conduct approximate the divine example. Often closely related to this idea of imitating the gods is the idea of being grateful to the gods. Both imitation and gratitude can be described as appreciative responses. If one appreciates the gods as having in themselves a sublime moral excellence, one has grounds for imitating the gods as ideal standards. But if what one appreciates about the gods is not simply that they are good in themselves, but also that they have been good to oneself, that they are not only ideals but benefactors, one has grounds for responding to them gratefully, expressing one's gratitude in whatever ways may seem appropriate.

STUDY QUESTIONS

1. What do most ordinary religious people mean by religion?

2. What is meant by the phrase "anonymous Christian"?

3. What are some chracteristics of human response to the conviction that a god or gods exist?

4. What effect can one's understanding of God have on one's practical ideals and behavior?

5. What distinction is often made between ethics and morality?

6. What are some of the sources from which one may derive ethical principles?

7. What is meant by distinguishing divine laws or rules from divine commands or orders?

8. How can one's appreciation of a god's excellence serve as a basis for morality?

9. How does religious response to a god's excellence differ from a response to divine laws or commands?

10. How can a religious morality be based upon gratitude?

11. Name one specific way in which your concept of God affects your ethical beliefs.

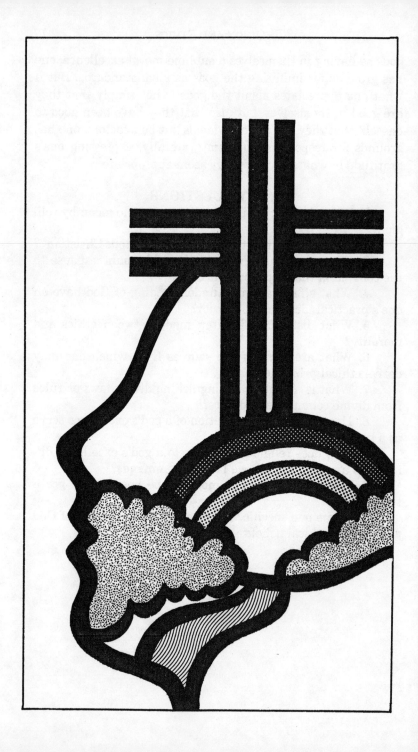

Chapter Three

CREATION AND REDEMPTION

CULTURAL ROOTS OF CHRISTIANITY

As is well known, the religion called Christianity came into being under historical circumstances that endowed it with an extraordinarily rich cultural heritage. Christianity's beginnings were deeply embedded in Judaism, and were crucially and indelibly influenced by the religious traditions and scriptures of Israel. The God of the Christians was identified with the God of Moses, and among the Christians' basic resources for understanding that God were the writings of what they came eventually to call the Old Testament, but originally called simply Holy Scripture, and regarded as the written record of divine revelation.

Although Christian beginnings are Jewish, we know that Judaism itself had by that time undergone considerable influence from outside its own biblical traditions, and notably from the Greco-Roman world. The Jews' own homeland was part of the Roman empire, and it had previously been part of the Hellenistic empire founded by Alexander the Great. Moreover, the Christian movement was very soon carried beyond the Jewish world, and made its greatest headway in Gentile cities of the Roman empire, of which, within only three centuries, it had become the official religion. Consequently, the cultural traditions of classical civilization had inevitably an early and continuing intense impact on Christian thought and behavior.

Finally, however, Christianity obviously cannot be adequately accounted for as the mere product of a union between Jewish and Classical cultures. It owes its fundamental identity to a unique feature. That critical component of what is indeed a very complicated religion is, of course, Jesus, the interpretation his followers gave to his person and life, and the efforts of them and their successors to refashion their own lives and persuade others to do likewise, in response to the message and meaning of Jesus Christ.

Christian ethics, like the Christian religion of which it is but one aspect, cannot be understood without taking into consideration all three of these contributory factors: that of Jewish biblical tradition, that of Greco-Roman Classical tradition, and that of Jesus of Nazareth and his dedicated followers. Some Christians have at various times sought to minimize one or other of these influences, usually with the intention of maximizing the third, the distinctively Christian component. It has been generally characteristic of Roman Catholicism to acknowledge and cultivate all three influences, in the conviction that they are, generally speaking, harmonious and complementary. This is true of Roman Catholic religious ethics no less than of other aspects of Roman Catholic Christianity.

COMMANDMENTS AND VIRTUES

This tendency to retain major elements from all three of Christianity's basic cultural sources can be seen very clearly in the persistent use by Christian ethical teachers of three traditional motifs. The first of these is the ten commandments, taken directly from the Old Testament. The second is the four cardinal virtues, prudence, justice, temperance, and fortitude, derived, mediately or immediately, from Platonic writings. And the third is the trio of theological virtues, faith, hope, and love, found in the New Testament. To a remarkable extent, these three motifs have furnished the framework of thought within which the oldest and strongest traditions of Christian ethics have been expressed and elaborated. Since the Reformation, many Protestants have virtually discarded that framework, and in very recent times it has been much less generally used and approved even by Catholics. But it seems true to say that wherever that framework of thought has been abandoned it has not yet been replaced by anything that could be plausibly described as either a traditional approach to Christian ethics or even a widely understood, much less a widely accepted approach.

REVELATION AND REASON; RULES AND TRAITS

In reviewing the three major components of traditional Christian ethics, there are two things one notices almost immediately. The first is that two of the components, namely the commandments and the theological virtues, come from biblical sources, and have been thought of as belonging to divine revelation. Whereas the other, the cardinal virtues, comes from pagan philosophy, and has been thought of as simply the conclusion of wise human reflection on human experience. Thus, traditionally, Christian ethics have readily combined ideas thought to be supernaturally revealed with ideas thought to be naturally discovered.

The second thing one readily observes about the three traditional components is that one of them, the commandments, comprises a list of negative imperative generalizations, a set of rules prohibiting specified categories of behavior. Whereas the other two components, the cardinal and theological virtues, are not rules of human conduct but traits of human character. In the one case, therefore, we have indications of what people ought, or more precisely ought not, to do. Whereas in the other case we have indications of how people ought to be. Thus, traditionally, Christian ethics have readily combined ideas about good conduct with ideas about good character.

CREED, CODE, AND CULT

Religion teachers often use the alliterative phrase, "creed, code, and cult" as a mnemonic device to suggest what seem to be three basic aspects of religions in general. The phrase is meant to remind us that most of the religions we know much about have some set of doctrines their adherents are expected to believe, some norms of conduct they are expected to abide by, and some rituals of worship they are expected to perform.

It is not easy to think of any two religions that would not have a certain amount in common under one or more of these three headings. Even among religions that are not known to be historically related, there is often considerable overlap in all three areas. Consider, for example, how many religions profess belief in some kind of salvation by god, advocate some ethic based upon benevolence, and cultivate some form of worship having to do with sacrifice.

IS THE CHRISTIAN CODE DIFFERENT?

When one undertakes on this basis to contrast Christianity with other religions, differences in the area of creed are easy enough to establish. What Christians profess to believe about the person and function of Jesus of Nazareth is obviously very distinctive. Certain differences in typical cult are likewise pronounced. Even with the current variety of denominational liturgies, what is called eucharist or communion has only remote and infrequent analogies outside the Christian churches. When it comes to code, however, differences become less clear-cut. It is not easy to formulate even a single rule of moral conduct, typically endorsed by Christians, that has not been advocated by many others as well, and in contexts not only of other religions but also of strictly secular morals.

Some, indeed, have considered it perfectly possible to extract the moral teaching of the New Testament and regard it as a universally commendable ethical ideal, quite independently of the religious beliefs originally associated with it. Some have considered that Christianity does not offer any unique ethical standards, but that it does offer distinctive religious motives for living up to ethical standards discoverable by believers and unbelievers alike. Still others, however, take the extreme opposite view, according to which Christian ethics are thoroughly distinctive, and in the lives of true Christians simply replace the sources of moral guidance available to unbelievers.

"NATURAL" AND "SUPERNATURAL" ETHICS

Roman Catholic tradition has generally steered a middle course between supposing, on the one hand, that Christian ethics are entirely unique or, on the other hand, that there is nothing unique about them. Here, as in many areas of its thought and action, Roman Catholicism has tended to prefer "both-and" to "either-or" propositions. Catholics have readily assumed that in Christian morality as in all of Christian living, both natural and supernatural forces are operative, and both reason and revelation are relevant, and that for the right conduct of life on earth, both are indispensable and mutually harmonious.

Throughout the greater part of Catholicism's history, this view of Christian morality and ethics has been more often taken for granted than explicitly defended in Catholic teaching. The reason for taking it for granted has been the belief that the same God stands behind both the natural and the supernatural influences that affect our lives, that the same God both endows human minds with ordinary reason and assists them with extraordinary revelation, because the same God is our Creator and our Redeemer.

CREATION AND REDEMPTION

A question naturally arises, however, when the Catholic position is expressed in this way. That is, if one and the same God is the source of all our ethical enlightenment and moral capacity, why should he operate as it were on two different levels, as implied by such contrasting terms as natural and supernatural, or reason and revelation? The main answer to that question is already hinted at in the final pair of terms mentioned in the last paragraph, the terms applied to God himself, Creator and Redeemer.

To refer to God as our Redeemer as well as our Creator implies that something went wrong, or goes wrong, or is wrong with the humanity God as Creator brought into being out of nothingness, which is put right again by God as Redeemer. Roughly speaking, to call God both our Creator and our Redeemer seems to credit God with having in the first place manufactured us and, in the second place, repaired us. And that raises the question of what did go wrong, or why repairs should be necessary.

The Christian answer to this question obliges us, of course, to recognize from the very start that Creation and Redemption can be likened only in a very superficial and inadequate way to what we normally understand as manufacture and repair. In ordinary experience we do, of course, constantly find that manufactured articles need sooner or later to be repaired. And we are aware of three basic reasons why repairs become necessary. One reason is defective workmanship: things that have been badly made break down easily. Another reason is inadequate materials: even the finest craftsman must work with components that, by the very laws of physics and chemistry, are more or less unstable. And the third reason is hard use: careless users damage things quickly, but even the most careful ones inflict a certain amount of punishment that will eventually take its toll.

FROM PERFECTION TO IMPERFECTION

The kind of God whom Christians call the Creator is not, of course, what we normally mean by a manufacturer. Because he is understood to be all-wise and all-powerful, it is impossible to attribute to him anything remotely comparable to defective workmanship. And because to create means precisely to make something out of nothing, there can likewise be no question of deficient materials. If, then, the human breakdown implied in calling God our Redeemer as well as our Creator can be compared at any point to the kinds of breakdown we are familiar with, it must have to do with hard use or misuse of what God has made.

But here again an obvious problem arises. For if God is the Creator of all things, he makes the users as well as the things that are used. Therefore, the users should be free of defects too; their use should not be capable of degenerating into abuse. But then how can human beings go wrong, if there is nothing wrong either with their maker or with what they are made of? If, before they go wrong, there is nothing already wrong with them, we find ourselves in the paradoxical position of looking to what is good and right for the explanation of what goes bad or wrong. This paradoxical position is the one that traditional Catholic thought has generally assumed.

STUDY QUESTIONS

1. What cultural traditions form the main historical roots of Christianity?

2. What additional factor gives Christianity historical uniqueness?

3. How are the traditional categories of "commandments" and "virtues" related to Christianity's cultural sources?

4. How are those traditional categories differentiated with respect to "natural reason" and "supernatural revelation"?

5. How do those traditional categories relate to the distinction between good conduct and good character?

6. What is the phrase "creed, code, cult" meant to express?

7. How different is Christianity thought to be from other religions with respect to creed, code, and cult?

8. How has Catholicism tended to regard the relation-

ship between natural and supernatural factors in morality?

9. What belief seems to be implied in considering God as both creator and redeemer?

10. What problem is raised by considering God to be both creator and redeemer?

11. In what way do you feel the Christian code is unique among ethical codes? Is the difference in content, motivation, or both?

Chapter Four

FREEDOM AND LOVE

PARADOX OF CREATED FREEDOM

The idea that humanity goes wrong not because of a defect in its basic makeup, but precisely because of a singular perfection in its makeup may be a paradoxical notion, but it is not entirely foreign to our ordinary experience. We commonly recognize that it takes a certain greatness in human beings for them to be greatly bad, as well as to be greatly good. As human individuals mature, for example, their capacity for behaving badly is progressively enlarged along with their capacity for behaving well.

In modern times especially, we have grown accustomed to praising education, and personal maturation in general, as enlarging the scope of human freedom. Intellectual improvement is said to broaden the mind, in the sense that it makes people aware of an ever-widening range of possibilities, and at the same time equips them with an ever-increasing repertoire of means for realizing new possibilities. And at the same time we are constantly reminded, sometimes subtly but also by phenomena as impossible to overlook as nuclear detonations, that among newly achieved human possibilities are possibilities for immense evil.

However, underlying all these ideas of human development as opening the way to new achievements, both good and evil, is the crucial idea of human freedom. Human development is thought to be unique precisely because human beings are thought to be more or less free to use their newly acquired powers of mind over matter as they see fit. Unless one subscribes to philosophical and psychological opinions that Christianity, and most of the human race, have always rejected, the difference between a very well programmed computer, or even a very well trained animal, and a very well educated human being is a difference not in degree but in kind. One can do a great deal with a well programmed computer or a well trained animal—including a great deal of damage to oneself or others. But what we mean by a well educated human being is not someone with whom one can do a great deal, but someone who can do a great deal. Humanists and Christians are in general agreement in finding the most impressive fact about human beings not simply their accumulation of power, but their freedom to direct the powers they accumulate. And being free to direct those powers, they are likewise free to misdirect them.

Thus the paradox of humanity's going wrong in virtue not of a defect but of a perfection, implied in the Christian idea of a God who is both Creator and Redeemer, is familiar enough even to secular thought. Freedom, generally acclaimed as humanity's most precious possession, is also generally perceived as humanity's most dangerous possession. In the Christian form of the same paradox, God in creating human freedom did not make something worse but immeasurably better; but being made better in that way is to be made capable of evil as well as of good.

THE MORAL GOOD OF FREEDOM

Even granted that a human perfection rather than a human flaw makes possible human wickedness, one may still be tempted to ask whether that perfection is, so to speak, worth the risk. Might we not really be better off deprived of freedom if by that very fact we were insured against malice? After all, conscientious persons have always insisted that it is better to do without even the most precious things, rather than do evil. Jesus himself tells us if our right hand scandalizes us to cut it off, and if our right eye scandalizes us to pluck it out. But surely it is our freedom that, in the last analysis, always "scandalizes" us. Does it not seem as though it would have been better if the Creator had plucked that out—or left it out—right from the start? Is is possible that human freedom does enough good even to compensate for all the harm it obviously does?

Even as this sort of question occurs to us, we tend to perceive that there is something absurd about it. The idea of getting rid of immorality by eliminating freedom is rather like the idea of getting rid of sickness by wholesale slaughter. A world without freedom would be indeed a world without immorality, but it would be equally a world without morality. What seems to be implied in the suggestion that we might be better off without freedom because we should then be without immorality, is that we should be morally better off. But we could not in fact be better off morally, because morality itself would no longer have any place in our lives. Freedom makes immorality possible only because it makes morality possible. The very fact of our considering immorality a bad thing is a consequence of our considering morality a good thing. And the kind of good thing morality is, is inseparable from freedom. A strictly compulsory morality, or a strictly automatic morality simply would not be what we mean by and value as morality.

FREEDOM AND LOVE

In calling God our Creator and Redeemer, and thereby implying that something went wrong with what God made us to be, we are first of all brought up against the mysterious reality of a human freedom which, because it is freedom, is capable of being misused. And secondly we are brought up against the basic Christian presupposition that human freedom not only can be misused, but has been and is misused, with moral consequences that make themselves felt universally.

But to speak of the misuse of freedom implies the further Christian belief that freedom is created not for its own sake, but for some definite purpose it is supposed to serve. Christianity's insistence on both the reality of human freedom and the misuse of human freedom raises the question of what, according to Christians, human freedom is for. What does freedom make it possible for human beings to do, which without it they could not do, and which God created them to do? This is equivalent to asking what, according to Christian belief, is the distinctive purpose God intends for human life.

The basic traditional answer to that question is well known, and it has been consistently expressed by Christianity since its biblical beginnings. The classical summation of God's design for human living is love: love of God and love of neighbor, in essential, inseparable conjunction. Whether the question is asked in terms of seeking to know God's will, or in terms of seeking to achieve humanity's purpose, the answer remains the same. You shall love the Lord your God with your whole heart and mind and strength, and love your neighbor as yourself. These words state, in the most general way, the substance of Christian morality and the standard of Christian ethics. In a sense, therefore, everything that follows in this book, in so far as it deals authentically with Christian ethics, is commentary on this basic Christian assertion. But at this point, what needs to be noted is the connection between this assertion and the significance of human freedom.

Christian tradition considers freedom the distinctive fact about human existence. Christian tradition likewise considers love the distinctive purpose of human existence. Not surprisingly, since the fact and the purpose are attributed to the same divine Creator, they are seen as profoundly interrelated.

That is, in a Christian view of things, freedom and love, in the last analysis, make sense only in terms of one another. Love requires freedom, and freedom is for the sake of love.

AMBIGUITY OF LOVE

Notoriously, one of the great problems about appealing to love as the ultimate norm of Christian ethics is the fact that the word love is now, and seems always to have been, an extremely ambiguous word. Love means, for different people and in different situations, all sorts of things. Later it will be necessary to make some attempt at specifying positively what love means in the ethically normative sense given to it by Christian tradition. But in the present context, one thing at least may be noted. The kind of love that is basic to Christian morality is a kind of love that is made possible by human freedom. Christian loving is always an exercise of freedom. If, therefore, one speaks of a kind of love that simply happens to people, one is not speaking of the kind of love by which Christian morality is measured. To speak, for example, of falling in love, in the sense of simply undergoing an experience, is certainly to speak meaningfully. But unless there is more to it than that, one is not speaking in the idiom of Christian ethical tradition. Christian love is not something that simply happens to human beings, it is something that human beings do, in virtue of the freedom given them by God.

Earlier, we observed that religion in its most general sense means how people respond to God. We observed also that ethics in its most general sense means how people think about right and wrong behavior. Hence, religious ethics means how people respond to God in their thinking about right and wrong behavior. What seems to be the simplest form of this kind of response is one that is founded on the belief that God has expressly enjoined a certain kind of behavior, and is properly responded to by accepting his injunction as a rule of conduct. Thus a Christian ethic based upon love is a proper response to a God who tells us, above all, to love.

GOD'S LOVE AS NORMATIVE

We also mentioned earlier another kind of ethical response to God. That is a response, not to God's commands or requirements, but to God's nature or character, considered as our supreme norm or model. We also noted that this idea of modelling one's moral behavior on God is often closely associated with ideas of gratitude to God. This approach to religious ethics also has its place in Christian tradition. And, most significantly, it leads Christian ethics in precisely the same direction as does the other approach, of obeying divine commandments.

Christians, believing in the kind of God they do believe in, and regarding this God as their Creator and Redeemer, are bound to ask, at some point, why such a God should do such things as creating and redeeming. For the kind of God Christians believe in is an infinitely perfect God. And to be infinitely perfect is to lack absolutely nothing. Therefore the God of Christianity is, to put it somewhat crudely, a God who has everything, who lacks nothing and needs nothing. So the question inevitably arises of how such a God could find any reason for creating. And indeed, many philosophers have believed that an infinitely perfect God must be so perfectly self-contained and, as it were, self-satisfied, that it is inconceivable why he should take an active interest in a world of imperfect creatures.

The kind of thinking that is involved here is, of course, based on ordinary human experience. The reason why human beings make things or do things is usually because they do not have everything, and want something they do not yet have. When we ask why certain deliberate human actions are performed, we expect to discover the answer in some human need or want that the action is intended to satisfy. And yet obviously this sort of answer cannot account for the actions of an infinitely perfect creator.

If therefore, any humanly intelligible answer can be given to the question of why or how an infinitely perfect God could

be a Creator or Redeemer, it has to be an answer in terms of
doing things otherwise than to satisfy needs. It has to be a
reason for acting which is not aimed at improving the condition of the one who acts. Certain psychologists, certain philosophers, and certain ordinary people seem to find it strictly
inconceivable that, at least in human behavior, there could be
such a reason for acting. Others, however, seem to find it
perfectly conceivable. And those who do find it conceivable
seem invariably to conceive it in terms of unselfish love.
According to this view there are indeed human actions which
are not undertaken to serve the interests of those who perform
those actions. There are said to be human beings who undertake activities simply to do good, and not necessarily to do
themselves good. There are said to be actions of pure benevolence and beneficence, determined not by self-interest but by
the interests of others. Even if such actions should, in fact,
benefit the persons who perform them, it is not necessary to
suppose that consideration of this fact enters into their motivation, or even into conscious awareness.

It so happens that I do believe genuinely unselfish actions
of this sort occur among human beings. But even doubting
that, it would seem hard to deny that, at the very least, some
human actions are much more nearly of this kind than others.
And in any case, even to deny the occurrence of such actions
seems to imply that such actions are hypothetically intelligible. And merely to have the idea of such unselfish actions is
sufficient to provide some basis for understanding how an
infinitely perfect God might involve himself in such an activity as creation.

At all events, ever since biblical times, Christians have
maintained not only that God wants us to love, but that God is
love. And they have connected these two statements in an
explanatory relationship. We love, because God first loved us.
Thus the Christian ethical emphasis on love appeals not only
to what Christians believe God wants, but also to what they
believe God is. To act as God wills is likewise to act as God

does. To obey God and to imitate God are, for Christian ethics, two aspects of a single reality.

SIN AND SINFULNESS

The idea that human beings, whom God created free to enable them to love, misuse their freedom, is in a very general sense the idea of sin. Sin, however, is not simply a synonym for wrongdoing. It identifies wrongdoing as not simply moral misbehavior, but as moral misbehavior that constitutes a wrong response to God.

Christian tradition talks about sin in two significantly different ways, corresponding to the two conventional phrases, actual sin and original sin. By actual sins are meant the concrete instances of wrongdoing by which human individuals respond wrongly to God. The idea of original sin is a less simple one, and a thorough treatment of it belongs not to religious ethics but to dogmatic and speculative theology. Nevertheless, an introduction to Christian ethics cannot leave this idea entirely out of account.

Despite various interpretations of original sin, and numerous controversies about it, one practical implication of what it means is typical of Christian approaches to ethics. Limiting our discussion simply to practical aspects of this idea of original sin, it may be said that Christian tradition envisages not only the possibility of individuals acting sinfully, but a general climate or atmosphere conducive to sinfulness in human society. Thus there is believed to be in the human environment itself a kind of bias towards sinful behavior. In the traditional Christian view, human freedom operates under a moral handicap, experiencing from the very outset a proclivity to sin.

Although this idea of sinful bias is assigned a dogmatic basis in Christian tradition, the idea itself has always been regarded as supported by ordinary human experience. That is, experience seems to confirm the belief that wrongdoing comes strangely easily to human beings, and that moral goodness, even when it is admired and desired, comes strangely hard.

It is not simply a matter of observing that human beings sometimes misbehave morally. Nor is it simply a matter of observing that they do so depressingly often. What is more significant is the observation that they seem to do so almost despite themselves. Not only does the moral behavior of our fellow human beings often disappoint us; our own moral behavior often disappoints us. Even in our better moments, there is generally an embarrassingly wide gap between the kind of moral behavior we admire and the kind we actually achieve. In our worst moments, that gap becomes positively horrendous.

Sometimes Christianity is criticized in this connection for cultivating what is frequently called a pessimistic view of human conduct. That, however, is not really the point. Christians are as temperamentally various as anybody else, and those of one temperament may insist on saying that people are "pretty good" while those of another temperament insist on saying they are "pretty bad." But this is rather like an argument between those who say a cup is half-full and those who say it is half-empty. The observed reality remains the same, even though observers' moods and attitudes differ. And what that reality seems to exhibit over a whole range of human moral performance from saints to villains, is that moral standards that are generally acknowledged are not generally achieved. Christianity has no monopoly on this observation, which has been expressed by wise teachers from every era and culture. "I see what is better, and I approve what is better—but I follow what is worse" is a classical pagan statement often associated with St. Paul's "I do not do the good I want, but the evil I do not want is what I do."

STUDY QUESTIONS

1. What is paradoxical about the Christian view that humanity, created by God, goes somehow wrong?

2. How is the idea of freedom related to the idea of morality?

3. What issues are raised by the suggestion that we might be better off without freedom?

4. What does Christianity typically suppose to be the basic purpose of human freedom?

5. How is the idea of freedom related to a distinctively Christian conception of love?

6. How is a distinctively Christian understanding of love related to the idea of God as a moral exemplar?

7. How does the idea of sin differ from that of simple wrongdoing?

8. What two quite different ideas of sin are both operative in Christian theology?

9. What aspect of belief in original sin is relevant to Christian ethics?

10. Has Christian understanding of original sin anything in common with non-Christian or non-religious thought?

11. Can you imagine a world without freedom? Describe a typical day in your life under those circumstances. Do you think your life would be better or worse?

Chapter Five

A GOD WHO SAVES AND RULES

SALVATION AND COVENANT

The foundations of Christian ethics, like the foundations of Christianity itself, are laid in the Old Testament. And, as is well known, the Old Testament differs from most of the world's great religious scriptures in being to a great extent an interpretative account of concrete events. For Israel's discovery of God was achieved not through mystical abstraction from the facts of history, but through practical attention to them. What those facts seemed to imply above all was that a uniquely powerful God had taken an intensely personal and benevolent interest in one of the least impressive human societies of the ancient Near East. The outstanding piece of historical evidence cited to this effect was a remarkable sequence of events that led these people from oppressive servitude in Egypt to a religiously based political sovereignty in Palestine.

It is no part of the business of this book to recall in detail, much less to analyze, the biblical narrative of those events. But it is indispensable to note that this story, with its religious interpretation of history, is the essential context of Old Testament religious ethics, and for that reason an essential key to all biblical ethics, including the biblical beginnings of Christian ethics.

Most significantly, the story does not begin with any notable ethical or religious achievement on the part of the people themselves. It is not even suggested that they were particularly good people. The outstanding fact about them was not their virtue but their predicament, as a group of despised and enslaved aliens in a land that had welcomed their ancestors. Their emergence from this predicament is not attributed to any heroism or ingenuity, or even piety on their part. It is attributed to a divine intervention so completely independent of human cooperation that it is described from start to finish in terms of the strictly miraculous. Thus, by his sole initiative and unaided power, God saved this people from misery and destined them for greatness. And by so doing, God committed himself to a lasting special relationship with this people. He chose them for his own.

The relationship between God and his people came to be spoken of in terms of a political analogy, as a kind of covenant, that is, a pact of alliance. Recent research on the kinds of covenants that existed in the ancient Near East has made this crude but eloquent analogy somewhat easier to understand. It seems likely that it reflects a particular kind of treaty whereby a powerful monarch offered protective patronage to a people who, in accepting the advantages of such a relationship, acquired the status and assumed the obligations of vassals.

LIBERATION AND SUBJECTION

The religious and ultimately the ethical significance of this political analogy is evident. It points to the fact that the covenant relationship between God and his people is not a mutual agreement concluded for their mutual benefit. Rather it is bestowed unilaterally by God for the unilateral advantage of his people. It does not represent simply their release from subjection. It represents their transition from one kind of subjection to another, from subjection under a maleficent tyrant to subjection under a beneficent God. The transition was not liberation, in the sense that it released the people from foreign masters to establish them as their own masters. It was liberation, in the sense that it released them from masters who governed them out of self-interest to establish them under the mastery of one who would govern them in their own interest. If there is a "liberation theology" in the Old Testament, it is one that conceives liberation as a deliverance not from heteronomy to autonomy, but from heteronomy to theonomy. Ideologies of popular sovereignty have simply nothing to do with the matter. The ending of Pharaoh's ruthless lordship and the beginning of Yahweh's merciful lordship were experienced by the people, and are expressed in their literature, as two sides of a single coin.

There is no suggestion of even a possible third option, whereby the people might somehow accept their emancipation from alien human rule, and yet refuse an absolute fealty to divine rule. To shake off the new yoke of divine sovereignty was understood to have only one possible outcome, which would be to assume once again the old yoke of human despotism. Much of the Old Testament narrative is the sad tale of how precisely that cause inexorably led to precisely that result, to the reestablishment of tyranny, first under domestic tyrants and then, rendered defenseless by their misrule, once again under tyrants from foreign lands.

THE LORD AND THE LAW

Given such an understanding of their history, and of the relationship with God that it implied, Israel's religious preoccupation with the idea of law is easy to understand. Since their salvation by God and their subjection to God were inseparable, their great privilege could in no way be detached from their great duty. Yahweh was Lord and his lordship was their salvation. Hence their salvation could be only as real and lasting as his lordship was real and lasting. In their world as in ours, lordship is expressed as law, and the lasting reality of lordship is realized in the constancy of a people's obedience to the law of their lord.

Law is thus at the very heart of this religion founded on the experience of salvation. Law is the guaranty of a secure relationship with God, the convenant relationship based on an exchange of promises. The Lord pledges his protection to those who pledge loyalty to him, and by his protection incorporates them into a new community life. The Lord determines the pattern of that life, and publishes guidelines for its development. The law shows how to live together with the Lord. Sin, as breaking the law, estranges the sinner from the Lord and from the community.

There are several collections of legal material in the Old Testament. None of them are legal codes in the sense of comprehensive systematic collections of statutes. Different periods of history are reflected not only in different collections, but in different parts of the same collection. Changes of interpretation strive to preserve the laws' relevance despite changing circumstances.

Of all these collections, the most memorable and the most influential, for Christians no less than for Jews, is the Decalogue, or Ten Commandments, which until very recent times was memorized as part of the basic religious education of every Christian. Unfortunately, even when the Ten Commandments were commonly known by even very young Christians, they were often treated as a kind of detached sheet of instructions, rather than as part of a story, which is the way the Bible presents them.

THE TEN COMMANDMENTS

Although the Commandments are, in some form, older than our Bible, it is their place in the biblical narrative that gives them, for us, their distinctive meaning and principal value. The familiar sensational features of their context—

Sinai, the Lord's voice out of a storm, the inscribed tablets of stone—are all essentially stage props for a highly intellectual, basically theological drama. It is the dramatic expression of that concept, equally vital to Jewish and Christian faith, called the Covenant.

In exaggeratedly simple terms, what the Covenant means is the bond of allegiance by which the God called Yahweh unites himself in love to a group of human beings who, by that very fact, are transformed from being merely people into being *a* people, and not merely a people, but this God's, *Yahweh*'s people.

The Covenant, as the Bible never tires of reminding us, is the supreme triumph of divine generosity; it is Yahweh's gloriously free gift, his act of grace, his miracle of unmerited choice. The people, thereby consolidated into *a* people, Israel, did not produce the gift, nor do they in any sense deserve it. Their role in this drama consists entirely in their accepting the gift. And yet acceptance of it means, and from the very nature of the case must mean, a great deal more than mere passive acquiescence.

For a gift that takes the form of a bond of allegiance, establishing a loving union is only really accepted to the extent that it is preserved and retained. The whole value of a covenant—as with a treaty, or a marriage, perhaps our most familiar worldly covenants—resides in stability, in lastingness. And since this is a covenant that simultaneously fashions a people and fastens that people to their God, there are two factors on which its stability structurally depends. One of those factors is the bond, of fidelity and love, that holds the people to Yahweh. And the other factor is the bond, of fidelity and love, that holds the people together. Whichever bond should break, the Covenant must inevitably collapse—whether the people should fall away from Yahweh, or whether they should fall apart from one another.

If we conceive the structure of the Covenant in these terms, as the religious adherence of a people to their God,

inseparable from the social coherence of a people among themselves, it is easy to see the Ten Commandments for what, in a
permanent sense, they are. They are a means for making
explicit, in a general and practical way, what the preservation
of God's covenant gift entails. Just as there are two dimensions of attachment, between the people and God, and among
the people themselves, so, as the story is told, there were two
tablets. Inscribed on the first, supposedly, were requirements
for undivided religious allegiance—one God, excluding all
rivals and substitutes. Inscribed on the other were requirements of social unity—familial respect, sacredness of oath,
conjugal fidelity, security of life and property. They are mainly expressed as prohibitions, and what they prohibit are the
most universally familiar ways in which people become
strangers and enemies, to their God and to one another.

There is, of course, no magic to the number ten, and the
Commandments can be both validly expanded and validly
condensed. To the possibilities of expansion there are no limits. To the possibilities of condensation, however, there is a
limit, imposed by the very structure of the Covenant. If there
is a magic number, it is two. For the Covenant has two irreducible and inseparable dimensions, of which we are reminded
in the Old Testament by those two stone tablets, and in the
New Testament by Jesus' twofold law of love.

THE FIRST TABLET OF THE LAW

According to an ancient tradition, the two stone tablets
given by the Lord to Moses divided their contents unevenly,
thereby setting off from the rest the initial commandments
which deal specifically with conduct towards God. And according to an ancient interpretation, the whole series is to be
understood as ten imperative statements drawing implications for human behavior from the one great declarative statement that precedes them: "I am the Lord your God."

If he is the Lord our God we cannot have strange gods
before him. For to be our God is to be, for us, ultimately and

absolutely first. To put anything before what is first is a contradiction. Therefore to allow anything, ever, to take pre-eminence in our lives over the Lord is not only a refusal of what God asks, but implicitly a denial of what God is. Our God is our source and destiny, our ultimate motive and ultimate goal. And the discovery, at any moment of our life, that our ultimate motive or ultimate goal is really something else—whether prosperity, security, power, prestige, pleasure, or some totally preoccupying trifle—is to discover our "strange god," and our real God-lessness. The first Commandment, as soon as one explores its implications, reveals itself to be an all-encompassing commandment.

To take the name of the Lord our God in vain probably referred originally to magical invocations. But magic is only a crude form of something that is often done in subtler, more seemingly respectable ways. It is the pretension of making the God who is our Lord and end into a god who is our servant and means. It is the effort to use God, rather than serve him. It is therefore, by Judeo-Christian standards, a kind of invert-ed religion. Not surprisingly, religion is what such behavior usually pretends to be. Its perversity is revealed in the fact that, despite religious trappings, it exists for the sake of other purposes than God or relationship with God. Religion to bring in money; religion to bolster tyranny; religion to get high on; religion to feel sentimental over; religion to build prestige by; religion to make us think we know more than we can or should know—such are only a few of the more popular ways in which the name of God is taken in vain.

The original significance of the third commandment is not clear from biblical evidence. The word sabbath is related to a Hebrew word for rest, and to call the seventh day of the week sabbath is to designate a weekly holiday. Exodus treats the sabbath as a commemoration of God's "rest" after his six days of creative "work." An older interpretation, in Deuteron-omy, regards it as a day when rest was made possible for everybody, including slaves and even work animals, in a spirit

of compassion reinforced by the Israelites' experience of en-
slavement in Egypt. From early times, moreover, the sabbath
was conceived as a holyday as well as a holiday, an appropriate time for worship. Thomas Aquinas nicely combines the
themes by characterizing the day as an occasion when one
"should have leisure for God." Unfortunately, first Jews and
then Christians made the weekly observance oppressive and
absurd by attempting to legislate the precise limits of obligatory rest and worship. In reaction, the excellent idea of a
weekly "time out for God" increasingly degenerated into a
formalistic weekly duty of "going to church." The original
concept is nowadays more authentically realized in such practices as periodically making a retreat or day of recollection—
and giving one's dependents and employees opportunities to
do so. We are undoubtedly a lot worse off, both physically and
spiritually, for the fact that, in any but a technical and trivial
sense, the third commandment is largely disobeyed.

STUDY QUESTIONS

1. How does the Old Testament give us to understand
that Israel discovered its God?

2. Why, according to the Bible, did God save the people
of the exodus?

3. What, according to the Bible, became the basic relationship between Israel and God following the exodus?

4. What basically is meant by a covenant?

5. What sort of covenant, in political experience, seems
to have provided a basis for the religious idea of covenant?

6. In what sense is liberation an inadequate account of
what the covenant represented for Israel?

7. How is the Old Testament concept of law related to
the idea of the covenant?

8. What account of the law in the Old Testament has
had the most conspicuous influence on Jewish and Christian
ethics?

9. On what two general factors does the stability of the
covenant relationship depend?

10. How are these two general factors expressed by the distinction of "two tablets" of the decalogue?

11. How are these two general factors related to the New Testament's twofold commandment of love?

12. In what sense is the opening statement of the decalogue considered basic to all that follows?

13. In what sense does the opening statement of the decalogue imply the prohibition of "strange gods"?

14. In what sense can the first commandment be regarded as implicitly an all-encompassing commandment?

15. What was probably originally meant by taking God's name in vain?

16. What is the broader implication of taking God's name in vain?

17. In what areas of life might the prohibition of taking God's name in vain be practically applied?

18. What two different accounts of the sabbath rest are given in the Bible?

19. In what sense can these two accounts be combined in a practical understanding of the commandment?

20. What understanding of the sabbath commandment might be usefully applied in modern circumstances?

21. How was the sabbath commandment abused by both Jewish and Christian official interpretations?

22. One ancient interpretation states that the ten commandments are all implications of the statement "I am the Lord your God." How might this be so?

Chapter Six

THE SECOND TABLET OF THE LAW

HONOR TO PARENTS

To "honor your father and your mother" is presented in the Old Testament as both religious obedience and practical wisdom. Clearly the behavior this commandment calls for was thought of as being, under ordinary circumstances, sane, normal, natural behavior. For most of a person's life his or her father and mother were presumed to be the members of the family who had been around long enough for experience and reflection, and to have experienced and reflected enough to be competent and wise.

And yet the Old Testament is clearly aware that, however normal this status of parents might be, it is neither universal nor permanent. Some parents are bound to be less competent than even quite young children. And most parents, if they live long enough, will eventually be excelled by their children in a great many respects. And so it is insisted in the Old Testament that, however much parents may differ or change, the commandment declares God's will inflexibly. Parents are to be

51

honored always, whether out of admiration for what they have and give, or out of gratitude for what they had and gave, or out of sheer recognition of what they are, the source under God of our very selves.

Where the New Testament reiterates (in Ephesians) the fourth commandment, it observes that "it is the first commandment with a promise attached, in the words 'that it may be well with you, and that you may live long in the land'." It is true that this additional phrase is attached wherever the commandment appears in the Old Testament. But perhaps as much as a promise, these words are simply a shrewd prediction. At all events, our society, which has coined such a phrase as "generation gap" to describe a result of its widespread disregard of this commandment, does not associate that phrase with anything that could be called "well-being."

This commandment, like all of them, is made easier for some than for others. Many have had parents whom only a fool or a knave could find it hard to honor. But many others have not. And for some it is a commandment whose fulfillment requires little less than heroism. Both the Old Testament and the New attach a kind of footnote, appealing to parents not to exasperate their children. It is a very important footnote. But it is addressed exclusively to parents, which only some of us are. The commandment is what is addressed to children, which all of us are.

YOU SHALL NOT KILL

It is often pointed out that those of the Ten Commandments that do not have strictly religious application reflect a kind of universal moral consensus which finds expression in every stable civilization. But if it is true that every reflective culture condemns a sin or crime of killing, great variety exists, from time to time and from place to place, in the understanding of what this sin or crime entails.

In our own culture, a superficial consensus of opposition to killing conceals very deep and basic differences, which come to light only when more specific issues are raised—such as the killing of non-combatant civilians for military convenience abroad—or the killing of unborn offspring for social convenience at home. It should come as no great surprise that over the vast span of time and culture from Exodus to the Sermon on the Mount, the Bible's prohibition of killing has not been understood and applied with perfect clarity and uniformity. In this as in other cases, the Bible's broad ethical directives can be effective only if they are a stimulus and are not a substitute for prayerful and careful moral reflection, the hard and serious work of a religious conscience.

Even to translate the fifth commandment is not easy. Some modern versions substitute "murder" for the too comprehensive verb "kill," but the Hebrew word is applied to many cases that we should never think of describing as murders. In fact, the meaning of the term developed considerably during biblical times. In early documents it seems to have referred chiefly to the kind of killing that provokes lethal retaliation. In this sense, the prototype of the killer is Cain, who acknowledged the social implications of his deed in the words "anyone who meets me can kill me." Within the moral perspective of a religious covenant that depends on the stability and integrity of God's people, it is easy to see why emphasis should be placed on homicide as not merely an isolated act, but a stimulus to the familiar pattern of vengeance and counter-vengeance that tears societies apart and plants in their survivors inveterate habits of hatred and fear, the wellsprings of further violence. In this perspective, every fatal shedding of blood holds the explosive potentiality of a far bloodier chain reaction called vendetta.

In later usage, the moral language of killing points less exclusively to the outward act and its social consequences, and directs attention inward, to the motives and dispositions that are manifested in murderous deeds. Killing is thus associated less with its effects than with its subjective causes, as expressing anger, jealousy, malevolence. Consequently, the same

term of disapproval is applied to a killing that takes vengeance as to a killing that provokes vengeance. One can see in
these developments a definite foreshadowing of moral reflections on killing which come to vivid expression in the New
Testament, but which have not even yet become generally
integrated with the moral thinking of either Jews or Christians. Thus we find attributed to Jesus a condemnation not so
much of outward murder as of an interior murderousness, so
that whether hatred finds its outlet in violent words or violent
deeds is less important than the hatred itself, which is the
main target of moral denunciation. And we also find attributed to Jesus a total moral rejection, not merely of unfair
retaliation, but of any retaliation whatsoever. It may be some
indication of where we stand in the development of biblical
morality that such teachings as these attributed to Jesus are
by most Christians both speculatively admired for their seeming nobility, and practically ignored for their seeming fanaticism.

Underlying the whole domain of biblical morality which
is represented by the fifth commandment, whether it be fo-
cussed on social tranquillity or interior benevolence, there is
also a characteristically biblical evaluation of life in general,
and human life in particular, as something that derives from
God with peculiar immediacy and is therefore endowed with
peculiar sanctity. Thus the symbolic description of creation
shows us God fashioning a human likeness out of raw clay,
like a ceramic artisan, but then making his artifact come to
life by an infusion of his own breath or spirit. One finds
accordingly that biblical writers express a religious awe for
life, as for the blood, in which life was believed to reside.
Therefore the taking of life and the shedding of blood have
moral overtones of a distinctively religious kind. Killing is not
only a matter of critically injuring the peace of society, or of
exhibiting the virulence of a hate-filled mind. It is a kind of
sacrilege, the profanation of that element in creation which is
closest akin to its divine source.

YOU SHALL NOT COMMIT ADULTERY

One of the purposes of these pages is to bring our thoughts about the ten commandments into somewhat closer contact with what they mean in their biblical contexts. So it might seem appropriate at this point to observe that where the ten commandments refer to adultery what they mean is precisely that—adultery. But even that statement does need to be qualified. For in Israel during biblical times adultery did not mean precisely what it means to us. The reason it did not was because of the deplorably low social status and limited human rights accorded by that society to women. Adultery was, in fact, defined as an offense against a husband, caused by the sexual infidelity of his wife who, along with her male accomplice, were the only ones who could be considered guilty of this sin. The sin was likewise a crime, whose seriousness can be estimated from the fact that it was punishable, and frequently punished, by death. It is not until the New Testament, however, that we find a husband's betrayal of his wife described as adulterous, and this development reflects a more generous view of the social dignity of women.

Once allowance is made for the strong masculine bias of Old Testament culture, the intention of the sixth commandment is clear enough. Its intention is to protect the unique intimacy of that marital union which is described in the creation narrative as "two in one flesh." The importance of avoiding what has too often been done, namely regarding the sixth commandment as a general condemnation of sexual misbehavior, is that this grossly misrepresents what the commandment is actually about. The value which the sixth commandment exists to safeguard is not sexual continence. It is marital fidelity. And the commandment pertains to sexual continence only inasmuch as sexual incontinence can disrupt marital fidelity.

This is not, of course, to say that the Old Testament is morally indifferent to the sexual behavior of the unmarried. Fornication and other sexual abuses are repeatedly denounced. But they are not, as such, dealt with at all by the ten commandments, and they clearly rank much lower in ethical importance than infidelity between husbands and wives. The extreme seriousness with which adultery is viewed is an index of the extreme seriousness with which marriage is viewed. For in the moral perspective of the Old Testament, the summit and perfection of human sexual morality is a faithful and fruitful marriage. And precisely for that reason, the lowest abyss of sexual immorality is adultery. The logic of the moral thinking here involved is that which is often expressed in a slogan of classical ethics: The corruption of what is best is what is worst.

What the ninth commandment adds to the sixth is attention to the subjective side of adultery. But, as its wording makes plain, its concern is still with marriage, and not with any vague eroticism or venereal fantasies. Its purpose is to extend moral blame from deliberate acts to deliberate motives, and therefore from adulterous behavior to adulterous attitudes. The same extension is attributed to Jesus in the Sermon on the Mount, when he condemns lustful contemplation as itself an interior form of adultery. And in connection with the basically marital values that underlie the sixth and ninth commandments, it is important to observe one further way in which Jesus extends the significance of adultery. For in every one of the relevant Gospel texts, it is in terms of adultery that Jesus condemns divorce.

Although Jesus takes his stand against divorce in opposition to a long tradition of permissiveness (once again, limited to males), the basis of his stand is precisely the traditional importance assigned to marital fidelity. Jesus, therefore, appeals even beyond Moses to the intention of God himself, who created "man," "male and female," to be "two in one flesh"— united by God's will, and therefore not to be parted by any mere human wilfulness.

There is, therefore, quite as much logic as rhetoric in Jesus' describing as an adulterer one who divorces his or her spouse. For the evil of adultery and the evil of divorce are here perceived to be the same evil, the evil of infidelity in a human relationship intended by the creator of the sexes to be a paragon of fidelity. And it is precisely as a paragon of fidelity that marriage assumes in Christian theology its sacramental significance, as symbolizing the relationship of indissoluble love that joins Christ to his Church.

YOU SHALL NOT STEAL

The tendency, in interpreting the ten commandments, continually to broaden their scope of application over the course of time is strikingly illustrated by the seventh commandment. For one thing, the verb steal is a more exact rendering of the Hebrew than we generally suspect. For, as we are reminded by the related noun, stealth, stealing does not imply simply wrongful appropriation, but wrongful appropriation accomplished sneakingly, secretly, or deceptively. The same is true of the biblical wording of this commandment in Hebrew. More than that, however, modern biblical scholarship has found good reason to suppose that in its original form the commandment not to steal referred to a very special kind of stealing, namely the stealing not of things, but of persons, or what we might call kidnapping. That one of the commandments should have been directed specifically against the stealing of people may seem by our standards impractical or suggestive of highly primitive social conditions. Nevertheless, as soon as one recalls the vast slave-trade in which this country was so deeply involved little more than a century ago, and the immensity of moral and physical evil that has derived from it, even the most primitive meaning of the seventh commandment may seem to take on more than a little contemporary relevance. And to observe how frequently our news headlines report the taking or holding of hostages may bring that ancient moral imperative even closer to home.

Even within quite ancient times in Israel, the understanding of this commandment was spontaneously extended to include the whole range of what we might categorize as dishonest appropriation. Nevertheless, the implication of secrecy, or subterfuge, in both the English word steal and its Hebrew equivalent, points to a prominent feature of the kind of misappropriation that is most conspicuous in biblical moralizing. For in biblical times, as in our own, it was not by the undisguised violence of banditry that most morally wrongful appropriation was accomplished. Most of what the religious moralists of the Bible condemned as equivalent to stealing was behavior that, from a different and more widely shared point of view, was judged to be simply good business, shrewd commercial dealing. This becomes especially evident from the time when the great prophets assumed their extraordinary role as spokesmen for God to the social conscience of his people.

Archaeologists have pointed out that excavations of ancient Palestinian towns exhibit striking features dating from that same period which heard the beginning of a sustained prophetic outcry for social justice. Remains of town dwellings from before the eighth century B.C. show them to have been generally quite similar in size and arrangement, whereas in the eighth century ruins one perceives clear separation between the variously elegant houses of the rich and the far more numerous, densely clustered hovels of the poor. The period in which this revolution in urban housing patterns occurred is known also to have been a period when unprecedented wealth flowed into Israel. The Israel of the early prophets was not poorer, but far richer than the Israel of earlier times. And yet the number and proportion of grievously impoverished people had outrageously increased. The land of the prophets had, like our own land, a problem of grave poverty that was caused not by a lack of wealth but by a lack of something very different that the prophets ceaselessly called for—justice and mercy.

The prophetic writings, with their tone of moral outrage, are so rich in concrete imagery that the situation they describe is unmistakable. Alongside the wretched orphans and helpless widows they depict the wives of the elders and officers of God's people, and angrily anticipate the day when a just God will strip them of all their lavish self-adornments and let them experience the humiliation their greed has inflicted upon others. Beside the cluttered slums they set the smug accomplishments of land-grabbing realtors who exploit the misery of debtors to expand their holdings. They bring us to the marketplace where complacent merchants and bankers conspire to disguise the badness of wares, ingeniously short-change customers who have no shrewdness in such matters, and set the prices highest where the needs are greatest. The prophet Amos sums up the moral atmosphere of contemporary commerce in a satirical reconstruction of the Saturday night musings of a grain-merchant: "When will the sabbath be past so that we may open our wheat again, giving short measure in the bushel and taking overweight in the silver, tilting the scales fraudulently, and selling the dust of the wheat; that we may buy the poor for silver and the destitute for a pair of shoes?"

Misappropriation meant for the prophets making one's own what justice and mercy, not mere legality, would require us to leave for another. Stealing means dissimulated or disguised misappropriation. And throughout most of civilized history, the most popular and effective disguises found for such misappropriation have been various forms of business arrangement. The motive for such arrangements, the motive for so much of the world's most feverish activity, is precisely what the tenth commandment, completing the seventh, forbids. It is interesting to try to imagine what business would be like among people who actually obeyed the tenth commandment!

YOU SHALL NOT BEAR FALSE WITNESS

It is characteristic of human lives to be guided not simply by natural forces and instinctive reactions, but by intellectual convictions. There are, however, different kinds of intellectual convictions, and on one kind we depend far more heavily than on any other. That is the kind of intellectual conviction known as belief. Beliefs are mental principles that we hold, not because we have confirmed them by any carefully controlled experiment or concluded them from any rigorously logical argument, but merely because somebody has assured us that they correspond to reality. Usually, the somebody who assures us has derived his own conviction in much the same way from somebody else's assurance. And if one were to track down such chains of belief, many of them would extend very far indeed before reaching a point where they originated in anything resembling an experimental or logical proof. However earnestly we cultivate a supposedly healthy scepticism, and however resolutely we try to ascertain important judgments for ourselves, we are all absolutely compelled, for nearly all the practical activities of a normal human life, to rely not on demonstration, but on simple faith.

Merely to drink one's morning beverage in the serene assumption that the cup contains coffee and not cyanide is to make an implicit act of faith in all sorts of people, most of whom one has never even heard of. There is simply no alternative, short of personally recapitulating the entire history of analytic chemistry. And long before we could apply such a process to verifying the nontoxic character of our simplest meals, we should inevitably perish of starvation. And it is the same with nearly everything of fundamental importance in our lives. From beginning to end, human lives proceed very little by steps of logic, and very largely by leaps of faith. To do otherwise would be fatal, and to try to do otherwise would be madness.

In all these leaps of faith, our belief that something is true is founded on a more basic belief that someone is truthful. The only thing that keeps the most basic activities of our lives from coming to a bewildered and terrified halt is a trait of elementary sanity that depends completely on an aspect of elementary social morality. The context of that morality is the almost constant interaction that society demands between believers and believed. That interaction depends on two indispensable virtues, called trust and truthfulness, or faith and credibility.

Where either of those virtues is generally lacking, society is impossible, and if either of them were totally lacking, life itself would be impossible. Of all the ominous clichés that have found their way into our modern idiom, none perhaps has more terrible implications than the popular phrase, credibility-gap. For a credibility gap is a tear in the most basic fabric of society. The society in which such gaps are permitted to multiply is irrevocably doomed. To watch the widening of such gaps in any society, a business, a friendship, a family, a nation, or a church, is to observe the progress of an absolutely lethal disease.

Within political society, the last stand of trust and truthfulness is taken in the law court. Here society's demand for "the truth, the whole truth, and nothing but the truth," motivated by society's need for justice, is imposed most solemnly and publicly. A case at law is an emergency. It implies that all simpler, more private appeals for honesty have failed. We recall St. Paul's horror that Christians could ever reach the point of confronting one another as adversaries in a secular law-court. If, even at this point, credibility gaps cannot be bridged, political society verges on chaos.

In the society that formulated the ten commandments all this was well understood. There was no distinction between secular and sacred society, and a courtroom witness was enjoined to tell the truth in the presence of God and God's people. An oath, which still lingers among us as a legal formality, was imposed to remind the witness that God would judge him by his truthfulness. It was to this situation that the eighth commandment chiefly pertained, as a warning against that ultimate credibility gap that a just society cannot survive. And it was implicitly a warning against all those antecedent credibility gaps without which courtroom proceedings would be unnecessary. For the way to court is always thickly strewn with infidelities and insincerities, distrust and untruthfulness.

Jesus who died for our sins, died also by our sins and among our sins, and in the stories of his Passion the air is thick with the poison of false witness and the sickness of unbelief. "The chief priests and the whole council sought testimony against Jesus to put him to death." "Many bore false witness against him, and their witness did not agree." "Why do we still need witnesses?" asks, in vicious hypocrisy, the priest. "What is truth?" muses, in pompous futility, the judge. "I do not know the man," swears, in pathetic timidity, the disciple. For a human society that could not stop short of lethal perjury, Christ died.

STUDY QUESTIONS

1. What natural motivation normally reinforces the commandment to honor one's parents?

2. To what extent is the commandment to honor one's parents independent of spontaneous motivation?

3. What promise is attached in the Bible to the commandment of honoring one's parents?

4. What ordinary social wisdom may this promise express?

5. What seems to have been the original idea underlying the prohibition of killing?

6. How does Jesus' teaching modify the understanding of the prohibition of killing?

7. What distinctive evaluation of life in general is evidenced in the Bible?

8. How is the understanding of adultery in the Old Testament related to the social status of the sexes?

9. What considerations seem to have influenced the Old Testament's strong condemnation of adultery?

10. How has the ninth commandment come to be understood in relation to the sixth commandment?

11. How can one account for Jesus' condemnation of divorce as equivalent to adultery?

12. What seems to have been referred to originally by the prohibition of stealing?

13. How does ordinary commercial enterprise become morally equivalent to stealing?

14. What social conditions were related to the prophets' pleas for mercy and justice?

15. What in general are beliefs and how significant are they in ordinary affairs of life?

16. What virtue is presupposed by trust, and what results socially from the absence of that virtue?

17. Why is truthfulness especially crucial in the context of the law court?

18. What is the traditional significance of the oath used in courts of law?

19. Of the commandments dealt with in this chapter, which did you discover in a new way? How?

Chapter Seven

JESUS AS AN ETHICAL TEACHER

BEGINNING WITH THE GOSPELS

One of the major intellectual developments in modern Christianity is what has been called the quest for the historical Jesus: the attempt by scholars to distinguish Jesus as he actually was from the interpretative accounts of Jesus set down in writing after his death. The project has relevance for the student of religious ethics inasmuch as it would obviously be of great interest to be better informed than we are concerning the ethical components of Jesus' own original statements. Still, it is evident that a reasonable understanding of Christian ethics is not something one must postpone until the quest for the historical Jesus has been pursued to its practical limits. For Christian ethics, as a tradition, is itself an historical reality. The written records of that tradition lead back in time to the New Testament. The New Testament, when examined critically, points back to previous documents, and oral traditions, which were expressions of earlier stages in that same tradition. And of course all of this points still farther back, to

Jesus of Nazareth, in whose words and deeds the tradition had its original basis and impetus.

Practically speaking, Christian ethical tradition has looked back, at every stage, to the Gospels as to an ultimate reference point. Nor was this merely because of an incorrect assumption that the Gospels are older than any other New Testament literature. It is rather because the Gospels seem to bring the reader closer than does anything else to Jesus Christ. And it is to Jesus as presented in the Gospels that most people have responded, over the past twenty centuries, with the faith that makes Christians and leads them to adopt a way of life that includes a distinctive ethical orientation. Thus in our earliest post-biblical Christian literature we find ethical teachings referred most frequently to the Gospels—because of their concrete presentation of Jesus—and especially to that Gospel material in which Jesus is presented most conspicuously as a moral teacher. We find a primary preference in this regard for the Gospel according to Matthew, and a secondary one for the Gospel according to Luke, both of whom add a great deal of ethical material to the Gospel according to Mark, most of whose other contents they reproduce. Within the Gospel according to Matthew, the Sermon on the Mount was esteemed from very early Christian times as a unique distillation of distinctively Christian ethics.

CALL FOR REPENTANCE AND ETHICAL PRESUMPTIONS

Two of the Gospels cite the beginning of Jesus' preaching in essentially the same words, calling upon his hearers to repent, because the kingdom of God (or kingdom of heaven) is at hand. The word usually translated "repent" is sometimes rendered as "reform your lives," which is more precisely what the word means. What the phrase calls for is not regret over a misspent past, but decisive personal reform, in the present and for the future. This repentance or reform is not solely an interior transformation, but a change in the whole pattern of one's external living. We are reminded of this by the Gospel according to Luke, in which John the Baptist, whose initial message is the same as that of Jesus, goes on to demand of his hearers "fruits that befit repentance," or, as we might say, appropriate results. Moreover, John leaves no doubt about the practical seriousness of repentance when he goes on to cite examples of what he means, such as sharing one's possessions with the poor, and refraining from the kinds of fraud and violence that certain stations in life make both easy and profitable.

One of the things to be noted about the passages in which Jesus, like John, begins his preaching career with a call for repentance, is that they obviously presuppose that people understood what repentance was all about. And to presuppose that is obviously to presuppose that they had valid ideas about morality. One does not start out by telling people to reform their lives if one has come to teach them the abc's of ethics. The initial call for repentance implies that, as far as Jesus was concerned, the people were not ethically ignorant even though they were ethically remiss. Hence the Gospel excludes from the outset any notion that Jesus came to teach ethics to people who either knew nothing about it or had it all wrong. It also excludes from the outset any notion that Jesus was indifferent to whether or not people fulfilled their moral obligations. By the call to repentance, Jesus is telling the people to live up to ethical standards of which he knows them to be aware, but also knows them to be negligent. Leaving aside for the present the question of whether or not Jesus teaches any ethics of his own, it is evident from passages like these that he takes a certain amount of ethics for granted, and insists on people's living up to it.

REPENTANCE AND THE KINGDOM

The same passages also call our attention to something of the utmost importance to Jesus' ethical preaching, and therefore fundamental to all of Christian ethics. Jesus calls for moral reform for the specific reason that the Kingdom of God is at hand. And anyone who reads the Gospels even casually must be aware of how constant and emphatic a refrain is this announcement of the Kingdom of God in Jesus' preaching. It should be pointed out that the meaning of the word here translated Kingdom has two aspects, only one of which comes across in that English rendering. It means not only the realm of God, but also the reign of God: that is, not only whom or what God rules, but also the effectiveness of God's actually exercising his rule. Hence the Kingdom means God's subjects being ruled totally by God. And the coming of the Kingdom means the coming about of that state of affairs.

Consequently, the announcement of the Kingdom's coming has a twofold import. First, it is a message of hope and reassurance for those who are loyal to God. For it means to them that the God who loves them is to take complete, immediate charge of those he loves. It means they shall not always be left to endure the tribulations of a perilous world, and suffer the abuses and negligences of their fellow human beings. But the message is also, and by the same token, one of dire warning for those who are disloyal to God. For the complete exercise of God's reign can only be real if it entails the complete exclusion of all who resist that reign. Given human freedom, resistance remains possible. But given divine sovereignty, resistance is doomed to defeat. Therefore the call to repentance is a call for God's enemies to become his friends, for the rebels to resume loyalty, for usurpers of divine prerogatives to acknowledge divine Lordship. But, as the Gospel narratives proceed, it becomes ever clearer that even the message to God's enemies, warning though it is, is itself a message of hope and reassurance. For we find again and again the insistence that even to those who behave as God's enemies, God himself remains a friend, constantly ready to forgive, ever intent upon reconciliation.

But this account of the meaning of the Kingdom's coming must be qualified in one very important respect. For the way it has been described thus far, for simplicity's sake, can introduce a serious oversimplification. That is, by referring to the real world of human beings as comprising those who are loyal and those who are disloyal to God, one may be led to forget that both loyalty and disloyalty exist not only among human beings collectively, but also within human beings individually. Individuals are not simply loyal or disloyal, they are loyal and disloyal, loyal in one way but disloyal in another, loyal at one time but disloyal at another. And so we find another characteristic theme as the Gospel narratives proceed: the constant assault of Jesus on moral complacency based on delusions of self-righteousness. The call to repentance meets its gravest obstacle precisely in those who assume it is not directed to them. Hence Jesus' severe polemics against proud self-approbation, and his relentless probing of hypocritical pretenses.

LAW AND LEGALISM

Since Jesus was a Jew, preaching to Jews, his references to the coming of God's complete control over his people naturally employed the terminology in which Jews habitually expressed such ideas. And as our brief discussion of Old Testament background indicated, such was the terminology that represents God as a king over his people. And such terminology leads naturally to the closely related idea of God's law, as the outward manifestation of the ruler's will, and therefore the objective standard of his people's obedience. Consequently, any traditional Jew spontaneously translated a divine call for repentance into a divine summons to obey God's law. To say that one must repent, and to imply at the same time that one might ignore the law would be not merely offensive to Jews, it would be unintelligible to them. Nor is there the slightest evidence that Jesus ever did say or imply anything of the kind. And yet it remains unmistakable to a reader of the Gospels that Jesus' attitude towards the law occasioned perplexity and controversy.

In order to understand this apparent ambiguity, it is

necessary to recall both what the law was and how it came to be viewed. It was the attempt of religiously inspired human beings to express in their human words how a life should be lived in grateful devotion to God. Like all attempts to deal with God in human thoughts and words, it was always inadequate. From the very start it had drawn on the moral and legal traditions of other, more ancient and more cultivated peoples, and attempted to select and organize elements of that wisdom in conformity with the unique religious experience of Israel. Such sacred summaries as the Decalogues were the products of gradually developed understanding, over the course of constantly changing experience. But even when the wording of such summaries became fixed, the understanding and practical application of them continued to develop. And it was always perceived that problems arose which could find no easy solution by simple inference from written traditions. As new solutions to new problems gained approval and authority, the written traditions were expanded to include them. Much of this expansion of the law can be perceived in the pages of the Old Testament. Much more of it is recorded outside the Bible.

JESUS FOR AND AGAINST THE LAW

The main trouble that commonly results from this expansion of law into increasingly detailed stipulations has been given the name of legalism. In the making of law, legalism is chiefly manifested as an attempt to formulate general regulations for every conceivable moral choice. In the obeying of law, legalism is chiefly manifested as an attempt to determine every moral choice on the basis of existing regulations. In either case, legal formulations increasingly dominate moral perspective, limit moral options, and replace moral insight. Law thus tends to become an end in itself, rather than a means to an end. And when this happens, law can easily frustrate the very purposes that brought it into being.

Thus we find in the Jesus of the Gospels both an insistence on respecting the law and a refusal to absolutize it. Although there were fanatical legalists among the rabbis of his day, many others tried conscientiously to interpret the law in humane and reasonable ways. Yet we find Jesus on more than one occasion doing what most rabbis could only call setting aside the law. Thus, it was commonly taught that the law forbade working on the Sabbath, and since medical treatment was work, it too was forbidden. Nevertheless, exceptions were made for what we might call emergency cases, conditions urgently requiring immediate treatment. But Jesus, in curing a paralytic on the Sabbath was, after all, doing something that could certainly be postponed for a few hours without notable harm. And in his refusal to wait, Jesus did indeed set aside the law, in the conviction that performing an act of mercy was simply more important than following the Sabbath regulation. His saying on a similar occasion that the Sabbath was made for man, not man for the Sabbath, typifies his steady refusal to allow law to defeat its own purposes. Nor did Jesus limit himself to ignoring certain prescriptions of the law in certain special cases. There were aspects of the law he simply denounced and rejected, as for example the law of equal retaliation expressed in the maxim, "an eye for an eye and a tooth for a tooth."

Nothing is more instructive for understanding how the Gospels present Jesus' attitude towards the law than its remarkable freedom from bias. That is, one cannot find in the Jesus of the Gospels an habitual tendency to either tighten or loosen the law's requirements. Sometimes he does one and sometimes the other. Among the rabbis of his time, in dealing with the law, some were notoriously liberal and others were notoriously conservative. Jesus, as he is described to us, was neither the one nor the other. Of Jesus' critical approach to the law, as represented in the Gospels, nothing is more characteristic than its many-sidedness.

The same Jesus who regarded the law of retaliation as too severe, regarded the law of divorce, even in its strictest interpretation, as too lax. The same Jesus who thought the law against Sabbath violation went too far, thought the law against homicide did not go far enough. The same Jesus who was willing to dispense with occasional oaths, was unwilling to dispense with habitual veracity.

Jesus certainly did not habitually deride or disdain the law. But he certainly did treat it as imperfect, and as imperfectly consistent with even its own basic inspiration. To maintain that Jesus had no respect for the law disregards the evidence of the Gospels. But the Gospels offer abundant evidence that Jesus' respect for the law was by no means uncritical.

STUDY QUESTIONS

1. What is the quest for the historical Jesus and how important is it for Christian ethics?

2. To what biblical writings have the main traditions of Christian ethics principally referred?

3. What is the basic idea of repentance as called for in the Gospels?

4. What practical illustrations of repentance are furnished by a Gospel account of John the Baptist's teaching?

5. What does the call for repentance imply concerning the uniqueness and originality of New Testament ethics?

6. What special reason for repentance is characteristically cited from Jesus' preaching?

7. What are two basic aspects of what is referred to as the kingdom of God?

8. What twofold import does the announcement of the kingdom's coming have for Jesus' heavens?

9. In what sense does the coming of the kingdom imply an urgent requirement of repentance?

10. What moral disposition is especially assailed in the Gospels as incompatible with the needed repentance?

11. How does reference to the kingdom lead naturally to considerations of law?

12. What complications are evident in the Gospel accounts of Jesus' attitude toward the Jewish law?

13. What, practically speaking, was the law of the Jews supposed to be?

14. In what sense was the law not a fixed body of definite regulations established once and for all?

15. What is meant by legalism and how does it tend to come about?

16. What is wrong with legalism from a religious point of view and how is Jesus represented as reacting to it?

17. Is Jesus described in the Gospels as habitually relaxing or intensifying the demands of the law?

18. What does Jesus' stand regarding law have to teach us?

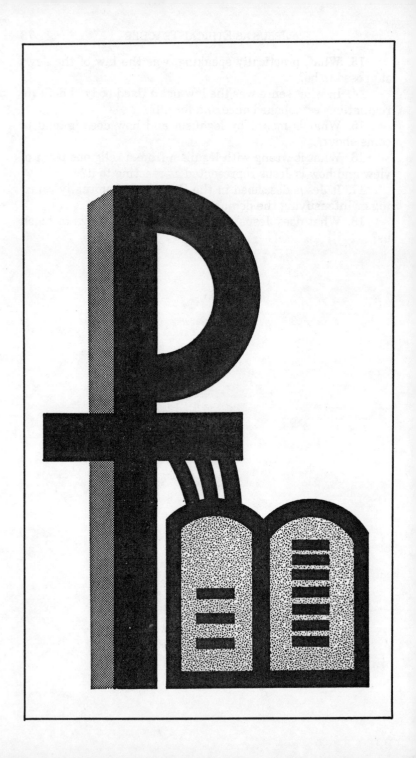

Chapter Eight

JESUS' SUMMATION OF THE LAW

SERMON ON THE MOUNT

Although ethical teachings of various kinds can be found in many different parts of the Gospels, one part of one of the Gospels has always been thought of by Christians as a kind of distillation of the kind of moral teaching uniquely characteristic of Jesus. Just as the Ten Commandments are thought of as epitomizing the basic moral outlook of the Old Testament, so in the New Testament, the Sermon on the Mount has always had a similar status. And indeed, to suggest such an analogy is evidently intended by the Gospel according to Matthew. For a comparison with the other Gospels leaves little doubt that these three famous chapters have put together as a single discourse teachings attributed to Jesus which originated in a variety of different contexts. In other words, originally scattered teachings have here been organized into an artificial literary unit for the convenience and instruction of readers.

The very setting in which this synthetic "sermon" is placed suggests a parallel between the great law-giver Moses on Mount Sinai and Jesus, delivering moral pronouncements from a hilltop where, it is noted, he taught as one having authority, and thus quite differently from contemporary rabbis. Implicit in this parallel is the idea of a new law delivered by God through a new Moses, thus suggesting the idea of a new convenant which did, of course, take firm hold in Christian thinking.

Such ideas, however, naturally raise a question of whether or not this new law is intended precisely to supersede, and consequently abolish, its Mosaic predecessor. Affirmative answers to that question have often been given, especially in the light of St. Paul's strongly-worded statements of opposition between the demands of the Jewish law and the meaning of Christian faith. But to use Paul indiscriminately as a guide to the Gospel's intentions is a dubiously sound practice, and if one takes the Sermon on the Mount according to its own terms, such an interpretation becomes hard to sustain. Indeed the interpretation seems to be anticipated and rejected in the lengthy passage that begins with Jesus' warning not to suppose that he has come to abolish the law and the Prophets, and proceeds to condemn, in terms of final judgment, even minor detractions from the law's scope of obligation. And significantly the passage concludes with a demand that the hearers be far better than the Pharisees and teachers of the law.

Since this demand to excel the Pharisees immediately follows a passage of emphatic insistence on keeping the law, it seems implausible to infer, as some have done, that being better than the Pharisees means being unconstrained by the Pharisees' typical diligence about the law. Somehow, therefore, this passage must conceive the surpassing of the Pharisees in such a way as to commend rather than discredit conscientiousness in observing the law. Some indication of what this conception might entail is furnished by the passage that immediately follows.

INTENSIFICATION OF THE LAW

The basic structure of this passage is provided by a series of six contrasts, drawn by Jesus, between that which is identified as ancestral teaching and what he puts forth as his own doctrine. The development of some of these contrasts occasions the introduction of other, loosely related material, which somewhat disrupts the continuity of the passage as a whole. Within the basic structure, Jesus' hearers are reminded of six traditional moral teachings, all pertaining to the Old Testament, and two of which are explicit in the Ten Commandments. The first five are prohibitions of murder, adultery, divorce without a document of release, perjury, and immoderate vengeance. The sixth is a positive injunction, to love one's neighbor and hate one's enemy.

In dealing with these moral doctrines, Jesus neither rejects nor mitigates any one of them. Rather in each case his own teaching is basically harmonious but decidedly more demanding. Thus he condemns not merely murder and adultery, but their inner roots of malevolence and lasciviousness. He does not merely oppose inconsiderate divorce procedure but, appealing beyond Moses to the creative plan of God himself, he flatly condemns divorce itself. Instead of denouncing the telling of lies under oath, he denounces insincere speech of any kind, and rejects the whole system of oaths which furnished pretexts for insincerity. Instead of disproportionate retaliation, Jesus condemns all violent resistance to injury. Although the commandment to love one's neighbor is found in the law, the commandment to hate one's enemy is not, and its addition may represent an ironic statement, consistent with the parable of the Samaritan, of what loving one's neighbor had come to mean in actual practice. In any case, what Jesus calls for, and identifies with behavior suitable for children of God, is the extension of love precisely to those who are most alien and even hostile.

Throughout this entire passage of the Sermon on the

Mount, we find that Jesus' response to statements of the law is never a simple yes or no, but always a "yes, but ... " which he proceeds to elaborate. Jesus restates the law, in instance after instance, in ways that, while preserving its positive exigencies, probe the depths of its motivation, and stretch the limits of its application. In a phrase which has gained currency, Jesus radicalizes the law, that is to say, he gets to the roots of its validity. It is in this radicalizing, this insistence on getting beyond superficial matters of external conformity to the very heart of the law's matter, that Christian tradition has understood the meaning of Jesus' requirement to be better than the Pharisees and teachers of the law.

In much of the rest of the Sermon on the Mount, we find Jesus vigorously denouncing the cruder manifestations of a kind of religious ethics in which such radicalizing has little or no part. It is a religious ethics essentially devoid of inner depth: so exclusively preoccupied with external conformity, and so fully satisfied with outward appearances, that virtue becomes indistinguishable from pious ostentation, and the cultivation of perfection degenerates into an art of hypocrisy.

Whatever else the New Testament may contain relative to the law of the Old Testament, and that best-known part of it we call the Ten Commandments, what the Sermon on the Mount chiefly implies in this connection is a solemn warning. It warns about what happens when any formulation of what is believed to be God's law is allowed to eclipse God himself, when legal terms of the covenant displace from people's minds the very meaning of the covenant, and when living within the letter of the law replaces the goal of living as children of a Heavenly Father.

THE RULE OF LOVE

Anyone who has even slight acquaintance with the ethical teaching attributed to Jesus in the Gospels can be expected to know, however vaguely or inexactly, that its characteristic predominant stress is on love. And people who recall even one relevant passage will usually cite some version of the twofold commandment, to love God with all one's heart, mind, and strength, and to love one's neighbor as oneself. We find this passage presented in the Gospels as a summation of God's law. Both parts of this double formula exist separately in the Old Testament, and although only Jesus is known to have combined them in this way, insisting that the second part is "like" the first, the idea that love is basic to religious morality was by no means unknown to Jewish rabbis.

Although there can be no doubt that the love of God was the central motif of Jesus' own life, and of the kind of life proposed to his followers, it is the love of neighbor that is dealt with most reflectively in the Gospels. Part of the reason for this is related to Jesus' characteristic insistence that failing in the love of neighbor inevitably entails failing in the love of God. Part of the reason also is because loving one's neighbor is something very easily and very frequently misunderstood. Hence in the teachings attributed to Jesus, we find not only insistence on loving one's neighbor, but deliberate elucidation of what this means. Considered logically, misunderstandings of what it means to love one's neighbor have two basic possibilities. That is, one might misunderstand the meaning of either of the two basic terms: the meaning of love, or the meaning of neighbor.

Loving means all sorts of things to us, and many of them have nothing at all to do with what Jesus had in mind. Clearly he was not calling for any warm glow of affection or for amatory raptures. He was not asking anyone to fall in love with anyone else. This is evident in all his examples, which have nothing to do with eroticism or even with what we normally mean by friendship. Friendships and love affairs are special events in anyone's life. They cannot be sustained indefinitely nor can they be generated at will. Neither can they be extended universally. To wish always to be everyone's friend or lover would be an absurd wish and a futile policy. And yet what Jesus is calling for in the name of love is clearly a policy, and not a relatively rare and fortuitous social experience.

From that point of view, Christian tradition has frequently interpreted love as benevolence. But if we take benevolence in its literal sense as wishing well, there is clearly more to it than that. For wishing is a weak word, which we often apply to completely ineffectual and impractical attitudes of mind. Christian benevolence, on the other hand, is essentially practical. It is wishing well, in the sense that it is a willing or wanting the neighbor to be well in such a way that it tries habitually to contribute to well-being. Thus benevolence, in the Christian sense, is linked inseparably to beneficence, as will is linked to effort.

The same idea of love is indicated by the simple criterion Jesus furnishes of how one is to love one's neighbor, namely, as oneself. Normal people do not love themselves passionately. But they do love themselves habitually and practically. And they manifest their habitual, practical self-love by their constant alertness to what they judge to be their own best interests. The cynical designation of the self as "number one" aptly conveys the crude experience of self-love as the tendency to give oneself top priority in all conflicts of interests. Jesus does not extol self-love as a virtue nor does he denounce it as a vice. Rather he perceives it as a familiar fact of life, and uses that familiar fact to indicate what love of neighbor actually means: taking the interests of others as seriously to heart as one takes one's own interest.

The problem of misunderstanding neighbor is related to the fact of self-love. Most people perceive themselves as so closely bound to certain other people that they spontaneously extend to those people something of their own self-love. Friends and lovers are thought of as so complementary to the self that loving them partakes of the spontaneity of self-love. Thus love is naturally extended to "one's own," although who are actually included in this highly personal category varies from case to case. But always, outside the circle of "one's own," no matter how large it may be, there are "the others." These others are either strangers to whom one is indifferent, or enemies to whom one is hostile.

An extraordinary amount of what the Gospels tell us of Jesus' words and deeds represents a concerted attack on loving "one's own," while excluding from love "the others," the strangers and the enemies, however identified. Jesus' own notorious intimacy with disreputable categories of people is central to the drama of the Gospel narrative. Moreover, Jesus teaches that this conduct of his reflects the kind of love that is God's own. And he is insistent that this divine standard of non-exclusive, or all-inclusive love is to characterize the behavior of his followers.

JESUS ON PARTICULAR MORAL QUESTIONS

To look to the Gospels for any detailed presentation of Jesus' teaching on a complete catalogue of ethical issues is a disappointing enterprise, and a foolish one. In any time and place such issues are innumerable, and with changing circumstances they are altered and multiplied endlessly. It is of course true that certain broad issues persist, and that in the course of time traditional moral wisdom develops certain broadly valid approaches to them. But, as already noted, Jesus himself was heir to a very rich tradition of religious morality, and his basic respect for and frequent recourse to that tradition is manifest. Nevertheless, in his time, and in the later time and different circumstances in which the Gospels were written, as in our own time, there were particular problems that attracted particular attention and elicited various opinions. We find Jesus dealing directly with a very few such problems, and indirectly with a few more.

Thus Jesus was presented with the question of divorce, hotly debated between liberal and conservative schools of rabbinic thought. The main force of Jesus' response, which appears in all accounts despite their variations in detail, is a resounding condemnation of divorce as contrary to the will of God. We find him faced with the moral implications of riches and poverty, and emphatic in his warnings about the corruptive influence of wealth and the pursuit of wealth. Questions of political morality were bitter in enemy-occupied Palestine, but Jesus is portrayed as refusing either to adopt a revolutionary ideology or to hold any brief for imperial establishment. In another context, we have already alluded to several particular instances of Jesus' impatience with certain applications of rabbinical legalism.

From the Gospel accounts of Jesus' dealings with these and other particular ethical issues, there is much to be learned. But nothing could be clearer than that such dealings were incidental to his ministry, and occurred only randomly in the course of it. In the background of Jesus' ethics is the law of God as expressed in the traditions of his people. And in the foreground, as the constant pattern of his life and the persistent motif of his teaching, is the all-encompassing love of the Father, given as a life to be lived by his children.

STUDY QUESTIONS

1. What section of the Gospels has been most referred to as epitomizing Jesus' ethical outlook?
2. How does the setting of the Sermon on the Mount suggest a parallelism between Jesus and Moses?
3. What interpretation of Jesus' attitude toward the Jewish law has often been based on St. Paul?
4. What interpretation of Jesus' attitude toward the Jewish law is suggested by the Sermon on the Mount?
5. What contrasts appear in the Sermon on the Mount between Jesus' demands and those of the Mosaic law?
6. What is meant by saying that in the Sermon on the Mount Jesus tends to radicalize the law?
7. What are some features of Jewish religious morality that Jesus denounces in the Sermon on the Mount?
8. Against what abuse of the law does the Sermon on the Mount typically warn?

9. What is the characteristic positive emphasis of Jesus' moral teaching as presented in the Gospels?

10. What classic summation of Jesus' understanding of the moral law is derived from the Gospels?

11. What aspects of the commandment to love one's neighbor are especially open to misunderstanding?

12. How are such misunderstandings counteracted by Jesus' teaching in the Gospels?

13. How is love of neighbor characteristically interpreted in Christian ethical tradition?

14. What clarification is introduced by the idea of loving one's neighbor as oneself?

15. What understanding of neighbor do the Gospels tend to reject as too limited and how do they correct it?

16. To what extent do the Gospels represent Jesus as giving explicit instructions for specific moral issues?

17. What are some specific moral issues that Jesus is represented as treating and how does he deal with them?

18. Do you think that Jesus should have given detailed prescriptions on specific ethical issues? Why or why not?

Chapter Nine

NEW TESTAMENT PERSPECTIVES ON ETHICS

THE NEW LIFE AND THE OLD LAW

Although Paul's writings are older than the first three Gospels, they are of course dependent on oral and written traditions about Jesus like those on which the Gospels are based. However, the Gospels present Jesus' ethical teaching as part of a narrative which reaches its climax and reveals its deepest significance only at the end, with the account of the crucifixion and resurrection. Thus whereas in the Gospel the events of Holy Week are recounted only after the ethical material has been presented, Paul explicitly presupposes those events. Accordingly, Paul's ethical material is characteristically introduced after he has declared God's saving action in Jesus Christ. For Paul the Christian's moral life is part of that transformed life which has become reality precisely because Christ died for our sins, and because the saving power that raised him from the dead enables all those for whom he died to triumph over sin and death.

To accept this revelation of divine mercy with joy and confidence, allowing it to take possession of one's whole being and reshape one's whole manner of life is what Paul means by faith. From this faith everything else follows. Hope follows from it in virtue of the confidence that what God's mercy has begun in Christ will be brought to completion in all those who belong to Christ. To live on the basis of this faith and in the prospect of this hope is the essence of what in Paul's teaching might be called general religious ethics. And the distinctive quality of such a life, for Paul as for Jesus the keynote of Christian ethics, is love.

For Paul as for Jesus, this love is not simply a human duty which God imposes. Rather it is a divine gift which human beings receive and, having received it, manifest. God is the original example and the original source of love. It is made uniquely visible and uniquely effective in the life, death, and resurrection of Jesus Christ. And in virtue of its effectiveness it becomes intimately part of the lives of those who accept God's gift. From an ethical point of view, love precisely is the new life of a humanity united with God through faith in Christ. The Gospels presented Jesus at the outset of his mission as declaring that the kingdom of God is at hand. Paul, regarding Jesus' mission as accomplished, declares that the kingdom of God is among us. And from an ethical point of view that present kingdom of God is the reign of God's love in human lives.

Paul's favorite way of expressing the participation of human lives in the life of God is by reference to the Holy Spirit. Spirit is, in general, the principle of life and of the actions that give expression to life. The Holy Spirit, God's Spirit, is the principle of divine life and of divine action. That Spirit that was so plainly and powerfully in Christ, is to be given by God to Christ's followers. In them as in Christ it is to be the principle of a new life, reshaped to conformity with God's own life, fashioning lives of Godlike, Christlike love.

Paul, like Jesus, leaves no doubt that the love he refers to is no mere stirring of emotion or partiality of affection. In a famous passage he describes a love that is, in the first place, patient and kind. It is not jealous, boastful, arrogant, rude, obstinate, irritable, or resentful. Its joy is in what is right, never in what is wrong. And, like Jesus, Paul tests the authenticity of this love by its all-inclusiveness, extending beyond the comfortable circle of friends, reaching out to the strangers and the enemies. And always for Paul there is one vivid point whereby the character of this love is displayed—the cross of Jesus Christ, who was obedient unto death and died for his enemies.

One element of Paul's teaching has caused considerable confusion about his ethics. That is his denunciation of the idea that the law of the Jews is the essential means of salvation, and his contrary emphasis on the primacy of faith. Conscious of his mission to the non-Jewish world, Paul struggled long and bitterly against acceptance of the belief that Christianity presupposed, even in the cases of Gentiles, a prior commitment to Judaism. In the heat of this debate, passages occur which, taken by themselves, might seem to reject the whole value of obeying God's law in favor of simply affirming the sufficiency of faith. But it must be remembered that for Paul faith is not a mere assent of the mind to a divinely revealed truth. It is a dedication of the whole person to embracing God's gift as a principle of total renewal. This renewal does not dispense with a religious ethics of obedience to God, but it puts it on a new basis. This is the basis of faith working through love, of putting on a new humanity, of living in the Spirit of God. And in Paul's letters to the new Christian communities there is no lack of insistence on the ethical commitment and moral strenuousness whereby faith works through love.

THE WORLD AND THE WORLD TO COME

Christians of the New Testament period thought of themselves as occupying the final and climactic chapter of human history. That chapter began with Jesus' coming as Savior. It would end with his coming as Judge. After that, God's reign would be inviolably and everlastingly complete. In the early years of Christianity, this final event was expected to happen very soon. With the passage of time, anticipation became more indefinite, but not less serious. And it was probably a common reflection then as later that, no matter how far off the world's end might be, death saw to it that the end of each individual's personal involvement in the world was never very far off. Consequently, it has often been noted that Christianity fostered a certain indifference to long-range worldly projects, which from a secular viewpoint might seem like lassitude. And at the same time, Christianity appealed for a concentration of humanity's limited time on living in a manner consistent with the reign of God. On both scores, there were undoubtedly exaggerations and fanaticisms among Christians, as well as among their worldly detractors.

Under the circumstances it was natural that there should develop among Christians, and especially among Christians who experienced secular hostility or secularizing corruptions, a sense of ultimate conflict with those for whom their faith had no reality. Thus we find, most conspicuously in the Gospel according to John, the idea of the world as an ungodly realm, wholly preoccupied with matters of no lasting value, and contemptuous of all that the reign of God was understood to mean. Put in still stronger terms, the world was Satan's realm, profoundly inimical to God and to the life of faith.

Ethically, this point of view had and continues to have complex implications. On the one hand, it fosters in Christians a precious freedom from secular ambitions and attendant anxieties that underlie so much of the meanness of the human condition. But on the other hand, it can also foster an indifference to worldly possibilities that greatly limits the practical scope of even the most authentically Christian ethics. For faith working through love in this world must do its work by the means this world affords. If despising the world leads to neglecting the means, love itself becomes stultified. Already in St. Paul, we hear ominous warnings against the idleness of Christians, whose unworldliness has become a pretext for irresponsibility that adds to the burdens of others. Thus from the very start, Christianity has had to seek a difficult balance, between a secularism of works without faith, and a quietism of faith without works.

Related to Christian preoccupation with the end of human history, and of individual human life, is another matter that has not been without effects on ethics. It is the matter of the opposite final destinies of the godly and the godless, the saved and the damned: the matter of heaven and hell. Despite the overwhelming emphasis of the New Testament on the good news of salvation, there has always been a tendency on the part of some Christians to focus on the darker implication of the Gospel. If salvation calls for faith, and faith is an exercise of human freedom, however much aided by grace, then faithlessness is a possibility and salvation is uncertain. To the extent that this possibility becomes a dominant consideration, hope is overshadowed by fear, and the force of the Gospel message itself is distorted into something basically threatening. Or, what is perhaps worse, the smug Christian finds a perverse vindictive satisfaction in anticipating the fate of those whom he considers his own enemies and God's as well. Thus certain elements present in the New Testament can be isolated and inflated to a point where they distort the whole central significance of the New Testament and pervert the whole character of a Christian life. Just as Christian belief has its heresies of thought, so too Christian ethics has its heresies of attitude and behavior. To accept the Gospel in faith is to respect its emphases and preserve its balance.

THE ETHICS OF A COMMUNITY AND A TRADITION

To preserve a balanced understanding of the Gospel has always been a task not simply imposed on individual Christians, but also assumed in their behalf by authorized teachers.

Some of the latter, as early as Paul himself, can be seen exercising that function within the pages of the New Testament. For in Christianity, the divinely assisted human teacher is the primary means of transmitting God's revelation, and even the New Testament itself is a product of such means. Moreover, since the Christian Gospel is rooted not in timeless abstractions, but in the historical events surrounding Jesus Christ and his mission, authentic teaching must of necessity be traditional teaching. Hence, in Christianity's earliest records we find both a recognition of authoritative teachers and a constant concern to insure the traditional authenticity of their teaching. This concern is made especially acute by the obvious necessity of communicating the Christian message intelligibly to a great variety of audiences, and of applying it practically to endlessly changing situations. This task of maintaining the Gospel's consistency without losing its adaptability was originally the task of apostles, evangelists, and prophets. With the development of a definite church organization, it became an important function of pastoral officials, most notably the bishops. And as Christianity's intellectual culture gained depth and complexity, the efforts of philosophers and theologians were applied to the same purpose.

Within Catholic tradition, there has always been a strong conviction that to interpret and apply the Gospel requires social and historical continuity. It requires reliable spokesmanship for the community of believers and the tradition of their belief. Not only is this conviction clearly evident in the New Testament, but so too is the development of its application. Thus in the so-called pastoral letters such as those addressed to Timothy, we find already a quite definite conception of official teachers, specially obligated by their position to exemplify and expound sound Christian doctrine and sound Christian morality, and specially assured of the Spirit's assistance in discharging this indispensable duty.

But publicly authorized teaching is not the only respect in

which the communal character of Christianity gives an uniquely social dimension to Christian ethics. For Christianity's understanding of its own communal nature goes far beyond what is normally understood as social communication. Thus in the New Testament we find frequent reference to a more profound connection between Christ and his followers, and among his followers themselves. The most striking expression of this idea is the way in which Paul likens that connection to the organic unity of a living body. A similar conception underlies the imagery of a vine and its branches in the Gospel according to John. Common to these figures of speech is the notion of a shared life, originating in Christ and animating all who believe in Christ. Such figures remind us that the principle of newness of life, the Holy Spirit, is shared but is not divided. Christian morality, as the outward living of this inner principle is always, therefore, communal, just as the vital functioning of one part of a living body is not isolated from the rest. Christian morality can no more be privatized than the Spirit of God can be privatized. The lives of Christians are complementary as the functioning of organic parts are complementary, and the consequences of how those lives are lived cannot be individually confined. As Paul summarizes, if one member suffers, all suffer together, and if one member is honored, all together rejoice.

STUDY QUESTIONS

1. Why does the relationship of moral teaching to Jesus' passion and resurrection appear different in Paul and in the Gospels?

2. What in general does Paul mean by faith and how is this related to hope, love, and Christian ethics generally?

3. In what sense does Paul present love as something other than a Christian duty or obligation?

4. How can the understanding of love be related to an understanding of the kingdom of God?

5. What relationship does the Holy Spirit have to Christian moral life?

6. How does Paul describe the concrete manifestations of Christian love?

7. How does Paul's understanding of faith influence Christian understanding of obedience to God's law?

8. Why did early Christians often tend to react negatively to involvement in worldly enterprises?

9. What contrasting effects can Christian indifference to worldly values have on ethics and morality?

10. What considerations led Christians to consider salvation as individually uncertain?

11. How can considerations of divine judgment lead to extravagances in Christian moral outlook?

12. How does the historical character of Christian revelation foster development of authoritative teaching?

13. What distinctive understanding of Christian community has influenced the social dimension of Christian ethics?

14. If you believed, as the early Christians did, that Jesus' second coming was immanent, how would your life be different?

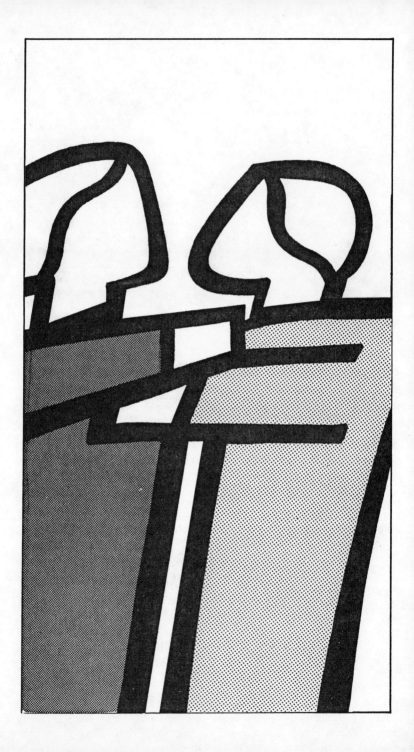

Chapter Ten

VIRTUES AND RULES

INNER ATTITUDES AND OUTWARD ACTIONS

One of the things that is often remarked by readers of the Sermon on the Mount, as we have already noted, is the tendency on Jesus' part to interiorize ethics. Jesus is not content with obedience to a series of rules forbidding certain kinds of overt behavior. He himself amplifies the requirements of traditional rules, but he does so in such a way that it becomes evident that he is not merely multiplying obligations, but calling attention to the interior dispositions from which prohibited behavior derives. Thus, it is not enough to exclude adultery as long as the underlying lustful mentality remains intact. Nor must murder only be done away with, but much more the contempt and cruelty that find expression equally in words of hatred or derision. Immoderate revenge is not the basic evil, but rather the spirit of vindictiveness itself. In these and many other passages of the New Testament we find the clear implication that what God requires and God's kingdom entails is not the performance or avoidance of certain actions, but rather the development of certain kinds of persons.

The same idea may be suggested by the New Testament's tendency to express its ethical standards in positive rather than negative terms. The outstanding example is undoubtedly to be found in the demand for love as a summation of God's law. Evidently, to love, as understood in the New Testament, entails the avoidance of all sorts of conduct that are simply incompatible with such love. And yet it is hard to conceive how any collection of prohibitions, however numerous and subtle, could ever add up to the same ethical teaching as is contained in the commandment of loving God and neighbor. The love enjoined by the Gospel is a disposition, an attitude, an orientation of behavior that is plainly irreconcilable with the kinds of conduct forbidden by the law. Nevertheless, the attitude involves more than simply refraining from the prohibited actions. It involves a transformation of character, a realignment of values, a complete redirection of moral vision.

PROS AND CONS OF PROHIBITIONS

It is not difficult to understand why human formulations of law might favor prohibitions. For it is only by such laws that human beings can hope to make objective judgments. A human judge can hope to determine whether or not adultery or murder has been committed. He cannot hope to make a similar determination of whether or not someone loves God and neighbor. For God, of course, no such problem can arise, and the law that Jesus formulates is one by which God alone is to judge. And it should be remembered in this connection that in Israel, moral and legal norms were combined, so that human judgment did have to be exercised on the basis of what was considered God's law.

In the same connection it should be noted that an ethical norm requiring one not to abstain from certain actions but to acquire a certain character, has an open-endedness that would be the despair of human adjudication. If the law says not to steal, then one who simply does not steal obeys that law, and obeys it perfectly. But if the law says to be merciful, who is to be considered obedient to such a law? One could always be more merciful than one has been, and so one is always more or less a violator of such a law even when one is more or less an observer of it. Probably the most meaningful observance of such a law would be precisely the general tendency to become more and more merciful. To the question, Have you committed adultery? one can answer truly and adequately, yes or no. But to the question, Are you chaste? the best one can do is answer yes and no, or more or less. Forbidden acts are events of one's history. Enjoined virtues are qualities of one's life. In Christian ethics there has been a strong tendency to emphasize such qualities of life. For it is precisely on an inner transformation of life, a newness of life, that Christian ethics is founded. And since the principles of Christian ethics are not required, like the precepts of Jewish tradition, to do double duty as humanly administered law, they do not have to be adapted to the capacities of human judges.

In view of this typical emphasis of Christian ethics on interior dispositions and positive ideals, it is not surprising that Christian ethical tradition has strongly favored what may be called an ethics of virtue as distinct from an ethics of prohibitive rule. This tendency appears in the usage, derived from the New Testament, of singling out faith, hope, and love as the outstanding features of a Christian life, the so-called theological virtues. It appears also in the eagerness with which Christian writers appropriated to their own uses the rich philosophical accounts of virtue that had been developed in Greco-Roman culture. The most outstanding result of this latter tendency was the Christian development of an elaborate moral theology organized within the framework of the three theological virtues and the four cardinal virtues. It is within this framework that Catholic moral doctrine achieved its greatest depth and scope of ethical understanding.

THE CARDINAL VIRTUES

From the time of the earliest known major writings on ethics in the Western world we find familiar references to four distinct qualities of human excellence. These are not the discovery or invention of any known philosopher. They seem to have been simply taken for granted as basic, indispensable ingredients of a humanly good life, for both individuals and societies. The fact that they were perceived as basic led to their later designation as "cardinal" virtues, from the Latin word "cardo," meaning hinge. As a gate both moves and hangs upon its hinges, human morality was thought to move and hang, that is, to depend for both effectiveness and stability, on these four qualities of life.

The cardinal virtues have a major role in the ethical writings of Plato, Aristotle, and many lesser figures in the history of ancient philosophy. And when, after its Palestinian beginnings, Christianity penetrated and increasingly dominated the Greco-Roman world, Christian moral teachers readily adopted this characteristic insight of classical ethics, which became as a result equally characteristic of traditional Christian ethics. In the middle ages it was made the fundamental motif of a system of moral theology developed by Thomas Aquinas, which predominated in Christian ethical teaching until the Protestant Reformation, after which it retained major influence chiefly among Catholics. It is only since quite recent times that even moderately educated Catholics have not in general had some basic familiarity with the ideas represented by the cardinal virtues. And recently there have been a number of signs, not only among Catholics, of renewed interest in the cardinal virtues, on the part of both scholars and popular teachers. Indeed a recent very widely read book on so un-theological a subject as economics concludes with the opinion that out of the whole Christian tradition there may be no lesson more relevant to our present economic crises than the doctrine of the four cardinal virtues. At all events, some treatment of this doctrine unquestionably belongs in anything claiming to be a modern presentation of Catholic ethics.

VIRTUES AS GOOD HABITS

Before saying anything more about the cardinal virtues, it may be advisable to recall what, in Catholic tradition, virtues are generally understood to be. Although there has been some rather complicated theorizing on this subject, the basic idea of a virtue is easily grasped by common sense. That is the idea of a morally good habit. Habits, of course, are not things we perceive. When we say someone has a habit of smiling, we do not imply that we have seen the habit itself. What we have seen are the smiles. And the smiling occurs frequently enough for us to assume there is something about this person that makes it easy to smile, and hard not to smile. We apply the same kind of thinking to less sheerly physical behavior. People who are regularly hesitant to work, and quick to leave work unfinished, are said to have a habit called laziness. People who regularly notice and try to satisfy the needs of other people are said to have a habit called benevolence or kindness. This habit of kindness we call a virtue, because we think of it as a morally good habit. And we think of it as a morally good habit because the actions that make us aware of it are what we consider morally good actions. Similarly, we classify morally bad habits, like laziness, as the opposite of virtue, called vice.

Notice that when we attribute a habit to a person we ordinarily do so because we have observed that person to behave frequently in a particular way. However, to say someone has a habit does not mean merely that he or she frequently performs a particular kind of behavior. It means that we think there is something intrinsic to that person which is revealed by such behavior. Obviously, the mere fact that someone behaves frequently or even regularly in a particular way does necessarily imply the existence of a corresponding habit. Students who frequently study may have no studious habits at all, but merely be avoiding the foreseen unpleasant consequences of neglecting school work. The regular pattern of behavior exhibited by prison inmates finds its principle explanation not in habit but in compulsion. Sometimes, of course, behavior exhibited by prison inmates finds its principal explamay generate a habit that will then keep such behavior going even after the external pressure is removed. But as every teacher and parent knows, this is by no means always the case.

VIRTUES INVOLVE HABITS OF MIND

To describe virtues as morally good habits is not the same thing as merely saying they are good habits, or helpful habits. No doubt it is possible to train human beings to do certain good or helpful things in much the same way that animals are trained to do good or helpful things. Nevertheless, the complex repertoire of extremely helpful habits to which a seeing-eye dog is trained does not constitute what is traditionally meant by virtue. And if some conditioning or brain-washing process produced comparably useful habits in human beings, we should not think of them as virtues either. For what we mean by a virtue is not merely some inner mechanism that causes certain desirable kinds of behavior to be repeated. An interior mechanism may indeed be necessary, but we do not consider it a part of virtue unless it is thought to be associated with a corresponding interior attitude. A mere routine practice of giving customers the right change does not constitute the virtue of honesty unless it goes with an attitude that acknowledges their right to the correct change, that considers fraudulence to be unworthy behavior. And indeed, we should normally consider virtuous a person who had the appropriate attitude, but was simply deprived by circumstances of all opportunity to express it externally. A person prevented by physical paralysis from performing any visibly kind action might nevertheless be a kind person, who would perform such actions if it were possible to do so. A brave soldier, stopped by a bullet from doing anything brave, is not necessarily deprived by the bullet of his bravery.

What all of this implies is that having a virtue (or, for that matter, a vice) does not primarily mean doing certain kinds of things. It means being a certain kind of person, who judges and decides in a certain kind of way. External behavior is merely our clue to the existence of virtues and vices in others. We may be aware of virtues and vices of our own which others have little reason to infer, because we have little occasion to express them publicly. People who ordinarily live very safe lives may possess a store of courage that goes entirely unnoticed until dangers at last arise in which heroic risks are readily undertaken. When Jesus in the Sermon on the Mount stigmatized as adulterous the man who lusts after a woman in his heart, he was calling attention to the fact that, even without lustful actions, lustful attitudes bear witness to vice. Indeed, one vice may be kept from outward expression merely by another vice, as sometimes only cowardice prevents the expression of hatred.

STUDY QUESTIONS

1. In what sense does Jesus' ethical teaching appear to require more than external obedience to rules?

2. How is this additional requirement illustrated in the Sermon on the Mount?

3. How can a preference for positive over negative ethical norms contribute to interiorizing ethics?

4. What advantage do prohibitive statements have for the formulation of human laws?

5. Why is it hard to determine whether or not positive ethical norms are conformed to?

6. How is the preference for positive ethical norms related to an emphasis on virtue?

7. Why are the cardinal virtues so called and where did the idea of such virtues originate?

8. Psychologically, how has Catholic ethics typically conceived the ideas of virtue and vice?

9. On what basis are habits attributed to persons and what is the attribution of them taken to mean?

10. How are virtues as morally good habits differentiated from other kinds of good habits?

11. Is it meaningful to speak of the existence of a virtue except in so far as it is outwardly manifested?

12. Why are prohibitions and exhortations about character both necessary for moral living? If either is omitted, what is the result?

Chapter Eleven

THE FOUR CARDINAL VIRTUES

PRUDENCE

St. Augustine has a typically catchy way of stating what, from a Christian viewpoint, the virtue of prudence might seem to be. He calls prudence a love that distinguishes well between what helps and what hinders its tending towards God. Thus prudence, as a Christian virtue, presupposes that the purpose of human life is to draw ever closer to God. Prudence does not discover that purpose, but accepts it on the basis of religion. What prudence is concerned with is what a person whose life is committed to Christian faith, hope, and love does, in the concrete circumstances of life, to bring his behavior into practical conformity with the implications of faith, hope, and love. Thus one might say that prudence is a religious person's ability to get down to business about his religion, the business, that is, of actually living in accordance with his supreme convictions. The task of prudence is the never-ending one of figuring out what to do about one's Christianity.

Here we obviously have to do with mental equipment, and if one examines traditional Christian writings on this subject it becomes abundantly clear that there is nothing very simple about the way this mental equipment is conceived. And there is no avoiding the implication that in the Christian tradition as regards morality, we are called upon to use our heads, and to use them faithfully and well. Slovenly thinking about moral questions is judged by Christianity to be a vice, and a very serious one. One might recall in this connection that parable of Jesus which describes the shrewdly calculating behavior of an unscrupulous employee, and concludes with the admonition that worldly people are "more prudent" or "wiser" in terms of their own worldly heritage of values, than are those enlightened by faith in terms of their very different heritage.

Numerous writers of ancient and mediaeval times undertook to subdivide prudence into a variety of distinguishable aspects. And although it would be hard to defend any of the resulting lists as the right one or the best one, the lists do remind us that prudence was thought of as anything but a simple psychological trait. According to one catalogue widely adopted by Christian theologians, eight distinct aspects of prudence are to be noted: memory, understanding, docility, cleverness, reasoning, foresight, circumspection, and caution. What such a catalogue means is that a person cannot be accounted prudent unless he is able to bear in mind past experience, comprehend current events, learn from other people, and figure things out for himself. Moreover, logical reasoning is essential to being prudent, and so is the ability to anticipate consequences, take account of circumstances, and circumvent obstacles.

Prudence, in short, represents the whole effectiveness of a human mind in coping with the moral problems of life. Its perfection would be a kind of ethical or moral genius, requiring an exceptionally keen, well-informed, and versatile mind. Prudence is not, therefore, a virtue whose operation is confined to a particular ethical concern, but one that is uniformly indispensable to all ethical functioning. Thus it has been traditionally maintained that, without prudence, no other moral virtue is even possible. But it has also been maintained that without certain other moral virtues, prudence itself is inoperative. Thus among the cardinal virtues, as among virtues generally, Christian tradition supposes a mutual dependence.

TEMPERANCE

Temperance is a word that, in the evolution of our language, has come upon even harder times than prudence. It easily tends to conjure up images that were realities within living memory, as of resolute ladies leading self-righteous onslaughts against barrooms and liquor shops under the banners of various Temperance Unions. The phrase "wise moderation" might do better service to the traditional idea, but I shall retain the traditional word.

Considerations relevant to temperance tend to arise in most people's minds even as they consider, in a practical way, the kinds of things that have just been said about prudence. For to most of us it seems fairly obvious that, even if most people do not think as prudently as they might and should, there are also plenty of people who think a great deal more prudently than they act. They "know better," as the saying goes, than to do things which, nonetheless, they persist in doing. We may call such behavior abnormal if we mean that it is irrational, but not, surely, if we mean that it is unusual. And since it is usual there must be other factors that frequently intervene between the relative prudence of people's deliberations and the manifest imprudence of their conduct. And of course there are such factors, and some of them are perfectly familiar to us.

Modern psychology has made us aware of some factors in this regard of which earlier generations had only obscure notions, and this is one of those areas in which newly discovered facts must modify certain ethical assumptions and conclusions. But the factors that were traditionally considered continue to be operative and are, moreover, deeply involved in the workings of more newly discovered ones. Traditionally, temperance was conceived of as exercising neither too much nor too little certain propensities that are human counterparts of basic animal drives. Such drives were perceived in ancient times as having a common motif of physical self-preservation, understood as the preservation not only of the individual but also of the species. The most conspicuous things animals must do to preserve themselves and their kind have to do with their digestive and reproductive systems, and one easily discerns how much of animal behavior can be described in terms of seeking and using opportunities to eat, drink, and mate, while avoiding obstacles to these pursuits.

Human beings have similar drives. But they seem also to have less automatic controls over them, more ingenious ways of complicating them, and a conscious awareness of other and greater purposes in life. Consequently, human beings have, on the one hand, to respect the real value and urgency of such drives and, on the other hand, to keep their satisfactions of those drives from becoming so excessive that they are both self-defeating and thwarting of higher human purposes. To discern the right measure between deficiency and excess is a task of prudence. The ability to live according to the right measure is what is meant by temperance.

COURAGE

Some of what has been said about the relationship of prudence with temperance is applicable also to its relationship with courage. There is no need to belabor this all-too-familiar point. Clearly, some of what our prudent deliberations show to be things we are plainly obliged to do are, nevertheless, things we do not quite dare to do. Like the timorous victim clinging to a window-ledge above the firemen's net, until finally overcome by smoke and flames, people may neglect, out of fear, their only and obvious way to avert moral disaster. The ability to behave otherwise is part of what is meant by the virtue of courage.

Courage is variously described as an ability to act well in

spite of danger, and as an ability to act well in spite of fear. There can, of course, be objectively grave dangers that in some persons arouse little or no subjective fear. Also, there can be very real fear in the absence of any real danger—as in cases of illusory danger, or neurotic fear—and such fears can make heavy demands on courage. Courage is not a synonym for fearlessness—which in some cases is merely symptomatic of a certain mindlessness—and in most instances fear is precisely what courage has to cope with. Sometimes it copes with it so powerfully that it effectively banishes or greatly diminishes the emotion of fear. In such cases it usually does so mainly by diverting attention from that which arouses fear to some other and far more powerful consideration. It is probably in this sense that we should understand the biblical assurance that perfect love casts out fear. But for all that, there is certainly no lack of courage in one who, though trembling with fear, does what should be done in spite of it.

Traditionally, a distinction has been made between what are sometimes called active and passive courage. Active courage is the courage to undertake what is, or seems, dangerous and fearsome. Passive courage is the courage to undergo what is, or seems, dangerous and fearsome. The distinction reflects the difference between courageously striving and courageously suffering. But in practice, what generally makes us fear to strive is the anticipation of what may or must be suffered in the very process of striving.

A more important distinction is that which contrasts courage as a moral virtue with the psychological trait we should normally call by the same name regardless of its relationship to morality. As there is a kind of honor among thieves, so also there is a kind of courage, but it is not the kind included among the cardinal virtues. It is not simply the ability to act in spite of danger or fear, but to act well in spite of them, to do what prudence discerns as right, in spite of what observation or imagination discerns as perilous. Because of a traditional awareness that what human beings find most ulti-

mately dangerous and fearsome is their so-called "last enemy," death, moral steadfastness in the face of death has always been regarded as the climactic manifestation of courage.
And here as elsewhere, it is not the absence of fear but the
overcoming of it that is decisive.

JUSTICE

In most of classical thought, the whole subject of social
morality was comprehended under the idea of justice. To live
justly was to do as one ought to do about others, whether
singly or collectively. It was to treat other persons and groups
of persons as they ought to be treated, to deal with them as
they deserve, to render them their "due." Here as elsewhere,
the moral judgments involved are the work of prudence. Thus
the prudent person discovers what is due to others, and the
just person accommodates his behavior to that discovery. Fail-
ures can, of course, occur in both processes. There are those
who render to others what they think is their due, but think
wrongly. And there are those who correctly perceive what is
due to others, but do not act accordingly.

Traditionally, three broad areas have been mapped out
for the workings of justice in human social conduct. First, and
most obviously, there is the kind of justice that is appropriate
to individual human transactions—whether they occur between actual individuals or between groups acting as individuals. Thus if a person, or a family, or a corporation sells
something, the buyer incurs an obligation to return something
of equivalent value for what has been bought. Ordinarily, the
acceptable equivalence is established beforehand, by some
kind of contract, however informal, in which case fidelity to
the contract becomes the determinant of justice. The case
would be similar if no actual exchange took place, but one
person simply deprived another—as by careless or malicious
damage—of some valued property. In such cases, restitution,
on a basis of equivalent value, is due just as plainly as in a
case of trade. This whole area of fair dealing in individual

transactions—which can, of course, become extremely complicated—is the domain of what is traditionally called commutative justice.

But there are other relationships of justice that are generated by the fact that societies, and especially political societies, have dealings of their own with those persons who are members of such societies. The very process of forming a state empowers and obliges the state, through the instrumentalities of government, to act upon the community and its members. How such action is to be carried out depends on the various ways political societies are fashioned and conceived. And an important reason for fashioning states in one way rather than another is to assure, as far as possible, that the state, or in practice the government, will act justly. In states that are well organized, laws regulate these matters, although a certain amount of governmental discretion has to supplement even the most perfect system of laws. Since, in our tradition, the purpose of political society is understood to be the common good, the justice of the state's actions as of its laws is judged by the service they render to the common good.

Two types of justice are distinguished on the basis of the two directions in which action can proceed between the individual and society. Either society acts upon the individual, or the individual acts upon society. Thus, in political society, the state is empowered and obliged to confer certain benefits on its citizens. Its doing so justly is the exercise of what is called distributive justice. The term legal justice is applied to the reverse process, whereby the citizens discharge their responsibilities to the state. Obviously, these two kinds of justice are complementary in securing the moral soundness of society.

STUDY QUESTIONS

1. How does St. Augustine describe the virtue of prudence from a Christian viewpoint?

2. What does prudence as a Christian virtue presuppose about the purpose of human life?

3. How is prudence related to the virtues of faith, hope, and love?

4. Why is the virtue of prudence incompatible with mental laziness or incompetence?

5. What are several distinct aspects of prudence that illustrate its complexity as a virtue?

6. What is the general relationship of prudence to other moral virtues?

7. What alternative phrase conveys the essential meaning of temperance as a virtue?

8. Why is temperance demanded for the practical exercise of prudence?

9. How was temperance traditionally conceived?

10. To what kinds of behavior has the need for temperance been especially related?

11. How does courage bear a practical relationship to prudence comparable to that of temperance?

12. What are some usual descriptions of the virtue of courage?

13. Why is courage improperly identified with fearlessness?

14. What is the difference between active and passive courage?

15. What is the difference between courage as a moral virtue and as a psychological trait?

16. In classical thought what was the role of justice with respect to social morality?

17. How is justice, in the most general sense, traditionally described?

18. In what respect does justice depend on prudence?

19. What are the three distinct areas in which justice was traditionally perceived to operate?

20. What are commutative, distributive, and legal justice and how are they related?

21. The Church has traditionally spoken about *four* cardinal virtues. Do you think this list should be contracted or expanded? What would you add or delete?

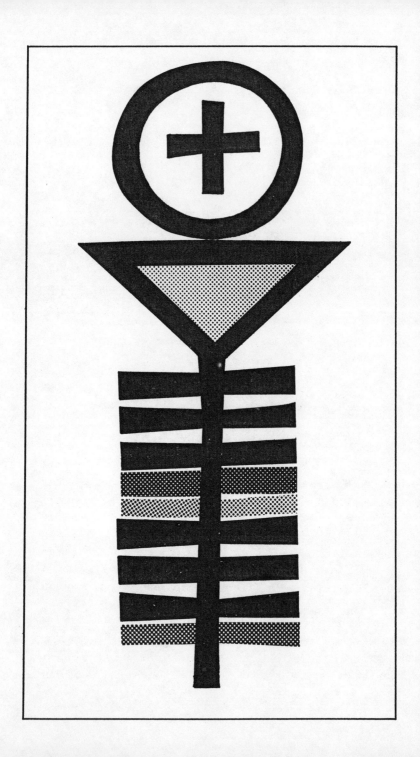

Chapter Twelve

FACTUAL BELIEFS AND ETHICAL CONCLUSIONS

SOUND MORAL JUDGMENT

Reduced to its simplest terms, moral life presents us with two fundamental aspects: first, knowing what is right and, second, doing what is right. We do not think of anyone as living a truly moral life who does not form definite judgments about right conduct. Even if someone actually did what we consider right, but did it without any conviction or decision, we should not regard such a person as any more moral than a robot, or perhaps a rabbit. But, neither should we consider someone to be living a moral life who formed convictions about what was the right thing to do, and simply ignored those convictions when it came to actual behavior. Moral living must, as it were, combine theory with practice.

As already indicated, that aspect of moral living which consists in knowing the right thing to do was associated in classical thought with the virtue usually rendered in English (from Greek via Latin) as prudence, although that word has acquired misleading connotations. The phrase "sound moral judgment" conveys the basic idea. And we commonly use that phrase to express not a momentary quality, but a habitual trait of character, that is, a virtue. If it is said of someone that he or she has sound moral judgment, what we understand to be meant is that the person in question regularly seems to know what is the right thing to do, not only in some narrowly defined circumstances but in a wide variety of situations.

The ordinary understanding of sound moral judgment also corresponds to the classical virtue of prudence in that it pertains rather to particular ethical decisions than to broad moral generalizations. To acknowledge, for example, that a person has "fine basic values" is quite a different thing from crediting him or her with sound moral judgment. For it is a familiar fact that some people whose ultimate values are irreproachable seem neverthless to have a very limited capacity for translating their values into practice. This is equally true whether one considers matters that affect a single individual or those that have extensive social implications. Admirable ideals do not lead invariably to admirable policies. Accordingly, it was traditionally said of prudence that it has to do not with ends but with means. And there can be little doubt that much of the ethical disagreement that exists in this world is among people who disagree not about what ultimate ends should be pursued, but about what means should be used to pursue them.

It should also be remembered, however, that an apparent agreement about means does not necessarily imply any agreement about ends. People whose ultimate values and purposes are very different may in certain circumstances decide in favor of an identical course of action. Soldiers who volunteer to fight on the same side may decide to do so for reasons that are morally worlds apart. The same holds true for soldiers who refuse to fight. And no one is unaware that two people may be prompted to marry, and even to marry one another, by principles that are morally irreconcilable. Two items, therefore, must be included in anyone's list of the outstanding follies in moral thinking. First, it is foolish to suppose that similar remote purposes must lead to similar conduct. Second, it is equally foolish to suppose that similar conduct must express similar remote purposes.

MORAL ARGUMENTS INVOLVE MORE THAN ETHICS

In fact, Catholic ethical tradition has characteristically taken the position that, as far as ultimate moral purposes are concerned, there really is no significant room for disagreement. That is, certain very general principles of morality are considered to be such that no normal person who is reasonably experienced could seriously deny or doubt them. On this view, all ethical disagreements presuppose certain broad ethical agreements. If that is true, the most constructive way to begin an ethical argument would be by establishing commonly accepted principles, and then trying to determine which of the contending positions is most consistent with those common principles.

Obviously, a certain amount of ordinary ethical debate is conducted on this basis. If, for example a bright child brings home a deplorable school report, one parent may think sympathetic encouragement is called for, while the other favors the prompt administration of a sound spanking. Both may be equally convinced that their sole purpose in the matter must be to foster the child's maximum long-range improvement, morally, mentally, and emotionally. But despite this common goal, their argument may be long continued and ultimately inconclusive, because they disagree on one or more other matters.

Moreover, the matters about which they disagree may or may not be ethical matters. They may be simply matters of fact, or they may be matters of opinion about subjects other than morality. They may, for example, disagree about the psychological effects of corporal punishment, and therefore about whether or not it is right to use it. Or they may disagree about the particular reasons why their child got a bad report, and therefore about how they should react to it. In a great many cases, what seem to be moral differences between people are found on closer inspection to be instead the moral results of quite other kinds of differences, most notably differences of information or opinion concerning sheer matters of fact.

As soon as one recalls how much seemingly ethical disagreement derives from disagreements about non-ethical, factual matters, another reflection must suggest itself. For everyone is aware that people differ greatly in their individual capacity to discover what is true, or likely to be true, in the factual domain. People differ widely in the quality and quantity of their experience. They differ widely in their education. They differ widely in their powers of understanding. And as far as experience and education are concerned, not only do individuals differ, but so also do whole ages and cultures. The fact that a New England judge of three centuries ago might have sentenced a neurotic old lady to be burned at the stake for witchcraft, whereas a contemporary magistrate would dismiss criminal charges against a similar defendant, does not imply that the modern judge has better moral judgment or greater moral integrity than his predecessor. What it does imply is that the modern judge, like modern people generally, is better informed and better advised about certain aspects of human psychology.

In all ethical discourse, therefore, it is imperative to find out whether what we are disagreeing about is, in the last analysis, what is right, or simply what is true.

PREJUDICE AND UNFAIRNESS

One area of discussion in which this distinction is both very important and very difficult to apply is the area we associate with the phrases social prejudice and unfair discrimination. Unfair discrimination is a moral failure, but social prejudice is an intellectual failure which may or may not owe something to moral negligence. As we are all aware, a great deal of unfair discrimination can be explained in large measure by a great deal of social prejudice. There are certain tribes that systematically exterminate all newborn twins. They do not do so out of sheer homicidal wickedness, however, but out of a sincere although tragically absurd belief that twins are monstrous and maleficent. Much of the racial discrimination in our own society has been deeply rooted in perfectly genuine although perfectly foolish beliefs about the genetic mental and moral inferiority of certain races to certain other races.

Under such circumstances, people can be expected to do better only if they are enabled to know better. They have to straighten out their facts before they can do very much about straightening out their morals. In this respect, education can render great services to morality without ever actually moralizing. And by the same token, mis-education and uneducation can do notable disservices to morality.

Perhaps it is needless to say that prejudices, even though they are essentially intellectual defects, are by no means always morally innocent. Some prejudices foster kinds of behavior that, for reasons of self-interest, people are not easily willing to give up. In such cases it is often perceived more or less clearly that to be disabused of certain erroneous ideas would logically necessitate abandoning certain pleasant or profitable practices. A complacent tyrant is seldom a severe critic of belief in the divine right of kings, and a prosperous slaveholder may cherish theories of the naturally servile character of certain peoples. Where these situations of advantageous prejudice prevail, there is often a positive effort to resist enlightenment and to preserve and foster convenient beliefs for which there is no respectable evidence. Here one is led to sin against the light by a recognition that certain areas of life remain most comfortable when they are kept in the dark. Ignorance and error are often morally, that is, immorally motivated. When they are, they take on a moral quality of their own from the motives that breed and nurture them. False and misleading propaganda must often be morally condemned on this basis.

FACTUAL ERROR IN MORAL TRADITION

Sometimes what appears to be an immemorial ethical tradition may be found on investigation to have been logically linked, throughout much of its history, with factual beliefs that better information makes simply untenable. In evaluating such traditions and deciding whether or not they ought to be respected and preserved, it is of the utmost importance to decide how dependent they are on simply erroneous factual assumptions. It may be that even when such supporting errors are eliminated, enough good reasons will remain to justify the tradition's continuance. But it is also possible that a reassessment of the factual premises may either greatly weaken the moral force of the tradition or entirely discredit it.

A good current example of this kind of moral tradition is the strong ethical opposition that has been maintained throughout most of our cultural history to sexual practices of masturbation. Whether or not masturbation is morally blameworthy or how morally blameworthy it is continues to be a matter of debate. But if one examines the history of this tradition in the light of currently validated information, one is struck by the fact that physical and mental consequences were frequently attributed to masturbatory behavior, even by medical authorities, that later and better research shows to be unsupported by any sound evidence. Among many writers of the past, belief in those consequences was said or implied to be the main reason for moral condemnation. There may, of course, be other, equally compelling and better evidenced reasons for morally condemning masturbation. But these other reasons have to be verified on their own merits, while a tradition of condemnation based on factual errors cannot be appealed to uncritically. In assessing traditional moral judgments, no less than individual moral judgments, factual presuppositions must be examined, and moral conclusions derived from fallacious beliefs must be either repudiated or established on more creditable grounds.

CHANGING FACTS AND MORAL TRADITION

There is still another important aspect to this matter of criticizing moral traditions by reevaluating their factual assumptions. For it may be that certain factual beliefs underlying certain ethical views were once verifiable but are verifiable no longer. An outstanding example of this kind of reassessment may be found in the Catholic Church's traditional moral judgment of the practice called usury, formerly understood to mean simply the lending of money at interest. This practice was strongly condemned in the Old Testament, and its condemnation was vigorously reiterated by the Church's ecclesiastical and academic authorities over the course of many centuries. Yet, as we know, the lending and borrowing of money at interest has by now long been the common and unashamed practice of Christians and Catholics generally, from papacy to peasantry. The tradition did a thorough about-face. But it did so on the basis of a reassessment of the social significance of money in an economic environment that has been dramatically altered in the course of history. Many of those who would defend the current approval of lending at interest would also defend its earlier condemnation as having been a morally sound judgment at a time when economic realities were greatly different. Obviously, to judge the rightness or wrongness of this radical change in traditional morality, one needs not only moral integrity, but a considerable knowledge of history and economics.

In our own time, ethical opinions about warfare show considerable revision, in a direction of increased severity, on the grounds that warfare is no longer the sort of thing it once was, with the result that moral principles that may once have been valid are simply inapplicable to the military realities of the present.

FROM IS TO OUGHT

Observing how frequently what appear to be ethical disagreements are traceable to differences not about morals but simply about facts may draw attention to some of the ways matters of factual belief and matters of ethical belief get entangled, and sometimes confused, in human thinking.

Philosophers often take note of how in many discussions there seems to take place an illogical transition from the realm of "is" to the realm of "ought." In this jargon, "is" represents statements about facts, while "ought" represents statements about moral obligations. And it certainly does seem as though one of the things people are constantly doing is making "ought" statements and backing them up with "is" statements. In the course of any day one may hear quite a few arguments to the effect that somebody *ought* to do something, because something *is* the case. To cite a minor, but nowadays rather frequent example, one person may say to another, "You ought to stop smoking," and, if asked why, give as his reason, "Because smoking frequently causes cancer."

But suppose the person who is told he ought to stop smoking because smoking is carcinogenic either enjoys quibbling or is not very bright. He might then retort along these lines: "What kind of sense does that make? Your argument says, (1) 'Smoking often causes cancer,' and (2) 'Therefore you ought to stop smoking.' But there is no logical way you can pull a moral duty out of a medical finding." If patience or whimsy enables this dialogue to continue, the first speaker may concede that the other is technically correct, and consent to rephrase his comment more or less like this: "One ought not to run a grave risk for a slight pleasure. But to smoke is to run a grave risk for a slight pleasure. Therefore one ought not to smoke." That, of course, is what most of us would suppose him to mean in the first place. But stating it more fully does bring to light that the only way the factual belief about smoking's causing cancer could logically support a moral disapproval of smoking is presupposing another and more general moral disapproval, of running grave risks for trivial pleasures.

One can, of course, imagine this conversation's being carried still further. One could question the presupposition that people should not run large risks for small gratifications. And if that presupposition were defended, the defense would presumably bring in a still broader generalization, perhaps about a universal duty to take at least moderate care of one's life and health. But in any case, if a broader generalization were to contribute anything to the argument, it would have to be a generalization having to do with duty or obligation; in other words, an ethical generalization and not merely a factual one; an "ought" and not merely an "is".

FROM OUGHT TO OUGHT

Reflecting upon this sort of thing will probably suggest to us that a great many of our spoken ethical assertions do presuppose other, unspoken ethical convictions, of a more general character. And where this is the case it would appear that the less general ethical assertions can be only as convincing as the more general ethical convictions they presuppose. Thus we may imagine any particular moral assertion as the final link in a chain extending logically "backward" to broader moral generalizations, and consider such a chain to be only as strong as its weakest link. However long or short such chains of moral reasoning may be, they obviously must begin someplace. And in view of what has already been said about "is" and "ought," it would seem that their only valid beginnings would have to be "ought" statements, regardless of how many "is" statements might be subsequently drawn into the argument.

If such chains of moral reasoning can validly begin only with an "ought" statement, it follows that moral reasoning is, in an important sense, an independent domain of human thought. You cannot draw ethical conclusions from non-ethical premises, and at some point or other you have to acknowledge a set of ethical premises that are not conclusions at all, but are strictly original premises or, as they are often called, first principles.

This way of looking at the general field of moral thinking has been highly typical of Catholic tradition, which has often concentrated on trying to specify ethical first principles, and then trace lines of logical argumentation from those principles to particular ethical conclusions. Indeed, it has sometimes seemed as though certain Catholic moralists thought they had achieved a complete list of these ethical first principles, and thereby reduced ethics to a mere process of reasoning cleverly and practically from established premises. Yet there is nothing in this basic approach to ethics that could justify a denial that genuinely first principles might be newly discovered by anyone at any time.

Interestingly, among modern ethicists one finds some who seem to urge that there are fewer first principles than used to be thought, others who seem to think there are a lot more of them, and still others who apparently do not believe there are any at all. Of these three opinions, only the last seems rather profoundly alien to Catholic tradition. These are matters to which we shall return presently.

FROM OUGHT TO IF

Some readers of the preceding sections may have been distracted by their perception that people often seem to use "ought" statements in a sense quite different from the one thus far considered. That is, sometimes our "oughts" seem to imply presuppositions that are not ethical ones at all. If I say, for example, "You ought to visit Yellowstone National Park," I am not likely to be suspected of announcing a moral obligation. What then am I doing with this "ought"? The answer to that question begins to appear when, on being asked "Why ought I to visit Yelllowstone?" I reply to the effect that it is a very beautiful, interesting, or exciting place. Here, once again, I may seem to be illegitimately deriving an "ought" from an "is." And yet, to introduce some presupposed ethical generalization is hardly what the situation calls for. "One ought to visit beautiful places. But Yellowstone is a beautiful place.

Therefore one ought to visit Yellowstone" may tidy my logic but it obviously distorts my meaning. I am not declaring a moral obligation to visit either beautiful places in general or Yellowstone in particular.

I am presupposing not a duty, but a desire, taste, or inclination. I am presuming that the person I am talking to, like most people, enjoys beautiful places and in a general way relishes opportunities to visit them. What my "ought" statement about visiting Yellowstone really presupposed was a desire, implying some remote purpose, of visiting beautiful places. "But Yellowstone is a beautiful place. Therefore you would presumably like to visit Yellowstone." All the "ought" represents is my opinion that a visit to Yellowstone is a good way of fulfilling a purpose that I presume you have, more or less habitually, of enjoying beautiful places. If you reply that you find beautiful places boring, I have nothing more to say. Your attitude may arouse amusement or contempt, but it does not arouse specifically moral indignation or provoke an ethical debate. It is as though I were to say, "You ought to try the Pompano" and be told in reply, "I don't care for fish." There is nothing more to say except, "Sorry, I assumed you did."

Thus, a good many of our "ought" statements are really nothing more than suggestions of effective means for achieving purposes that we take it for granted other people entertain. Our moral "ought" statements, on the other hand, indicate necessary means for attaining purposes that we consider it morally wrong not to entertain. If we say, "You ought to share your superfluous wealth with your indigent neighbors," we are not satisfied by the reply, "I don't care for philanthropy." Such a reply will not end the argument, but intensify and prolong it.

Thus, "ought" statements sometimes are and sometimes are not ethical statements. Ethical "ought" statements, if they presuppose anything, presuppose other, more general "ought" statements. "You ought to pay a decent wage" presupposes "One ought to act justly." Non-ethical "ought" statements, on the other hand, presuppose "if" statements. "You ought to visit Preservation Hall" presupposes "If you like jazz ... "

To put it another way, non-ethical "ought" statements are based on hypotheses about particular non-moral values and purposes, while ethical "ought" statements are based on convictions about general moral values and purposes. To notice the difference is to notice the radical distinctness of moral thinking from other kinds of thinking that often employ similar language. A failure to perceive this often underlies the suggestion one sometimes hears that moral matters are essentially matters of taste, about which "there is no disputing." Sometimes ethical relativism is grounded in this kind of thinking. However, it is no less arbitrary to regard this kind of thinking as ethical thinking than it would be to regard duties and tastes as the same thing.

STUDY QUESTIONS

1. What are the two obviously fundamental aspects of moral living?

2. How is one of these aspects closely related to prudence?

3. In what sense has Catholic ethics presupposed a general acceptance of moral principles?

4. What factors may lead to practical ethical disagreement among persons holding the same ethical principles?

5. What is the relationship between unfair discrimination and social prejudice?

6. To what extent is prejudice, as an intellectual defect, exempt from moral criticism?

7. How can factual errors influence the validity of ethical traditions?

8. How can factual changes in the course of history influence the validity of ethical traditions?

9. What specific examples illustrate factual complications of ethical traditions?

10. What problem is conceived as the difficulty of logical transition from "is" to "ought"?

11. In what sense must moral reasoning be considered an independent realm of thought?

12. How do current opinions differ concerning the existence of ethical first principles?

13. How can "ought" statements be used without implying obligation?

14. Choose one ethical area not discussed in this chapter. How have changing facts affected the moral tradition on this subject?

Chapter Thirteen

ENDS AND MEANS

"THE END DOES NOT JUSTIFY THE MEANS"

One of the most persistent and widespread of our ethical clichés is a statement that has been made so frequently and dogmatically that it seldom arouses critical reflection. "The end does not justify the means" is a saying more like a proverb than a philosophical principle. Yet, as soon as one reflects on this saying, one is tempted to react by asking, "If the end does not justify the means, then what in the world does?" For surely it is precisely ends to which all of us normally appeal whenever we feel the need of justifying means. The violence done by a dentist to our oral anatomy and general comfort would surely seem unjustified were it not for the end he and his patient have in view of remedying some unhealthy condition. The weariness and frustration even good teachers inflict on students is tolerable only because inseparable from means to a desired end called education. Indeed, in the rough and ready ethics of decent people everywhere, few principles seem to hold a place more honored in practice than the contradiction of the one just referred to. Throughout most of life's moral decision-making it is precisely by ends that means are justified. What then, has induced human beings to make proverbial a principle that seems to go against ethical common sense, declaring that "the end does not justify the means"?

SOME ENDS JUSTIFY SOME MEANS

Clearly enough, although many of life's morally irreproachable decisions are based on the supposed justification of means by ends, so also are some of life's most reproachable ones. The ambulance driver who endangers lives by exceeding speed limits and neglecting signals would explain his dangerous behavior by the end he has in view. But so too would a driver who in similar fashion was merely rushing home to his cocktail hour. In both cases what accounts for the means is the end. But whereas in one case most people would concede that the end justifies the means, in the other case they would not.

To declare that "the end does not justify the means" seems to state a partial truth. What seems implied in a vast number of ordinary and unchallenged moral reactions is that sometimes the end does justify the means, but sometimes it does not. Perhaps the main value of the saying is to remind us that at least some ends do not appear to justify some means. But that raises the important and difficult question of what ends justify what means. The kind of answer one hopes to find is an answer with sufficiently general validity to be applied as a standard to a wide range of moral perplexities.

The basic form of these perplexities is that of a situation in which we are trying to do something good, or at least not downright bad, and perceive that the only or most effective means of doing it involves notable badness. To try to end a war by dropping a nuclear bomb on a populous city is a familiar case in point on the grand scale. To try to end a pregnancy by aborting a fetus is an equally familiar case in a more narrowly personal context. To try to end a tiresome visit by declaring untruthfully that one has an urgent appointment elsewhere is a milder example of the same kind of thing. Of the many people who approve and practice all three of these kinds of behavior, few appear simply to dismiss moral considerations from their minds in doing so. Characteristically, they entertain real moral regrets about the means they advocate using, but consider those means justified by the ends they are intended to serve. Their state of mind resembles that of the parent who accompanies spanking with the trite but often true words, "This hurts me more than it does you." The means are admittedly deplorable, but the end is too important to forego even if no more acceptable means can be found.

ENDS AND MEANS IN THE BALANCE

Among people who approach any of these issues with ethical concern, at least two considerations seem universally present. In the first place, the end itself must be morally acceptable. Whether or not good ends justify bad means, no ethically serious person supposes bad ends justify anything at all. And in the second place, there seems to be universal recognition that some proportion has to be preserved between ends and means. To employ nuclear assault to end or avert major war is an ethically arguable decision, defended by conscientious people. But to do the same merely to punish private offenders or intimidate some remotely threatening adversary would outrage the most liberal conscience. Abortion to avert the consequences of rape often seems morally acceptable to people who would find the use of abortion to preserve a girlish figure simply detestable. Similarly, to lie about one's social availability to the neighbors is a different matter from doing the same to one who has traveled a great distance hoping to enjoy brief companionship of a supposed friend.

All these examples illustrate two things about which there seems to be general agreement. First, to justify any means, one's end or purpose must be good or innocent. Second, ends that are only slightly good will not suffice to justify means that are decidedly bad. According to some people, that is all that can be said with any confidence on this subject. Others, however, especially within Catholic tradition, deal with these matters much more elaborately.

CONSEQUENCES THAT ARE NEITHER ENDS NOR MEANS

The question of justifying means by ends envisages one form, probably the most familiar one, of a larger question that cannot be formulated quite so neatly. That is, many of the things we do have multiple consequences which may be variously good, bad, or indifferent. And of these consequences, some may be related to one another as ends and means, while others may have no such relationship. When a surgeon performs an appendectomy, the resultant scar was neither his end nor a means to it, but it was a consequence of his action. When a man works in his garden through a bright summer day, the resultant sunburn was neither his end nor a means to it, but it was a consequence of his action. When a pianist practices all night before a concert, the disturbed sleep of his neighbors was neither his end nor a means to it, but it was a consequence of his action. Thus, most of the things we do result not only in the accomplishment of certain ends and the employment of means to those ends, but also in a great many other effects which, even though entirely incidental to our real purposes, may be inevitable consequences of the actions we perform. Our question about when, if ever, an end justifies a means must be broadened to ask when, if ever, it is morally justifiable to perform an action that results in bad consequences as well as good ones.

In answering this question, some attach great importance precisely to the distinction between bad consequences that are means to the end for which an action is performed, and bad consequences that are not means but might be called side-effects. This distinction is sometimes related to another one that is frequently emphasized, between bad consequences that are intended (or "directly willed") and bad consequences that are merely permitted (or "indirectly willed"). It is from this point of view that Catholic moral theologians during recent centuries worked out various formulations of the so-called "principle of double-effect." Although recently a number of Catholic scholars have tended to withdraw their allegiance from this principle, the principle is still widely accepted and has profoundly influenced certain areas of Catholic ethical thinking including official teachings. Under the circumstances it seems incumbent on a book of this kind at least to indicate what this principle is and why doubts have been raised about its adequacy.

THE PRINCIPLE OF DOUBLE-EFFECT

A typical formulation of the principle of double-effect is expressed by listing four conditions under which it is considered justifiable to perform an action having both good and evil consequences.

(1) The immediate action performed must be good or indifferent.

(2) The foreseen evil consequence must not be intended in itself.

(3) The foreseen good consequence must not be an effect of the evil consequence.

(4) The foreseen good consequence must be proportionate to the foreseen evil consequence.

Although this principle has for a long time been widely accepted in Roman Catholic moral theology, it remains true that in applying it to identical ethical questions, different thinkers have often reached different conclusions. Presumably, therefore, it is not perfectly evident just when the four conditions are concretely realized. And that would seem to imply that the very meaning of the conditions is not perfectly clear.

ACTIONS GOOD OR INDIFFERENT "IN THEMSELVES"

One source of confusion in applying the double-effect principle is the fact that where the first condition requires the immediate action to be good or indifferent, the goodness re-

ferred to is moral goodness, whereas where the other conditions refer to good and evil consequences, goodness and evil
are understood in a broader sense, as including physical as
well as moral evil. Therefore, using this principle seems to
oblige us, in accordance with its first condition, to determine
the moral goodness or indifference of the initial action before
going on to any consideration of intentions and consequences.
However, to many people it seems scarcely possible to speak
meaningfully about the moral goodness of an action except
with reference to intentions and consequences.

Thus the principle of double effect must assume at the
very start the whole burden of a debate over whether or not it
makes sense to talk about certain kinds of actions as morally
good or bad "in themselves," that is, independently of intentions and consequences. This debate is considered elsewhere in
these pages. Roman Catholic tradition has long tended to favor
the idea of moral absolutes, in the sense of believing there are
kinds of behavior whose moral goodness, badness, or
indifference can be specified even before examining intentions
and consequences. However, this tendency in Catholic moral
teaching has recently become the object of much
reexamination, many qualifications, and some outright
rejection. Thus the once firm adherence of Catholics generally
to the principle of double-effect is shaken by the same winds of
doubt as their general acceptance of the idea of moral
absolutes.

INTENDING AND PERMITTING

The second condition of the double-effect principle introduces a psychological notion whose importance to ethical
thinking is beyond dispute. An early and important part of the
character development of any child is the discovery of how
important intentions are to morality. "I didn't mean it" is a
significant moral plea in any household, just as it is a significant legal plea in any courtroom. Most of the time, however,
in these ordinary domestic cases, the claim that no wrong was
intended is based on a claim that no wrong was anticipated.

The child who leaves the chicken coop open and claims not to have intended the chickens' escape is likely to make good such a claim only on the assumption of unusual ignorance or distraction. But in Roman Catholic tradition, the principle of double effect is regularly used in cases in which bad effects are clearly anticipated, but are said nevertheless not to be intended.

Thus it is often supposed that a belligerent force that rains bombs onto a populous city need not intend the slaughter, certain to take place, of the city's non-combatant inhabitants. Similarly, a surgeon who removes the uterus of a pregnant woman is often said not to intend the abortion which inevitably results. One moral theologian even asserts that in whipping his own children he does not intend their feeling pain.

Even these few examples may sufficiently indicate that the concept of intention involved in the principle of double-effect is an elusive one. Some of the applications of this concept are hard to reconcile with common language or common sense, and easy to interpret as instances of sophistry. The word generally used to describe a morally acceptable attitude towards the foreseen evil consequences of our actions is "permitting." But distinguishing between evil consequences we justifiably permit and those we unjustifiably intend seems often to become a mental game lacking clear, reasonable, and agreed-upon rules. Nevertheless, it is important to maintain in principle that a good person can remain consistently opposed to evil even at times when his or her way of pursuing good makes it inevitable that some evil will occur. In trying to make practical use of this distinction between intending and permitting evil consequences of our actions, we seem often to be led from the second to the third condition of the principle of double effect.

EVIL CAUSES OF GOOD EFFECTS

The third condition appears clearer than its predecessors. It does seem possible, given an ordinary popular understanding of cause and effect, to determine in at least many cases whether or not the good consequences of my action are actually caused by some of its bad consequences. Thus, I may get a splendid candidate into public office, and keep a dreadful one out, by stuffing ballot boxes. Or I may get some thoroughly admirable bills made into law by bribing certain congressmen. Or I may satisfy some woman's genuine longing for motherhood by an act of adultery. Or I may prevent transmission of a female sex-linked hereditary disease by performing hysterectomies on everyone diagnosed as having it. Or I may curtail the anti-social activities of a sex offender by compulsory castration.

Some of the actions described in the preceding paragraph would presumably be ruled out by the first condition, as not being morally good or indifferent "in themselves." Thus election fraud, bribery, and adultery would easily find their way onto conventional lists of actions that are plainly wrong. Hysterectomy and castration, however, are more likely to be perceived as physical evils which, under certain circumstances, constitute morally and medically sound procedures. Some have gone on to argue that if such surgical mutilations are justifiably undertaken for the patient's physical health, they might also be justifiably undertaken for broader social purposes. Among Catholic moral theologians, however, this position has usually been opposed on other grounds which will be discussed in another place.

WEIGHING GOOD AGAINST EVIL CONSEQUENCES

It is the fourth condition of the double-effect principle with which most people tend to feel most at home, and the basic insight it embodies readily commends itself as common sense. If one is to justify performing some action from which both good and bad consequences result, it clearly will not suffice to bring about a few trivial good effects at the cost of a multitude of grave evils. To "intend" a slight good does not entitle us to "permit" an enormous evil. Prevention of major evils takes moral precedence over the pursuit of minor goods.

One of the most noteworthy developments in recent Catholic thinking on moral questions is a fast-growing tendency to treat this last condition of the double-effect principle as the one really crucial condition for solving the kind of problem that principle addresses. The difficulties, both theoretical and practical, raised by consideration of the first three conditions gives special attractiveness to the idea of concentrating on the fourth condition. To do so does not require us to suppose that moral evil can be justified by a sufficient quantity and quality of physical good. Neither does it require us to declare invalid or irrelevant the distinction between intending and permitting evil consequences. But it does require us to admit the possibility that physically evil effects, even if intended, might be justified if they were sufficiently outweighed by good effects of the same action.

COMPARING THE CONSEQUENCES

Current developments in Catholic thinking about actions that produce both good and bad effects are clearly moving in a direction that judges the moral quality of these actions by considering the goodness and badness of their results. The basic underlying notion is that actions that produce a lot more good than evil are good actions, whereas actions that produce a lot more evil than good are bad actions. Actions that seem to produce good and evil effects more or less equally are hard to assess, and one must simply do the best one can.

Despite the quality of common sense that people seem to find in this approach, it too offers difficulties, both practical and theoretical. Of the practical difficulties the one most often noted is the problem of how to measure good and bad consequences against one another in any reliable, objective way. The problem is especially acute when the consequences to be compared belong to completely different orders of value. How can one weigh the deaths of construction workers against the growth of construction projects, the expansion of knowledge against the diminution of privacy, the incentives of private enterprise against the inequities of capitalist society, the cost of winning wars against the cost of surrendering sovereignty? There is no easy calculus for solving such problems but neither is there any ethical system in which such problems never arise.

Of the theoretical difficulties, the outstanding one has already been alluded to in other contexts. That is, to what extent is it possible to judge the morality of certain kinds of actions even before weighing their concrete effects? Are there indeed certain things it would be wrong to do even if the physically good results of doing them enormously outweighed the bad results? There is perhaps no single issue that haunts the deliberations of serious moralists more than this one.

STUDY QUESTIONS

1. In what sense can it be reasonably claimed that the end does not justify the means?

2. In what situations do conscientious people tend to be morally concerned over whether or not the end justifies the means?

3. What must be true of an end before the question of its justifying certain means can even be raised ethically?

4. How do the relative goodness of an end and the badness of the means affect the justification of means by end?

5. Can all the consequences of human actions be classified as either ends or means?

6. Are consequences that are neither ends nor means relevant to ethical evaluation of an action?

7. For what purpose is the principle of double effect employed in ethics?

8. How is the principle of double effect typically formulated?

9. How does use of the double-effect principle raise the question of actions good or bad "in themselves"?

10. To what extent is intention normally considered relevant to moral evaluation of actions?

11. How does the distinction between intending and permitting tend to become confusing?

12. What is a practical difficulty about determining the relative proportion of good and evil consequences?

13. What is the main theoretical difficulty about basing ethical evaluation on the comparision of good and bad consequences?

14. Is the double-effect principle a good criterion for evaluating moral behavior? If so, why? If not, how should it be amended?

Chapter Fourteen

MORAL GOODNESS AND HUMAN HAPPINESS

SCHOOLS OF THOUGHT IN ETHICS

To the question, how does one decide what is the right thing to do, many different answers are given. The more persuasive answers have laid foundations for major schools of thought in ethics. Many of these schools of thought have long histories and complex developments that can be appreciated only through concentrated study. However, the characteristic outlooks and major assumptions of some of these schools of thought closely correspond to notably different ways in which ordinary people tend to make their moral decisions. Like the character in Molière's comedy who was astonished to learn he had been speaking "prose," lots of people would be equally surprised to learn that their moral deliberations marked them out clearly as stoics or epicureans, deontologists or teleologists, naturalists or idealists, and so forth.

In the following pages I wish to indicate a few of the types of ethical thought that continue to thrive, however anonymously, among us. I hope to do this, as far as possible, without using either historical references or conventional labels, so as to neither exceed nor distract from this book's limited purposes. Despite my intended avoidance of historical references, I would venture the historical opinion that, for all the talk we hear about "new moralities" there is not one among the ethical systems currently vying for popularity that has not been around for quite some time.

THE PURSUIT OF HAPPINESS

One of the oldest traditions in ethics, and one taken up strongly by Christian and Catholic tradition, begins by asking in a very general way what human life is driving at. Only if we know, in that sense, what we are for, can we hope to know what our opportunities and activities are for. And only on that basis can we satisfactorily organize and criticize our activities. It seems reasonable to suggest that if human life has some governing purpose, then human deeds should be approved or disapproved according to how well they line up with that purpose. If human life had no governing purpose, or none we could hope to discover, there would be little hope of demonstrating any "right" way for human beings to behave.

One obvious way to propose an answer to the question of what human life is driving at is by generalizing about conscious human motivation. It is in this way that the question has often been answered by saying that what human life is driving at is happiness. Everything we do seems to be aimed ultimately at preserving, increasing, or simply obtaining happiness. Even when we choose, in the popular sense of the phrase, to "make ourselves miserable," we do so on the supposition that the misery itself is a way to some kind of happiness. We willingly toil and suffer in the belief that our toil and suffering are, for some reason, prerequisite to a happiness the prospect of which makes such things endurable. Accordingly, a great deal of the popular moralizing that goes on around us takes the form of an effort to persuade people that something they are trying to do or trying to get will not bring them happiness or that the happiness it does bring will be not as much or not as good as a happiness they might otherwise achieve.

HAPPINESS AND MORAL GOODNESS

If, indeed, everything people deliberately do is part of a universal pursuit of happiness, if this indicates happiness to be the purpose of human life, and if ethics takes the position that human conduct is right or wrong according as it does or does not serve the purpose of human life, then the function of ethics is clear. The job of ethics is to show people how best to pursue happiness, showing them in the process how some of the things they do are poorly conducive to happiness. Thus one venerable and very influential school of thought in ethics takes as its foundation what some philosophers of the last century called the "greatest happiness principle." That is, the ethical rightness or wrongness of behavior is gauged by its relative conduciveness to the greatest happiness. Practically speaking, what this means is that the right thing to do at any given moment is whichever of the possible alternatives can be expected to result in the greatest net increase of happiness.

One naturally asks, "Whose happiness?" If one answers that question to the effect that the right thing to do for any given individual is whatever will bring greatest happiness to that particular individual, this position becomes sheerly egotistic. Understood in the same way it obviously opens the way to endless conflict, since there is every chance that what two or more persons decide is most conducive to happiness will be available to one of them only if it is unavailable to the others. Although some people contend that for each individual to pursue his or her own best interest would, in the long run, be best for everybody, such a view seems more wistful than realistic. Although Christian and Catholic tradition has often closely related ethics to the pursuit of happiness, it has not generally identified the happiness in question with each individual's independent satisfaction of his or her own desires.

Still, there is one sense in which Christian tradition might be thought of as fostering a kind of ethics of individual self-interest.

BEING GOOD AND BECOMING HAPPY

It is well known that Christians, and Catholics in a rather special way, hold that those who do God's will enjoy God's blessing. Moreover, the fullness of God's blessing is understood as entailing happiness which is everlasting and unimaginably superior to even the most ecstatic occasions of natural happiness. There can be no doubt that in Christian tradition a strong link is forged between being good and becoming happy. And this is especially the case in Catholic tradition where a doctrine of merit presents the prospect of ultimate happiness as not only a gift bestowed by God, but also in some sense a reward deserved from God.

Christianity does, therefore, typically associate ethical righteousness with acquiring happiness in the long run. This association must be included among the traditionally central, basic beliefs of Christians, and as part of what is implied in considering the virtue of hope as integral to Christian living. Just how the association of ethical righteousness with ultimate happiness is conceived is, of course, an extremely important theological question, but not one to be dealt with at this point. The present emphasis is confined to the notion that in Christian thought being good and becoming happy are, in the last analysis, inseparable.

However, it is very important to perceive the difference between a theological conviction that moral goodness is linked to human happiness, and an ethical position that sees the pursuit of human happiness as precisely the way to moral goodness. In practice, it is the difference between saying that if one pursues maximum happiness one will thereby be doing the ethically right thing, and saying that if one does the ethically right thing, one will thereby be pursuing maximum happiness. The Christian belief that one who does the right thing, equated of course with God's will, shall achieve ultimate happiness does not, of itself, offer any indication of what the right thing, or God's will, might happen to be. Very different is the ethical assertion that seeking to bring about the greatest happiness is precisely what doing the right thing means.

LOVING AND PURSUING HAPPINESS

Some Christians do seem to confuse these two very different ways of linking moral goodness to human happiness. But some who do not confuse them are nevertheless eager to combine them. And in Christianity itself they seem to find a plausible basis for doing so. For, as we have frequent occasion to recall, Christianity's most insistent and fundamental ethical demand is for love. And whatever else may be implied in the Christian understanding of love, it seems reasonable to suppose that its most obvious practical implication must be precisely a pursuit of happiness. For to love, in any but a trivial or sub-moral way, is surely to want and to seek the happiness of whomever one does love. Hence it might well seem that the best way to translate the Christian ideal of universal love into practical ethics would be precisely by adopting the "greatest happiness principle" as a comprehensive moral norm. That is, if in all one's conduct one seeks to do those things which promise to contribute most to human happiness and least to human unhappiness, one might seem to be living a life of love in the most practical possible way. Although there is nothing new about Christians' understanding love as a striving to make people happy, modern times have witnessed a widespread, systematic tendency to find in the "greatest happiness principle" an adequate practical key to Christian ethics. Consequently, some reflection on the strengths and weaknesses of this principle is indispensable to a modern account of Christian ethics.

HOW TO TELL IF ONE IS LOVING

One of the great advantages Christian ethics is thought to have by many people is its capability of being boiled down to a single idea, the idea (as Christians conceive it) of loving. Concrete ethical decisions can become so very complicated that it is reassuring to have some single principle as a basic reference point from which to take one's moral bearings. Thus it is sometimes said that in the midst of his or her ethical confusion over what is the right thing to do, a Christian can always straighten matters out by translating that question into one that asks what is the loving (or perhaps the most loving) thing to do. However, as soon as one begins thinking about it, doubts are likely to arise about whether it is really very much easier to give a conclusive answer to the one question than it is to the other.

On innumerable occasions, one could plausibly represent a long list of ethical alternatives as being, every one of them, a loving thing to do. Any action that does anybody any kind of genuine good can, to that extent, be called a loving action. And a great many of the actions we have trouble choosing among do different kinds of real good to different people. If one includes loving oneself among the ethical duties of a Christian —as many, and probably most Catholic moral teachers have done—almost every course of action that is not wantonly malicious can be brought within the category of loving actions. Thus it may seem as though all the Christian's love ethic enables him to do is to substitute for the question "What is the right thing to do?" the question "What is the right loving thing to?" and thereupon resume his original perplexity.

It is here that Christians may find themselves strongly attracted to something like the greatest happiness principle. For although there may be a wide range of loving things to be done, one might perhaps find a way to decide which of these loving things is in some meaningful sense more loving than the others. And if one understands as loving deeds, deeds that contribute to the happiness of others, one might give this question some practicality by asking which of one's options seems likely to contribute the most happiness to others.

COMPARING HAPPINESSES

However, as soon as one begins trying to apply this norm to the ordinary options of life, its practicality becomes less obvious. It may seem practical enough if one does not look too far ahead. Thus, if I ask whether I should, on my day off, enjoy a late sleep in the morning, or rise early to prepare breakfast for the family, the latter may seem evidently more loving, as designed to give more happiness to more people. But perhaps I am so genuinely tired, that my own happiness at getting some rest would be far greater than my family's at having me fix breakfast. Or even if I leave myself out of the calculation (as some would judge a Christian ought to do), I may know that the loss of needed rest is very likely to make me dull and inefficient and even irritable later on, and thus occasion greater unhappiness eventually than the little happiness it immediately affords.

Clearly such speculations about the relative net happiness to be expected from even such simple options might often go on indefinitely and inconclusively. And if one tries to apply similar calculations to more momentous choices—such as vocational alternatives—the prospects of a confident solution on this basis may become exceedingly dim. Further complications arise if one compares not only the different amounts of happiness but also the different choices. Should I give my savings to the poor, or spend them on an education otherwise unattainable? Should I work longer hours in behalf of my clients, constituents, patients, students—or should I share more leisure with my family? Whether or not one should ask oneself questions like these, it is clear at least that on the basis of comparing different prospects of happiness, some of them are not going to yield compelling answers.

Perhaps one could conclude that when convincing answers to such questions are forthcoming one should act upon them, and that otherwise one should simply do one of the more than trivially "loving" things and let it go at that. This would be a kind of adaptation to the love ethic of an ethical strategy called "probabilism," that was developed (amid considerable strife) over a long period of Catholic moral theology. Such a norm would recommend that if, after due investigation, one found serious probability that either of two alternative courses of action was an ethically good thing (or, in terms of a love ethic, a loving thing) to do, one should feel free to do either of them. Another strategy, also strongly supported in Catholic tradition, called "probabiliorism" would require one to choose an alternative that showed greater probability of being a morally good choice. In their original form, these ethical strategies were employed to distinguish between right and wrong or good and bad choices, not good and better or more and less loving ones. Nevertheless, their basic purpose, of relieving people of hopeless quests for moral certainty, has wide applicability.

DOING MOST GOOD AND MATTERS OF HOMICIDE

Quite apart from practical difficulties of comparing different prospects of happiness, the principle of always preferring the course of action that generates the greatest amount of net happiness encounters another kind of difficulty which pertains more directly to ethics than to the psychology of bewildering choices. Let us suppose, for example, that a group of terrorists kidnap a group of school children and announce that they intend to kill all of them unless a certain political enemy of theirs, who happens to be in local protective custody, is promptly put to death. An unqualified adherent of the greatest happiness principle might reasonably conclude that a lot more happiness would result from the survival of the children than from that of the politician. Suppose further that it is perfectly possible under the circumstances for someone to arrange for the politician's "suicide" to take place in his detention cell. Probably the only way an adherent of the greatest happiness principle could disapprove of the politician's murder would be by supposing that the long range effects of such action would ultimately cause greater unhappiness than the (presumably otherwise unavoidable) slaughter of the children. Such an argument just might seem persuasive, but it would be no surprise if in certain circumstances it did not.

Consider another case that partially resembles the preceding one. The driver of a streetcar approaches a point where the tracks fork, at which point he can control onto which track his car proceeds. Just beyond this point, but closer than the distance in which it is possible to stop, the driver sees sprawled on one track an intoxicated pedestrian. On the other track, at the same distance, he sees wrestling together a group of very small children, oblivious of his horn-blowing. An adherent of the greatest happiness principle might find this an easy, though a sad choice, and opt for the course that spares the children and slays the drunk. From any ethical point of view it would be hard to argue convincingly against this decision.

There are a number of reasons why a conscientious person might approve the choice made in the latter case much more readily than the one made in the preceding case. Among these reasons, one of the most pressing would be the fact that in the former case downright murder was committed (albeit for praiseworthy motives), whereas in the latter case it was not. Most people are convinced that there is a crucial difference between committing murder, even to prevent someone else from committing more extensive murder, and killing one person in the process of avoiding killing, in the same way, a number of people. Most people would accordingly judge that whereas the drunk was a victim of impersonal tragic circumstances, the politician was a victim of personal injustice. Even one who judged that the action of murdering the politician was, in the situation, fairly readily excusable, would probably also judge that the action of the streetcar driver simply required no excuse. And to excuse an action does imply that the action is considered not merely unfortunate, but wrong. But if the only thing that makes any action wrong is its foreseen failure to result in a net maximum of happiness, then in the murder of the politician there is apparently nothing wrong, nothing to excuse, nothing ethically different from the case of the streetcar driver.

DOING MOST GOOD AND BREAKING PROMISES

Let us turn to simpler and less dramatic cases. Suppose I have promised a mediocre student that I shall meet him after school to discuss an academic project in which he is not very diligently engaged. Shortly before the meeting a telephone call from some old and very dear friends tells me they have a very brief stopover between planes and that nothing would please them more than for us to take the rare opportunity for a brief reunion. It may be plain to me that meeting the student will give him very moderate happiness and that missing the appointment will cause him only minor inconvenience. On the basis of the greatest happiness principle, my choice may seem clear. And yet it would hardly be fanatical for me to judge that that choice would be wrong for the simple reason that it would mean breaking a promise. Yet if there is any validity at all in that point of view, it depends on a belief that there is something ethically wrong about breaking promises and something ethically right about keeping them, independently of comparing foreseen consequences for human happiness. And on that basis one might understandably judge that keeping a promise, with somewhat less resultant happiness, might be right, and breaking a promise, with somewhat more resultant happiness, might be wrong.

To fill out this picture more fully, suppose we change the preceding case to one in which I disregard my appointment because on my way to it I encounter someone who is alone and seriously injured, and do what I can to make him comfortable and get him suitable assistance. No one is likely to accuse me of having done the wrong thing in breaking my promise. Here, as in the case of meeting the old friends, I have decided to neglect my promise in order to make a greater contribution to human happiness. The difference is that in this case the foreseen contribution is so extremely much greater. If one judges the two cases differently, it is not on the basis of believing that promises are to be kept only when keeping them is likely to result in greater happiness than could result from breaking them. It is because, although I believe promises are to be kept simply because they are promises, I also believe this genuine moral obligation to keep promises can be over-ruled by a graver ethical obligation to give vitally needed assistance. It is not, therefore, that I consider the greatest happiness principle to be the sole basis of all moral obliga-tions. Rather, I consider that it may come into conflict with other, quite distinct moral norms, and that in such circum-stances one should abide by whichever obligation seems in the circumstances genuinely graver. The decision as to which is graver may draw some assistance from general considerations, but must rely in the last analysis on individual moral discre-tion, the concrete exercise of that personal moral judgment which is sometimes referred to as conscience (a term with inconveniently many meanings).

DOES THE GREATEST HAPPINESS PRINCIPLE MAKE SENSE?

As a parenthetical consideration, it may interest those who enjoy logical games to consider how much sense can really be made of the classic utilitarian or consequentialist formula that enjoins us in all our actions to seek the greatest happiness (or greatest good) of the greatest number. How, in using this formula, is one supposed to organize the two com-bined goals of producing as much happiness as possible and making happy as many people as possible? Supposing happi-ness to be somehow at least roughly measurable—which must be supposed if the formula has any use at all—how is one to determine the relationship between total quantity and overall distribution? Suppose I can produce 100 units of some kind of happiness, and parcel it out in all sorts of ways. Is it better to deliver one unit to each of 100 people than all 100 units to a single person? Or should it be 2 to each of 50, or 4 to each of 25, and so on? Or suppose instead I can either settle a 100 unit lump of happiness on one person, or make a much wider distribution of no more than 90 units of happiness? To try to effect as much happiness as possible is one policy. To try to make as many people as possible happy is another policy. Is there any rational way to combine them as a single policy? Is "the greatest happiness of the greatest number" more than empty rhetoric?

STUDY QUESTIONS

1. What general questions are the various ethical schools of thought attempting to answer?

2. What line of thought leads some schools of ethics to focus on the idea of happiness?

3. What is meant by the greatest happiness principle?

4. On what interpretation of the greatest happiness principle is it essentially egotistic?

5. Is there any sense in which Christianity might seem to foster concern for individual self-interest?

6. How does Christian tradition tend to link moral goodness with human happiness?

7. How might an ethical emphasis on love suggest an emphasis on the pursuit of happiness?

8. In what sense is Christian ethics sometimes regarded as being extremely simple?

9. Why is a general determination to do the loving thing sometimes unhelpful as an ethical norm?

10. How practical is an ethical determination to do the more or most loving thing?

11. What are some practical ways of dealing with doubts about what is the more loving thing to do?

12. How might the greatest happiness principle lead to morally quite different decisions to take human life?

13. How might the greatest happiness principal lead to morally quite different decisions to break promises?

14. Why does applying the greatest happiness principle raise questions about the validity of other ethical principles?

15. What logical questions arise concerning the meaningfulness of seeking the greatest good of the greatest number?

16. What are some of the elements of human happiness as you define it? How does your definition relate to moral goodness?

Chapter Fifteen

MORAL PRINCIPLES AND NATURAL LAW

PLURALITY OF ETHICAL PRINCIPLES

One of the main purposes of the preceding discussion has been to invite criticism of the idea that, by seeking in all our actions to bring about a net maximum increase of human happiness, the demands of ethics can be fully satisfied. There is no intention of implying that this is not a useful ethical norm. What is suggested is that it is not a sufficient one. For occasions do seem to arise in which a course of action that entails such violations of elementary justice as the taking of innocent lives or the breaking of apparently binding promises does seem likely to result in more happiness than any other available course of action.

If this line of criticism is valid, what it suggests is that a norm like the greatest happiness principle is a principle, but not the sole principle for the ethical guidance of our lives. The kinds of moral experience represented by the few examples cited intimate that there are other principles, such as respect for an individual life or fidelity to a reasonable promise, that cannot in theory be absorbed within the greatest happiness principle, and that can therefore in practice come into conflict with it. Real life can pose such real questions as: "Should I do what is likely to produce the greatest happiness, or should I spare an innocent human life?" "Should I do what is likely to produce the greatest happiness, or should I keep my word?"

There are those who maintain that to follow such principles as respecting life and keeping promises does result, generally speaking, in a net maximum of happiness. This may be true, generally speaking, but there is no practical way of determining whether it is or not, and there is every reason to doubt that it is invariably true. Hence the question inevitably arises of what should be done in cases where it does not seem to be true. There are those who maintain that precisely in order to bring about a net maximum of happiness, certain other principles ought to be followed even when we cannot really perceive that following them is likely to bring about the greatest happiness. This latter view implies the assumption that by following certain other principles we are really, even if unwittingly, following the greatest happiness principle. Some Christians would justify this assumption on the theological grounds that God will ultimately reward with supreme happiness those who respond conscientiously to what they perceive as their moral obligations. But at this point it is clear that the greatest happiness principle is no longer envisaged as a universally practical guide for moral life, whereas for such practical guidance we must rely not on one principle alone, but on a number of principles. And since the concrete applications of these different principles do not always harmonize, we must also rely at times on quite particular moral judgments of our own.

THE NATURAL AND THE REASONABLE

Catholic tradition concerning moral principles has long been associated with the idea, which is older than Christianity, of natural law. This phrase has been understood in a number of different ways, with the result that it has generated much confusion and controversy. All that is feasible in a book of this kind is to try to express as simply as possible some ideas about natural law that seem basic to a persistent and central way of thinking among Catholic moral teachers.

God is believed to create purposefully. The things he creates he intends to be and act in definite ways, and his intention finds expression in the created things themselves. It is not as though God first made purposeless objects, then assigned purposes to them, and finally got them going in accordance with those purposes. What a thing is is inseparable from how it is and how it is designed to act. Hence, created things have certain tendencies, and these tendencies are part of their very being.

Thus different kinds of things are said to have different natures, corresponding to the different ways they are designed to act. One discovers the natures by observing the things together with their activities. And in the course of such observation, one discovers large areas of regularity and predictability. On this basis, one designates classes of things having distinctive similarities of form and function. Such observation, in its discovery of patterns, is readily interpreted by one who believes in God as the uncovering of a plan, of which the observed patterns are, so to speak, the realization. This plan, built in as it were to created realities, is natural law. It is thought of as natural inasmuch as God's direction and control operates from within the things that he creates. It is thought of as law inasmuch as it derives from the directing mind and controlling will of God. As applied to the non-living world, or to plants and animals, this way of thinking has much in common with elementary natural science, with its descriptive laws and classificatory schemes based on regularly recurring phenomena.

With regard to human beings, however, the notion of natural law becomes more complicated. Human beings have, of course, many aspects of form and function in common with sub-human beings. Hence, the findings of physics and chemistry, of biology and animal psychology are extensively applicable to human beings. Yet at the same time, human beings are put into a distinctive class precisely because there seems to be something quite special about them. And in classical and Christian philosophical tradition, this something special has long been identified as rationality. Hence the familiar definition, rational animal, the first term of which implies that the distinctively natural thing about human beings is their tendency to reason and act in accordance with reason, or at least think they ought so to act.

Thus it appears why traditional Catholic moral teachers seem sometimes to be claiming an ethics of natural law, but at other times to be asserting an ethics of right reason. Natural law implies acting in accordance with nature. But since human nature is a rational nature, for human beings to act naturally involves their acting rationally. Thus Thomas Aquinas, whose ethics employ a natural law basis, is able to say that all vices are unnatural vices, because he understands vices to be habits of irrational behavior and human behavior to be naturally rational. Yet in his day as in ours, people were accustomed to apply the phrase unnatural vice to only a small number of vices, notably to deviant sexual behavior. Thomas explains that this popular usage refers to departures from natural tendencies that human beings have in common with other animals, but that it is no less unnatural to violate distinctively human, that is, rational tendencies.

PRACTICAL REASON

From what has been said it appears that in the tradition we are examining, following the natural law implies, for human beings, following the guidance of reason. And the question naturally arises of how reason is supposed to provide the requisite guidance. Traditional answers to this question generally begin by pointing to a distinction between speculative reason and practical reason. This distinction can be related to the one discussed previously, between "is" and "ought," or between the factual realm and the moral realm. Thus speculative reason has to do with factual truths, whereas practical reason is concerned with what ought to be done. Obviously, human beings do form judgments and reach convictions about what ought to be done. Their capacity for that kind of thinking is what practical reason refers to.

If practical reason is part of human nature, and if its function includes discovering what, in the moral sense, ought to be done, one obvious conclusion might seem to follow. That is, different individuals who are said to have a human nature, and therefore supposed to have a practical reason, might be expected to show at least general basic agreement about what ought to be done, that is, about moral principles. And of course, they do.

At this point, certain objections naturally arise having to do with whether or not there really is general basic agreement about moral principles. For surely it is true that not all people hold to an identical set of moral principles. It has often been pointed out that not only are there individual differences in this respect, but there are broad cultural differences as well. Even in antiquity, travelers' tales about Amazons and cannibals raised doubts concerning the universality of Western ethical views of the subordination of women and the respect owed to the dead. And the less fanciful information provided by explorers and anthropologists in modern times has greatly increased popular awareness of the ethical diversity among human groups. Such findings have even led some to endorse theories of what is called ethical relativism, the view that what is right and wrong varies from one society to another, and that there is no validity to absolute statements of what is right and wrong.

It does not of course follow logically that because certain peoples think something to be wrong which other peoples think to be right, there can be no absolutely true statements concerning rightness and wrongness. Ethical statements, like other kinds of statements, might correspond to the truth even if all peoples thought otherwise. But in fact, ethical relativists tend to be also ethical subjectivists, for whom there is no real difference between being right or wrong and being considered right or wrong. Catholic tradition has been consistently opposed to unqualified forms of either relativism or subjectivism. That is, Catholic tradition has regularly maintained that there are moral norms applicable to all, and that human minds discover such norms but do not simply invent them. And even on a less theoretical plane, Catholic tradition has always supposed that there really is general knowledge of such norms.

This is not to say, however, that Catholic tradition has claimed that all valid ethical principles are known to everybody. Indeed, its classic spokesmen have been quite conservative on that score, proposing only very few principles as being acknowledged by most people everywhere, and seldom venturing to propose a definitive list even of those. The general tendency of this tradition is to consider some very broad ethical principles to be generally known, while considering other, more particular principles as matters of limited awareness and widespread doubt. It is unfortunately true that in rather recent times some Catholic writers, mainly of seminary textbooks, seemed to imagine the natural law was rather easily reducible to tidy comprehensive handbooks. Although such simplemindedness is no fair sample of the tradition, it did precipitate much of the anti-traditionalism that is now in evidence. On the whole, it is much more the view that there are valid ethical generalizations, than any extensive listing of what they are, that truly characterize Catholic tradition. Hence, although the reality of a natural moral law has been traditionally affirmed among Catholics, much of the content of that law has been endlessly debated.

THE PRIMARY PRECEPT OF THE NATURAL LAW

According to Catholic tradition, natural law has one so-called primary precept, on which all the rest of it depends. The usual way of formulating this primary precept is to the effect that what is good ought to be done or sought, and what is evil ought to be avoided. In thinking about this statement, one is likely to reflect that it seems to be a mere tautology, a saying of the same thing in different words. For what is traditionally meant by the good is precisely that which ought to be done or sought, and what is traditionally meant by evil is precisely the contrary. Although this reflection is correct, one should not too easily conclude that the statement is simply trivial. Perhaps the real point of it can be brought out more clearly by putting it somewhat differently, saying that there is such a thing as the good, meaning what ought to be done or sought, and there is also such a thing as evil, meaning the contrary. In other words, what this first precept represents is precisely that basic human awareness of good and evil which underlies all ethical thinking. It expresses the realization that there are moral aspects as well as factual aspects to reality, and that therefore the human mind must deal with "ought" questions as well as with "is" questions. The primary precept is not really a precept at all; it is a way of expressing in words the very dawning of moral consciousness.

It is therefore misleading, though unfortunately not uncommon, to treat this primary precept as the starting point for logical arguments. To formulate such arguments as: Evil is to be avoided, but adultery is evil, therefore adultery is to be avoided, is hardly to express what any normal human mind does in ethical deliberations. To know that adultery (or anything else) is evil is precisely to know that it ought to be avoided. It is absurd to pretend that one might first come to know that adultery is evil, and then go on by a process of argumentation to reach the further conclusion that it ought to be avoided. What the primary precept declares is that there are things that ought to be done, which we call good, and other things that ought to be avoided, which we call evil. In saying that adultery is evil, one is simply putting it into the latter category. One could not put it into that category if one was unaware of the distinction between good and evil, and in that sense the primary precept of the natural law is indeed presupposed by every ethical judgment. But that does not, of course, answer the question of how one is supposed to know whether adultery or anything else is good or evil.

FURTHER PRECEPTS OF NATURAL LAW

As this tradition is elaborated by its most influential representatives, notably Thomas Aquinas, the elementary notions of natural law are based on elementary tendencies of human beings. Of these the most elementary of all is said to be an inclination common to all natures, the inclination to self-preservation. That is, all other tendencies presuppose a basic tendency to stay in existence, to avoid destruction or annihilation. And evidently there could be little point in pursuing other goods for oneself if one did not in some prior sense seek to keep oneself in being.

Beyond this tendency considered common to creatures in general, there are other fundamental tendencies that human beings share with other animals. Among these the one most often cited is the mating tendency of male with female and the closely related tendency to produce and raise offspring. This is often considered analogous to the previous tendency as being directed to the preservation rather of the species than of the individual.

On the distinctively human plane are tendencies that depend on the operation of humanity's distinctive attribute, reason. Traditionally this is exemplified by the human tendency to discover truth concerning God—or, as modern jargon might have it, about ultimate meaning and value. Also commonly cited in this connection is the tendency to develop distinctively human society. Hence, on this level, natural law urges the overcoming of ignorance, and of whatever behavior causes offensiveness in communal living.

Thus natural law for human beings is typically unfolded according to distinguishable levels on which human beings naturally exist. This does not mean, however, that there is one natural moral law for human beings as mere creatures, another for them as animals, and still another for them as rational persons. For human reason is intended to influence human existence on every level. It is for reason to prescribe for self-preservation, and for sexual and parental behavior, no less than for the quest of truth and the development of community. That all these things are naturally good appears from observing natural inclinations. But what ought to be done about these naturally good tendencies is the task of reason to discover. Consequently, natural law ethics is not simply a matter of doing what comes naturally. Rather it is a matter of determining what it is reasonable to do about what comes naturally.

So, for example, normal tendencies shared by human beings with other animals indicate that the mating of the sexes is good. But it remains to be determined how this good purpose ought to be pursued consistently with other good purposes. How is that which is good on the basis even of animal nature to be treated as good on the basis of rational nature? To bring the natural and the rational into a distinctively human harmony is the basic program of natural law ethics as developed in classical and Christian tradition.

STUDY QUESTIONS

1. What might lead one to doubt that pursuing maximum happiness corresponds to a sufficient ethical norm?

2. What are some other ethical norms that might appear to have independent validity?

3. Is it possible or demonstrable that following such norms leads to maximum happines?

4. Is the idea of natural law derived from Christian sources?

5. What theological convictions underlie traditional Christian use of natural law ethics?

6. Practically speaking, what is meant by attributing different natures to different things?

7. Why are seemingly natural patterns of activity thought of in terms of law?

8. What complicates the application of natural law to the realm of human action?

9. Why do natural law ethics and right reason ethics tend to be associated in Catholic tradition?

10. In what sense might all vices be thought of as unnatural?

11. On what basis are some vices distinguished from others as unnatural?

12. Broadly speaking, what is the basis for distinguishing between speculative and practical reason?

13. Why does natural law ethics seem to imply some general agreement concerning ethical principles?

14. What evidence casts doubt on the assumption of general agreement about ethical principles?

15. What is meant by ethical relativism?

16. Does the fact that some consider right what others consider wrong compel one to accept ethical relativism?

17. Does Catholic tradition maintain that all valid ethical principles are universally known?

18. What is traditionally referred to as the primary precept of the natural law?

19. What seems to be the significance of this primary precept?

20. In what sense is the primary precept a starting point for ethical argumentation?

21. On what elementary tendencies of human beings have basic natural law principles been traditionally established?

22. Is the practice of natural law ethics reducible to simply doing "what comes naturally"?

23. What is the relationship between natural law and human reason? What would happen if one were to exist without the other?

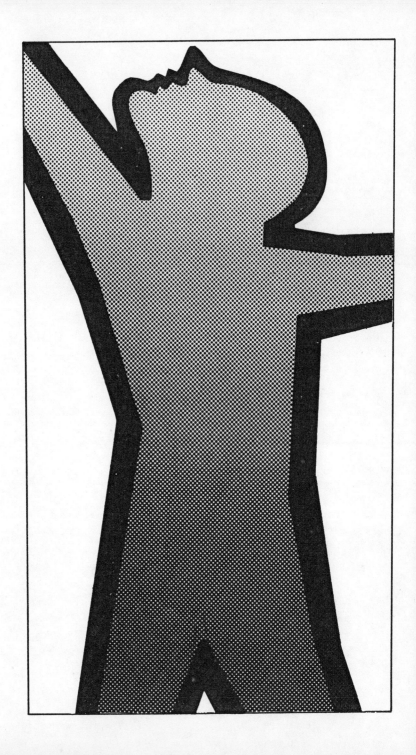

Chapter Sixteen

THE EMERGENCE OF ETHICAL
PRINCIPLES

FROM THE IS OF NATURE TO THE OUGHT OF LAW

It may be noted that a great deal of ground is covered, although in extremely general terms, by those very basic aspects of natural law cited by Thomas Aquinas: self-preservation, sexual and parental conduct, pursuit of ultimate truth, and cultivation of communal life. It would not be easy to think of significant moral issues that do not pertain to one or more of these headings. Nevertheless, what these headings refer to are basic universal tendencies of human beings, considered as such to represent fundamental human goods or values. Thus far, no ethical principles have been indicated beyond the very general assertion that goods or values such as these ought to be pursued in accordance with reason.

It is at that point that the tradition moves from the realm of is to the realm of ought, from observing how people behave to declaring how they ought to behave. That move cannot be justified by strict logic. The normal tendencies of human beings are matters of fact. The assertion that those tendencies ought to be pursued in a rational manner is a matter of ethics. Moreover it is a matter of basic insight. If someone simply denies either that human behavior should be rational or that it should be directed by basic natural inclinations, there is no way such a denial can be proved wrong. Any ethical tradition has to begin with some starting point that is itself ethical. Catholic tradition has tended to begin here, with the assumption that natural goods, as evidenced by natural tendencies, ought to be pursued, and that the pursuit of them ought to be governed by reason.

A SELF AMONG SELVES

Where does one go from there? I should suggest that of the basic areas of natural law referred to previously, two in particular furnish the initial context for most people's ethical thinking. They are, self-preservation and communal living. Both of these areas are already familiar parts of people's environments by the time they are capable of ethical thinking. Everyone is an individual who, from the very dawn of life, experiences both dangers and safeguards to self-preservation. Pains and pleasures, precariousness and security, are intensely present from the moment of birth, and efforts for self-preservation are pathetically evident even in the cradle.

All these primitive experiences occur, of course, within a community, but a practical awareness of community comes only after a certain amount of maturation. When it does come, what it involves is a recognition that the self one is habitually trying to preserve exists in intimate and inevitable relationship with other selves, who are also self-preserving individuals. Each of these individuals thus finds himself or herself depending for self-preservation itself on a lot of other individuals who are in essentially the same position. It seems very likely that this is the setting in which morality first becomes a conscious factor in human life: the point at which self-preserving individuals become aware, as such, of one another, and of their dependence, as such, on one another. In this context, the human being discovers that self-interest and respect for the self-interest of others must go hand in hand. Thus a primitive life that strives merely to seek pleasure and avoid pain, starts to become the life of a consciously social being who tries to enter into mutually satisfactory relationships with others. Naive egotism begins to give way to more enlightened reciprocity, to a sense of fairness in human transactions, to an awareness of the rights and obligations inherent in mutually satisfactory relationships. There comes a point fairly early in most lives when primitive complaints to the effect that "I don't like it" give way to very different kinds of complaints to the effect that "It's not fair." And with the understanding that something may not be fair to oneself, there is established a basis for understanding that something may also be unfair to others.

Much of this emergence of ethics in the experience of society is easy to observe among children and to remember from one's own childhood. At one time or another, phrases like the following can be heard among even the youngest in any schoolyard. "You promised you would, so you have to!" "Don't take more than your share!" "It's the least you could do, after all I did for you." "She can't do all that, we'd better help her." "Don't be mean, he didn't do anything to you!" "They broke ours, so they should let us use theirs."

These concrete imperative statements obviously do not express mere wishes and pleas. They are principled statements, despite the fact that most children who make them would be unprepared to formulate the underlying principles. It is, of course, true, as the examples themselves suggest, that the reason why such principled imperatives are expressed is usually to get someone else to behave as the one who expresses them desires. But, regardless of their motivation, they are in fact taken quite seriously by those to whom they are addressed, and they in turn will readily invoke similar principled imperatives when the situation changes. The very fact that children are so quick to argue or make excuses testifies to their common acknowledgement of ethical principles as valid norms. Sheer undisguised disdain for such principles implies a degree of depravity that takes time to develop, hence is found chiefly among adults or older children.

As one reflects on such statements, what they appear to indicate is the widespread early recognition of certain familiar principles of beneficence and justice. Common to them all is an acknowledgment that other people are morally comparable to oneself, so that the principles constitute a common ground for mutual understanding and the settlement of social conflicts. This supposes that deeds that would be judged wrong if one were the object of them, must also be judged wrong if one is the doer of them. This underlying assumption suggests the "golden rule," cited not only in the Gospel but also in records of moral wisdom from countless ages and cultures, of treating others as one would have others treat oneself. Such thinking is obviously in close continuity with the idea of loving one's neighbor as oneself.

It is scarcely possible to specify just what principles or how many principles of this sort are recognized commonly by ordinary people in the course of their social experience. And one can argue interminably over the extent to which such principles can be combined and included under more general principles. The typical phrases recalled above suggest such principles as the following: Promises should be kept. Common goods should be evenly distributed. Favors deserve gratitude. One should help people in need. Unprovoked injury is wicked. Damages require compensation.

NATURAL LAW AND RELIGION

Principles such as these are usually already operative to a considerable extent in most people's ethical thinking early in life. They are generally well established long before any explicit seeking of God, or of ultimate truth and value, is feasible, and very long before there is any possibility of assuming the roles of spouses or parents. When these further stages of maturity are reached, the practical scope of principles already recognized is enlarged to accommodate these new dimensions of life. In addition, further principles may be recognized, especially such as pertain to religious duties and intellectual integrity. Just as earlier principles concerning social fairness suggest the duty of loving one's neighbor as oneself, so these further principles point to the duty of loving God above all. And once God is understood as the ultimate source of all truth and value, the whole domain of morality assumes a religious aspect. Moreover, belief in a wise and benevolent creator powerfully reinforces that crucial starting point of natural law ethics, the supposition that one should pursue in accordance with reason those things whose goodness is attested by natural tendencies. God's law is perceived behind natural law because God's love is perceived behind nature.

What the advent of religion means to the ethics of natural law is more, however, than simply reinforcement. Religion often makes its entry by a kind of extension of the dynamism of natural law, towards something beyond created nature to which the tendencies of human nature point the way. Human beings who pursue those good created things towards which their natures tend, and who pursue them reasonably and in that sense ethically, discover the inadequacy not only of their success, but even of their very goals. Human beings discover in themselves a capacity for truth and goodness which they perceive cannot be fulfilled by any quantity or quality of created satisfactions. Augustine's prayerful testimony to a God who made us for himself, with hearts that are restless until they rest in him, gives memorable Christian expression to this idea. But it is an idea that has often been expressed by non-Christians as well, some of whose thought has been abundantly utilized by Christian theology. Disputes over whether or not it is correct to speak of a natural desire for God, or of natural religion, is of little relevance to our present line of thought. What is relevant is the widely attested experience that an attitude characteristic of natural law ethics tends to carry human aspiration beyond the pursuit of limited values and partial truths, to absolute goodness and perfect truth.

Belief in God, and in a God who represents the ultimate origin and goal of all human endeavor, not only reinforces ethics, but enlarges the scope of ethics. It introduces a factor to which everything else in the whole domain of ethics must be totally subordinate. If everything to which human nature tends derives from God, then God's goodness is implicit in every good. If everything that gratifies nature is God's gift, then all appreciation should be rooted in gratitude. And if the seeking of God's gifts leads to awareness of human nature's tending towards their giver, then the reasonable seeking of any good must be consistent with the seeking of God. And yet the seeking of God cannot be like the seeking of any other good. God cannot be a passive object of his creatures' activities, if he is himself the source of all their activities. Any tendency that leads towards God has to be a tendency that derives from God. To move towards God is to be moved by God, and the only meaningful quest for God must take the form of submission to God. The cultivation of that submission is the moral life of religion, the ethics of adoration, the homage of an adoring mind and an obedient will, the loving of one's Lord and God with all one's heart and mind and strength. This first and greatest commandment is the summit of Christian ethics and, once that summit is reached, it is the source of all the rest of Christian ethics.

NATURAL LAW AND SEXUAL RELATIONSHIP

Among the basic situations in which fundamental principles of natural law are said to be discovered there is also the mating of the sexes and the raising of off-spring. Here too, natural tendencies are regarded as indicating good human purposes, and the reasonable pursuit of those purposes is what ethical principles seek to formulate.

There can be no serious doubt that moral development is profoundly affected by the fundamental conditions of family life. Although conjugal and parental activities are undertaken rather late in moral lives, they constitute the setting in which other moral lives begin. Ordinarily it is in familial relationships that the first lessons of social experience are imparted, and the first awareness of social possibilities is acquired. And the quality of those lessons and the clarity of that awareness depend crucially on the habitual behavior of a man and a woman. The family is both the nucleus of communal life and the life-stream of moral tradition, with the result that how spouses act towards one another and towards their children has remarkably far-reaching moral effects. It is not unlikely that the ethics of family life finds its basic directions in the same principles as communal life in general. But the family's high ethical sensitivity and its potentiality for extensive ethical influence commend it to special attention.

It is an understanding of sexuality as oriented towards family life that has traditionally shaped Christian ethical views concerning sexual behavior in general. Broadly speaking, sexual conduct has won Christian approval in so far as it has been judged conducive to the development of wholesome conjugal and parental relationships. It has generally been disapproved or viewed with suspicion in so far as it seemed to depart from that orientation. And because of the notorious capacity of sex to arouse passions that inhibit reason, great emphasis has usually been placed on upholding this objective standard for assessing the moral goodness of sexual conduct.

STUDY QUESTIONS

1. What is fundamentally assumed by typical Catholic natural law ethics?

2. What two basic natural tendencies seem to provide the initial context of most people's ethical thinking?

3. At what stage in the development of individuals does it seem likely that morality becomes a conscious factor?

4. What are some typical manifestations of ethical awareness commonly found even among young children?

5. What sort of comparison of oneself with others seems to be prerequisite for ethical thinking?

6. What are some basic principles that seem typically to emerge in the course of moral development?

7. How does belief in a wise and benevolent creator tend to support the starting point of natural law ethics?

8. In what sense does the pursuit of natural values seem in some cases to lead into religion?

9. Why cannot the seeking of God be essentially similar to the seeking of any natural good?

10. Why is submissiveness a basic feature of distinctively religious morality?

11. In what sense are sexual relationships a source of primary influence on personal ethical development?

12. What orientation of sexuality has typically dominated Christian ethical views concerning sexual behavior?

13. Why is the seeking of God different from the seeking of any other good?

Chapter Seventeen

CONSCIENCE

THE MORAL OBSERVER WITHIN

The word conscience derives from two Latin words meaning knowledge and with. The word's history shows that it referred originally to knowledge shared with someone else in a very special way. Actually the word implies a kind of myth, based on the idea or experience of someone's being "in on" one's private affairs. As a kind of primitive image of conscience, we may envision the presence of a kind of observer who, on occasions of our least public performances, does not miss a thing. It suggests the idea of an imaginary bystander, who sees our behavior for what it is, unaffected by our passions or pretenses. This silent companion who was "there" when we did "it," is afterwards in a position to remind us, with painful frankness, of what kind of mischief we were up to. (Of course our secret behavior might have been commendable, and the shadowy observer is capable of approval, but this is not the context implied by the oldest and most frequent usage of the word conscience.) An intimate associate, with

175

whom our alibis and excuses count for nothing, is the image evoked by the vocabulary of conscience.

If we take this image, and give it interior existence within our psychological makeup, the result corresponds closely to what seems to be the basic experience of conscience: a sense of there being a kind of interior critic within our minds, a part of us and yet disconcertingly indifferent to our selfish preferences and special pleadings. Fundamentally, this seems to be the experience of a kind of hindsight which passes judgment on things we have done with the firmness of an incorruptible eye-witness. But secondarily, conscience can also function by anticipation, passing judgment on things we have in mind to do, even before we reach the point of doing them. In this anticipatory function, conscience advises rather than accuses, dissuades rather than blames; its unspoken words become "You mustn't" rather than "You shouldn't have".

Common to both of these concepts of conscience, and to its moral understanding generally, is a notion which may serve for a very general description of the class of phenomena to which the word refers. It refers to the psychological experience of a kind of self-criticism which, although part of oneself, seems to have an objectivity that makes it independent of the self. Thus one aspect of the mind seems somehow to detach itself from the motives, interests, and wishes of the rest of the mind, and to reach verdicts which may be unwelcome and even strongly resisted. It is easy to see how this kind of common experience might give rise, as it has done, to the idea of conscience as a distinct entity, sufficiently separate from the rest of the self to confront it with its approvals and disapprovals. Thus in addition to the idea of conscience as something that the self experiences, and the idea of it as something that the self does, there arises also the idea of conscience as something that the self has. The result is an understanding of conscience as something the self, so to speak, lives with, and is compelled, willy-nilly, to listen to, like Pinocchio's Jiminy Cricket.

ORIGIN AND VALUE OF CONSCIENCE

Thus far we have merely considered what kind of experience our language about conscience points to. But having identified conscience to that extent does not yet tell us anything about its origin and development or about its value. Consequently, it offers no practical direction concerning what, if anything, one ought to do about conscience. Concerning its origin, many psychological theories have been proposed, of which the most influential are derived from either psychoanalysis or learning theory. Concerning its development, in addition to extensions of the theories just mentioned, theories of a very different and much less conjectural kind have been elaborated by developmental psychologists. About the value of conscience, one might look for enlightenment from philosophy and theology. Modern philosophy has made relatively little room for this topic, but in recent religious literature, not least among Catholics, it has figured prominently.

A kind of programatic statement for recent Catholic thought on this subject was made by the second Vatican Council, which said that in the depths of conscience a human being detects a law which is not self-imposed, but which demands obedience. This law is said to enjoin the doing of good and the avoidance of evil, and also to indicate specific things to be done or avoided. It is described as a law written by God in the human heart, as the foundation of human dignity, and as the basis on which human beings will be judged.

In this statement we find the same notion of conscience suggested by the history of the word, as an internal, yet somehow autonomous and objective moral censor, which commends or condemns the intentions and actions of the very person of whom it seems to be part. But we also find another notion, to the effect that this conscience is, or is regulated by a law of God himself. Hence the very highest ethical value seems to be assigned to conscience, on obedience to which one's ultimate judgment is said to depend. This notion is reinforced as the document goes on to describe conscience as the sanctuary where a human being is alone with God, and which reveals the law that finds fulfillment in loving God and neighbor.

The application to conscience of language of this kind can certainly be defended. But it can also be disastrously abused. For it is easily misunderstood to imply that what people ordinarily mean by conscience is an infallible oracle of God's will. Thus it might be supposed that any moral dilemma is readily solved by merely attending to that particular kind of subjective experience we have identified as what the language of conscience is talking about. The absurdity of such a conclusion is readily apparent. For persons who do rely on their experience of what we call conscience reach conclusions which not only often disagree, but sometimes vigorously oppose and condemn one another. If the voice of God is not self-contradictory, and is heard in conscience, it must be heard in some consciences but not in others, or at least better in some than in others.

In fact, after the exalted references to conscience already cited, the Council document goes on to say that conscience frequently goes wrong from invincible ignorance, and may in some cases grow practically blind as a result of habitual sin. These rather anticlimactic observations express the practical problems of conscience. For if the earlier statements warn that it is not right to go against one's conscience, these later ones acknowledge that conscience itself may be wrong or even ineffectual. To concede that consciences may be malfunctional or non-functional is implicitly to concede that consciences do not work like magic, but may be in need of direction, correction, or even revival. It is to concede the importance of criticism of conscience and of the formation of conscience.

FORMATION OF CONSCIENCE

One very important aspect of the formation of conscience is implied in the Council's statement of the problem. For if conscience may grow practically blind as a result of habitual sin, and if as the earlier statements indicated, to disobey conscience is precisely to sin, we must conclude that part of the task of the formation of conscience is discharged in the very act of obeying conscience. Like so much that is human, conscience is withered by frustration and neglect, and invigorated by use and cultivation. There can be little doubt that one of the most practical maxims for the formation of conscience is the simple advice that to act in accordance with such experience of conscience as one has results in making that experience progressively stronger, clearer, and more frequent. One who waits for a better conscience before doing anything about it, soon develops a worse conscience, in the sense of a weaker and more confused one, and winds up, practically speaking, with no conscience at all. A first rule for the formation of conscience is to make the most of what one has got, with the result that one will get more, and learn to make more of it.

Catholic tradition has defined conscience primarily as moral judgment concerning the rightness or wrongness of behavior. Understood in this way, conscience is sharply distinguished from mere emotion. And it is only in this sense of conscience that one is enjoined always to obey one's conscience, which is to say no more than that one ought not to do what one rationally judges to be wrong. Although there can be no reasonable alternative to this policy of conformity to conscience, the policy itself does not solve all one's problems. For one's intellectual conviction that some behavior is right or wrong may be completely sincere, and yet completely mistaken.

In addition, therefore, to nourishing the vitality of conscience by living consistently with the conscience one has at any given time, conscience must be developed in such a way that its judgments become progressively more reliable. This progressive improvement of conscience is a matter partly of maturation and partly of education. As with most human growth, the two processes are closely intertwined. The moral judgments of conscience are formed by reflective understanding of experience, and they are learned from a great variety of teachers in a great variety of ways. There can be little doubt that parental instruction, by reward or punishment, explanation, exhortation, and example, has immense influence, especially during the impressionable years of early childhood. With increasing age, the views and examples of one's peers assume increasing importance, and a whole barrage of cultural influences, some of them very subtle, come strongly into play. Consequently, in the development of conscience, as of mental capacity generally, the competence of one's teachers, whether formal or informal, is a decisive factor. A social environment in which conscience is largely ignored or widely abused represents a handicap to the development of conscience that can be surmounted by only exceptional individuals.

DIFFERENCES IN DEVELOPMENT OF CONSCIENCE

Reference to exceptional individuals reminds us that, even with similar environments and equivalent efforts, individuals do not develop uniformly. With moral judgment as with other mental functions, some persons can develop faster and farther than others. Our understanding of individual development in this respect has been considerably illumined by modern psychological studies. Research in this area clearly indicates that moral judgment is not simply a rationalization of emotional reactions. Neither is it based simply on the passive adoption of habits of behavior prevailing in a given environment. On the contrary, the traditional Catholic conception of conscience as an intellectual function is highly consistent with psychological findings. Such findings show a regular pattern of development in the way persons think about moral questions which is closely correlated with patterns of development in the way they think about other matters.

Careful research has demonstrated the existence of distinct stages in the development of moral judgment. These stages have been consistently verified in extensive studies involving a wide variety of cultures and a large number of individuals. There is good reason to believe that basic differences in the ways moral questions are dealt with correspond to differences in the extent to which individuals have progressed along a path of development which is characteristically human and genuinely universal. Psychological implications of this kind offer a valuable corrective to the fashionable kind of ethical relativism which denies that there is any firm general basis for moral preferences. It becomes possible to characterize moral judgments in a meaningful way as more or less mature, more or less adequate to human potentialities for moral evaluation, and therefore in the last analysis, as more or less good. And in fact there is considerable evidence that the kinds of moral judgment typical of the higher stages of development cope more adequately with real moral problems than do those belonging to less mature stages.

Once moral judgment is recognized as a developmental phenomenon in the domain of thinking rather than of feeling, moral education presents itself as an important practical undertaking. For in this as in other areas of mental life, development can be fostered or frustrated, accelerated or retarded, by deliberate factors as well as accidental ones. This conclusion finds evidence in data which indicate that, although there is one general pattern of development of moral judgment, there are striking differences in the average progress made within this pattern by members of different social groups. Broadly speaking, in societies that closely restrict the availability of different social roles, and narrowly limit their members' involvement in formulating and solving moral issues, development of moral judgment tends to be retarded. Contrariwise, social environments with opposite characteristics tend to be most effectively educating of moral judgment.

Those who, in any capacity, assume the immensely important task of educating the consciences of others, cannot afford to be altogether ignorant of basic psychological indications in this area. They need some awareness of stages of moral development in order to avoid dealing with others on levels so far above or below the levels they actually occupy that no effective communication of moral thinking is possible. And to the extent that they perceive moral judgment as partaking in the maturation of human mental capacity, they will be less ready to equate the formation of conscience with the crude indoctrination of rules, or the mere training by reward and punishment of desired responses. In moral education as in all education, the goal can and should be to encourage progressively more adequate thinking, enabling persons to think effectively for themselves. Good moral educators, like all good educators, make themselves most useful in the process of making themselves increasingly dispensable.

The formation of conscience, in the traditional sense of moral judgment, is one thing. Getting people to behave themselves is quite another. Both tasks are important and they are not unrelated. But they are as different as the task of a teacher and that of a policeman, as different as educating a person and training an animal.

MORAL PLATITUDES AND MORAL INERTIA

There is a psychological observation that may come to mind as one reflects on the difference between asserting general moral goals, on which normal people usually agree, and prescribing particular moral means, about which people so often disagree. That is, public recitations and acclamations of broad moral goals seem often to have a kind of narcotic effect on the consciences of those individuals who comprise the public. They tend to induce simultaneously a sense of moral righteousness and a condition of moral inertia.

Let someone proclaim fervently that human beings are created equal and endowed with certain rights, and, if the proclamation discreetly confines itself to rhetorical variations on that theme, large audiences are likely to go home satisfied and self-satisfied. They will, with a kind of moral voluptuousness, enjoy a sense of civic and ethical wholesomeness derived simply from participation in unanimous approval of the good. In such circumstances, the audience's experience is a deeply comforting one that seems to inflate flaccid egos and soothe chafing superegos. One tends to be amiably disposed to whoever has made such inner comforts possible. And one is understandably annoyed by persons or events that threaten to break that sort of spell.

Most significantly for our subject matter, one kind of person who seems very often to break such spells and to provoke such annoyance is the sort of person who ventures to draw practical inferences from those very principles that the public finds it so exhilarating to celebrate. One cannot but notice how often the sweetness of moral generalities seems to go sour when they are reduced to practical applications. Extol human rights and universal brotherhood and the world smiles with you. But take the further step of specifying social obligations and deploring unequitable practices, and smiles turn easily into frowns. Great moral truths are indeed beautiful, and to contemplate and celebrate them entails its own kind of aesthetic satisfaction. But to savor that satisfaction in its "purity," the moral truths have to be kept very general. As they are brought closer to particularity and practical urgency, they become too challenging for sheer enjoyment, too naggingly insistent to be simply admired. Universal human brotherhood is a lovely idea. But deriving from that idea personal obligations to treat certain actually existing human beings in a brotherly fashion is often a quite unlovely experience.

Thus we find, among the numerous paradoxes of moral living, that a certain kind of attention to moral principles can actually serve as a distraction and deterrent from the moral practices implicitly enjoined by those very principles. And there are certain kinds of religious, moral, and political orators who know this phenomenon very well, and exploit it very effectively. Ethical uplift can mesmerize. Moral banality can paralyze. And here again we are reminded that the virtue of prudence was wisely perceived to pertain rather to means than to ends.

STUDY QUESTIONS

1. What is the verbal derivation of the word "conscience"?

2. What imaginative basis seems to be implied in this derivation?

3. What typical experience seems to be referred to by the term "conscience"?

4. What field of study deals with the origin and development of conscience?

5. How is conscience understood and evaluated by the second Vatican Council?

6. To what abuses can this understanding of conscience easily lead?

7. What significant qualification does the second Vatican Council add to its evaluation of conscience?

8. What important aspect of conscience is implied by this qualification?

9. How has Catholic ethical tradition characteristically understood conscience?

10. What general factors seem chiefly to influence the development of conscience?

11. What are some important psychological findings concerning the development of moral judgment?

12. How are such psychological findings relevant to moral education?

13. What is the difference between forming conscience and simply getting people to behave in approved ways?

14. How can the preaching of very broad moral goals do a disservice to practical ethics?

15. Do you agree that deriving personal obligations from oral platitudes causes discomfort among people? Support your answer.

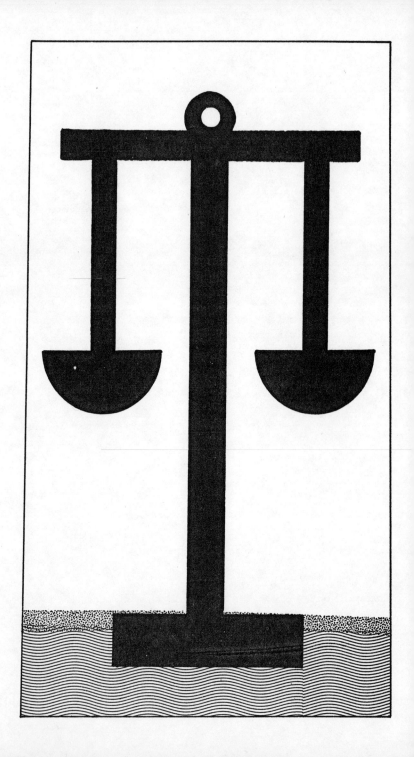

Chapter Eighteen

JUSTICE

CAUSING HAPPINESS AND DOING JUSTICE

If, as an earlier discussion was intended to suggest, one cannot reasonably proceed from an "is" to an "ought," from sheerly factual information to genuinely ethical decision, then ethical decisions must refer ultimately to certain fundamental "oughts," that is, to moral principles that are not simply derived from other moral principles.

In much of the preceding discussion, we have considered the attempt frequently made, in recent times even by Christians, to treat one moral principle as either the source of or a substitute for all others. On biblical grounds, that principle has been identified with the sovereign Christian norm of love. But the problem inmediately arises of how a general determination to love can be translated into practical directions for living. The most widely accepted way of doing this is to suppose that one is acting lovingly if one is always trying to bring about through one's actions as much happiness as possible.

However, as we have seen, to make this an exclusive

ultimate norm for moral action raises other problems. Such problems arise when the course of action that seems fairly sure to result in maximum happiness seems also sure to result in injustice. And although one could simply say that all such injustices must be reluctantly accepted as the unfortunate concomitants of being as loving as possible, most people are conscientiously troubled by that sort of conclusion. And in reflecting on why one is thus troubled, one is likely to conclude that justice cannot, in practice, be taken quite so lightly as all that.

But to draw that conclusion is equivalent to admitting that loving, in the sense of trying to cause maximum happiness, is not a completely adequate ultimate norm for moral living. It is to imply that justice is likewise an undeniable norm, which cannot be reduced to loving understood in that way. One may, of course, if one chooses, broaden one's understanding of love to include both these norms. One might then say that to love as a Christian should require that one try to cause the most and the the best happiness one can, within certain limits established by justice. Thus one would be asserting that the end does not justify the means, if the means are unjust even though the end is a maximum increase of happiness. Such an assertion has good claim to be regarded as a traditional presupposition of Catholic ethics, in which obligations of justice have always been regarded as having independent—or, theologically speaking, divine—authority.

THE BASIC IDEA OF JUSTICE

Justice is one of those terms with which we seem to get on very comfortably until we try to define them. According to an ancient and classical definition, justice is the virtue of giving to each person what is due to that person. But as soon as we go on to ask what is meant by something's being "due" to somebody we find ourselves saying equivalently that what is due to a person is what it is just for that person to have or to get. Thus it seems that we are talking in circles, and that our definition has not really clarified matters. Possibly the best way to clarify matters at that point is by considering some instances of what are generally recognized as matters of justice or injustice.

If I hire three equally strong men to help me carry a heavy object and, after they have all worked equally hard at the job, I pay one of them a great deal more than either of the others, I do not seem to have behaved justly. One of the men appears to have received more than his due, while the others have received less than their due. Examples of this kind suggest a feature that is often cited as essential to justice, namely, that similar treatment should be given to similar cases. But this also requires some clarification. For suppose, for example, that the two men to whom I gave less pay had brown hair, whereas the one to whom I gave more pay was blond. In that case my dissimilar treatment would in fact correspond to dissimilar cases. And yet no one would be likely to consider my behavior any the less unjust. For the difference of hair color is obviously beside the point. It is simply not relevant to any reasonable determination of how the workers ought to be recompensed. And so we have to modify our earlier statment to say that justice requires similar treatment for cases that are similar in relevant respects. Just what respects are relevant will obviously vary from one situation to another, and is not always as evident as one might wish. Indeed, it may be too seldom realized that doing justice frequently requires not only firm moral purpose, but hard, careful thinking. Justice, in other words, can make heavy demands on prudence.

JUSTICE IN DISSIMILAR TREATMENT

There are two ancient Jewish parables that may be worth recalling in this connection. One of them was part of a funeral oration for a brilliant rabbi whose career of excellent service was ended by death at a very young age, and just before the birth of his first child. The preacher told a story about a wealthy farmer who hired a group of day laborers at a standard wage. While it was still quite early in the working day, the farmer called one of the workmen aside, and spent the rest of the day strolling about, entertaining this man with pleasant conversation. At quitting time, the farmer paid all the workmen, including his conversational partner, exactly equally. Most of the workmen objected to this seeming favoritism, but the farmer silenced them by pointing out that the man he had called aside had been working so intensely hard that he had done as much work in a few hours as the rest of them had done in the whole time. The point was, of course, that God had called to himself a rabbi who, despite his youth, had already done what for most people would be a lifetime of service. And the hearers, of course, appreciated the point because they perceived that the fictional farmer had behaved with unquestionable, and instructive, fairness. Dissimilar treatment had been given to what only superficially appeared to be similar cases.

That parable is likely to remind us of another, curiously different one, attributed to Jesus. In that story a farmer hired workers in much the same way, but at different times. And some of them were hired so close to quitting time that they were able to do only a very little work. When the latecomers were given the same pay as the others, there was a complaint about unfairness. But the answer in this case was quite different from that in the preceding parable. For the farmer did not maintain that the latecomers had done work equivalent to that of the others. What he did maintain was two things. First he pointed out that he had not underpaid anybody; every workman received the agreed-upon wage. Consequently justice has been done. But he also pointed out that in paying the latecomers more, obviously, than they had earned, he was spending what was, after all, his own money, on an act of kindness. Consequently, something more than justice had also been done. What the complaints revealed, therefore, was an attitude not of justice, but merely of envy. Here the similar treatment given to dissimilar cases does not detract from justice, but it does go beyond justice. The farmer gave all that was due. Therefore he acted justly. If he had not done that much he would have been unjust, and he would also have been unkind as we normally understand kindness. Thus it appears that kindness, or love, is understood to include justice: one cannot be unjust without being unkind or unloving. But the farmer also gave more than was due. Therefore he acted more than justly. If he had not done that much he would have been less kind, but he would not have been less just as we normally understand justice. Thus it appears that kindness, or love, is understood not only to include justice, but also to exceed justice. Such has been the traditional view of Catholic ethics. But it should not be confused with a quite different view, that once love is made an essential part of ethics, justice becomes superfluous. To say that love demands justice is not to say that love replaces justice.

JUSTICE AND RIGHTS

If the idea of justice is that of a virtue whereby one gives to each one whatever is due, the idea of a right may be understood as designating what it is that is due, what it is that it would be just to give and unjust not to give to someone. Thus, if I sell you a dog whose value we have agreed to be $100, it may be said that $100 is due to me, that justice requires you to give me $100, or that I have a right to $100 from you.

Because rights are always related to obligations of justice, clarity in talking or thinking about rights depends to a great extent on being clear as to what the obligations are to which the rights correspond. Unfortunately, because people feel strongly about their rights, and talk passionately about them, a great deal of what is said about rights is confused and confusing. Faced with such confusion one of the most useful things one can do is to ask concerning any asserted right, what obligation corresponds to it, who are supposed to have this obligation, and what is the reason for supposing them to be thus obliged.

As soon as one begins thinking about rights in this way, it

becomes evident that there are not only many different rights, but also many different kinds of rights. Since most people who assert rights do not say what kind of right they are asserting, misunderstandings are constantly occurring in this matter, sometimes with disastrous effects. It is therefore much more than an academic exercise to consider an elementary classification of rights. Traditionally, most of this kind of classifying has been done in legal contexts, understanding rights as conferred by human law. But the ideas are equally applicable to rights believed to exist independently of human law, such as are called natural rights or human rights.

Rights in the strict sense of the word are distinguished first of all from liberties or privileges, understanding the latter to mean exemptions from specific duties. I have a duty not to go about punching people, but if someone physically attacks me I am liberated from that duty on the basis of self-defense. I have a duty not to enter private homes of other people, but if I am invited in I am liberated from that duty on the basis of consent.

Liberties such as these are often referred to as rights, but they are different from rights in the strict sense, which are usually called claim rights. These are rights on the basis of which demands can be made of others. Such are a worker's right to wages, a child's right to parental support, or a defendant's right to legal counsel. The possession of such rights is expressed in morally or legally based insistence, and to grant what is thus claimed is not the doing of a favor but the fulfilling of an obligation. Claims based on such rights are thus normally distinguished from appeals or requests based on other grounds, such as generosity or compassion.

Among claim rights one may distinguish between those whose claims are directed against specific persons, and those whose claims are directed against everyone in general. One may also distinguish between positive rights, obliging others to perform certain actions, and negative rights, obliging them to refrain from certain actions. And one may distinguish again between active rights, to suit oneself about doing something or not doing it, and passive rights, not to have others do certain things that affect oneself. Some examples will clarify these distinctions, and show that they often overlap in practice.

A seller has a claim right against a specific person, the buyer. If a customer runs off without paying for his $10 purchase, the merchant has no claim against anybody else, and even if someone else should give him a consolation present of $10, that would not alter his right to claim $10 from his customer. On the other hand, a homeowner's claim right to sole occupancy is directed against everyone without exception —although an invited guest or policeman with a search warrant might have the liberty or privilege of invading that right. The homeowner's right also exemplifies a negative right, the right not to have anyone enter the home, as contrasted with the merchant's positive right to have his customer pay up. The homeowner's right might also be called a passive right, a right not to be encroached upon by others. He also has an active right to occupy his own house or not as he pleases.

All rights in the strict sense entail obligation, since meaningful claims must be directed against somebody. As indicated, the classification of such rights is determined by who are obliged and how they are obliged. Rights, therefore, need to be clarified by reference to the obligations they entail. Take, for example, the much-cited right to life. Is it an active right, meaning that one may suit oneself about living or not living? Is it a passive, negative right, directed against everyone in general, meaning that no one may stop one from living? Is it a positive right, directed against particular persons, obliging them to do something in support of one's living? Or is it several of these? Or is it all of these? Until such questions are answered, the assertion of a right to life has little practical significance, and there is little point in going on to pursue the no less complicated question of just what life is understood to mean in this context. And the same may be said of a great many other rights that tend to be asserted more loudly than clearly.

RIGHTS AND REGULATIONS

Most reflection on the ethics of rights has taken place within the context of human law, and there are those who consider that the only kind of rights worth discussing are those that are established by human law. Obviously, some rights and obligations are simply legal contrivances, such as the right to drive on one side of the street and the obligation not to drive on the other. Most rights, however, even if conceded by law, are generally thought to require confirmation by ethics. Merely to reverse the laws against rape would not persuade many people that there were no longer any rights to sexual privacy and integrity. Thus, common estimation, like Catholic tradition, acknowledges both legal rights that are not natural rights, and natural rights that may or may not be legal rights.

It may also appear from the simple examples just cited that a right is a protection of someone's interest. But since what rights protect some people's interests from is precisely the conflicting interests of other people, rights also involve a restriction of interests. Thus, if my corner lot happens to be also your short-cut, my property right which obliges you not to trespass restricts your interest in the process of protecting mine. If you have an interest in smoking and I have an interest in breathing clean air, the question may arise of whether you have an active, negative claim right against everyone including me, or I have a passive, negative claim right against people like you. The establishment in public places of separate sectors for smokers and non-smokers represents a compromise regulation, establishing one right for one group and another right for the other group. Thus, conflicts of interests are often dealt with by human rules that recognize opposing rights under conditions that seek to minimize the practical effects of their opposition. A classical, and much disputed example of this sort of thing is the legal establishment of a right to commercialized fornication by licensing prostitutes and restricting the location of brothels, thereby attempting to protect the interests of both chaste and lustful citizens. The posting by local authorities on public beaches of signs requiring no nude bathing beyond some designated point represents a similar kind of regulative strategy to protect conflicting interests by conditional rights.

There are, of course, people who believe no one has a natural or moral right to smoke, fornicate, or go publicly unclad. And there are a lot more people who would deny a natural or moral right to do one or two of those things. For them, the question inevitably arises of whether it is ethically tolerable to establish legal rights to do things that there is no natural or moral right to do, or, as it is often expressed, whether the law may protect immorality. This issue will reappear in a discussion of the relationship between law and ethics; the present context may clarify certain aspects of that issue.

HUMAN RIGHTS

In the preceding discussion reference was made to natural rights and moral rights. For our purposes these may be treated as roughly equivalent, and as distinct from legal or institutional rights. That is, there are some rights that exist in virtue of rules made by human beings, of which the most influential are the laws made by political societies. But most people believe there are other rights that exist independently of human regulations. Among rights of this latter sort, reference is frequently made to what are called human rights. There has been much discussion of human rights in recent times, especially in connection with international relations. For if there are rights that are independent of the laws made by various nations, such rights would themselves have an international character, and might furnish some of the ethical common ground that nations so obviously need as a basis for peaceful and constructive relationship.

What are generally meant by human rights are rights that are considered fundamentally important, unconditional, unchangeable, and equally possessed by all human beings. In terms of our earlier classification, human rights are claim rights, and in practice they seem to be considered as negative or passive and as directed against everyone in general. There is no definitive list of such rights, and there is much disagreement about whether or not various rights should be included. Recent international deliberations do provide some examples about which there is, at least in theory, little dispute. Such are the right not to be executed without due conviction of a capital offense, the right not to be tortured, the right not to be enslaved, and the right not to be arbitrarily prevented from emigrating from a country. It is noteworthy that these and most other widely recognized human rights are negative. That is, they are rights not to be dealt with in certain ways. Some people regularly cite positive human rights, but there are problems about that which it is important to recognize.

One of the currently most cited examples of a supposed positive human right is a right to nourishment. The desire to assert such a right is intensified by growing awareness of cruelly uneven distribution of food among the world's people, and the appalling frequency of malnutrition and actual starvation. That this situation is an enormous evil can hardly be questioned. But saying that is not the same thing as saying there is a human right to adequate nourishment. Suppose, for example, that climatic conditions cause a famine, with the result that in some area large numbers of people suffer and die for lack of food. If there is a human right to eat, then these people have an unconditional unalterable claim against somebody. It would be easy to defend a negative, passive claim right against everybody, meaning merely that everybody is obliged not to prevent these people from eating. But the honoring of such a claim right would not be much help to these people.

The only helpful right would have to be a positive one claiming in effect a right to be fed. Clearly, it would be very difficult to maintain that they had such a claim right against everybody, meaning that everybody has an obligation to feed them. But if one tries instead to maintain that they have a claim right by which particular parties are obliged to feed them, it becomes a prohibitively difficult matter to defend any particular designation of the parties whose obligation to feed corresponds to the victims' right to eat.

This discussion is not simply a quibble. And the conclusion of it is not equivalent to saying that there is no ethical response which offers any solution to the plight of the starving people. It is to say that appealing in such cases to the idea of human rights has a way of bogging down short of any practical solution. Catholic tradition would, of course, maintain that there is an obligation in love or charity for those who can alleviate such suffering to make what contribution they reasonably can. Catholic tradition would also maintain that there are issues of social justice involved in such cases which entail real obligations both to feed hungry people and to create conditions that make it unnecessary to do so. These topics will be taken up presently.

UNJUST SITUATIONS AND UNJUST PEOPLE

One of the ways we use the term injustice tends to conceal certain problems that should be brought to light. The problems are related to the fact that in our language and some related languages, just, justice, and similar words have not always been, but have increasingly become strictly ethical terms. Thus, by justice we usually mean a virtue, and by injustice an opposed vice. We call someone just who is supposed to have this virtue, and one is judged to have the virtue from the fact that he or she habitually performs the kinds of deeds we call just deeds, and habitually refrains from the kinds of deeds we call unjust. In the same way, the results of just deeds are said to be just and the results of unjust deeds are said to be unjust. The important thing to notice in all this is that the way these terms of justice and injustice are applied takes its start from the idea of a human person who perceives and fulfills a certain kind of moral obligation, and does so habitually. Thus if I, as a parent, perceive my obligation to provide adequately and equitably for my children, and habitually fulfill that obligation, I am (to that extent) a just man, doing just deeds, contributing to a just state of affairs. If I were not in this respect a just man, doing just deeds, the state of affairs that depended on me, the resultant condition of my children, would be one of injustice. Someone who knew the full circumstances, including the state of my children, would know the latter to be the consequence of my unjust behavior: the injustice (in an objective sense) of their condition would be traceable to the injustice (in a subjective sense) of my character and conduct.

But suppose one did not know the full circumstances and only observed that several children seemed both very poorly and very unevenly provided for. Such an observer might naturally and properly call what he observed a situation of injustice. But if his use of that term implied that the situation must have been caused by some unjust person or persons, he might well be mistaken. The situation of the children might be beyond the power of the virtue of justice to remedy, and in no sense a result of the vice of injustice. It might be simply an unfortunate accident. It might be the result of the children's own folly or malice. And it might therefore be totally wrong for anyone to infer from the objectively unjust situation that it must be the result of someone's unjust behavior. In other words, although unjust people do produce unjust situations, they do not produce all of them. This point has both religious and ethical importance.

It has religious importance because it is abundantly clear that a great deal of what we should normally describe as objective injustice, such as grossly unequal opportunities for even the most elementary human satisfactions, exists long before anyone has a chance to exert either just or unjust influence. People are born with extremely unequal capacities to achieve or even to experience happiness. They are born into environments that offer extremely unequal opportunities. Even in a world peopled with uniformly philanthropic inhabitants, if it was otherwise the world we know, it would not be even remotely possible to furnish everyone with equal happiness or equal chances for happiness. In this sense, unjust states of affairs are among the primary data of human existence. And for much of this objective injustice no accusing finger can be reasonably pointed at any existing persons by whose unjust behavior it is produced. One may at this point invoke the idea of original sin, as a primordial moral and religious failing that leaves its traces in the world's evils. But whatever the theological merits of this doctrine, to blame the enormous native disparities of human well-being on some ancient malefactor raises more questions about justice than it settles. One must, then, either blame God for such injustice—and thereby discard all religiously based hope for even ultimate justice—or humbly acknowledge a downright mystery of evil, made bearable perhaps, but not explicable, by faith. The phrase, "mystery of evil," represents the Christian's traditional readiness to accept that perplexity while refusing that despair.

That same tendency, always to attribute unjust states of affairs to the unjust doings of some unjust persons, can operate as unconstructively in ethics as it does in religion. There is an inclination, especially among people of what might be called a "prophetic" disposition, to react to what they perceive as unjust states of affairs with moral indignation. Such moral indignation may be appropriate, if the unjust situation is evidently the product of unjust deeds by unjust persons. In such cases the indignation finds natural expression in admonitions or denunciations, which may possibly lead either to spontaneous reform or to pressure for reform. But there are other cases in which unjust conditions cannot be pointedly referred to unjust action or inaction. And in such cases, moral indignation is at least inappropriate and unhelpful, and it may also be itself unjust and damaging. It becomes especially damaging when awareness of unjust conditions leads to a quest for moral culprits, even when such culprits are unidentifiable or simply non-existent. A certain kind of moral sensitivity engenders a kind of vice that often passes itself off as a kind of virtue. It is a positive zeal to blame, an eagerness for prosecution. This appetite to blame and prosecute easily leads to sweepingly irresponsible allegations. It easily becomes so bent on finding culprits that it is content to find scapegoats. It easily assumes epidemic proportions, and generates a whole social climate of irrational hostility, masquerading as moral indignation, and unleashing senseless violence. No one familiar with even recent history can fail to notice how often times of greatly heightened moral sensitivity, especially in the realm of social justice, tend to coincide with times of mindless violence in word and deed. Confronted with unjust conditions in human society, it is horrible to remain apathetic. But it is no less horrible to become apoplectic. Good is never done by a blind hatred of injustice. Good is done by a clear-sighted love of justice. And the one never seems to lead to the other.

STUDY QUESTIONS

1. What moral principle has Christian tradition tended to regard as uniquely basic?

2. How does this principle tend to be understood in practice?

3. What difficulty arises when this principle is understod in this way?

4. What other virtue tends to be considered as basic as love?

5. In what sense does justice require equal treatment for all?

6. When is unequal treatment considered unjust treatment?

7. What is illustrated by comparing Jesus' parable of the laborers with a somewhat similar rabbinical parable?

8. How has Catholic tradition generally related love to justice?

9. How is the idea of right related to the idea of justice?

10. What is necessary to avoid unclearness in appealing to rights?

11. To what extent is the existence of rights dependent on human law?

12. What is the difference between rights and privileges?

13. What is meant by a claim right?

14. Distinguish positive from negative and active from passive rights.

15. Why is it necessary to clarify what is meant by a right to life?

16. How are rights related, positively and negatively, to interests?

17. What is generally meant by human rights?

18. What are the practical difficulties of asserting a human right to nourishment?

19. What other traditional Catholic ethical approach responds positively to the hunger problem?

20. What difficulties result from describing as unjust situations of painful inequality?

21. What are the implications of the statement that unjust people are not responsible for all unjust situations?

Chapter Nineteen

SOCIAL JUSTICE

THE JUSTICE OF SOCIETY

Social justice is an idea notoriously difficult to formulate satisfactorily, but very hard to do without in discussing ethics. Basically, what one is trying to do in talking about social justice is to investigate in what sense a society, as distinct from an individual person, can be called just or unjust, or more or less just or unjust.

It will be recalled that justice was classically understood as a virtue whereby one was habitually inclined to give others their due. Building on that foundation, traditional accounts of social justice consider it as that which makes a society just, and understand as a just society one that gives its members what is due to them. One obvious difficulty with this approach is that it leaves no room for considering in terms of social justice how a society deals with others than its own members, whether they be other societies or individuals. To describe as just a society that satisfies its members' requirements while at the same time trampling on the rights of others is certainly a morally misleading way to use language. Unfortunately, traditional usage does foster this deception.

Although it is instructive, up to a point, to liken societies to individuals, and consider their activities just or unjust much as one would consider the activities of individuals, the comparison obviously disregards important differences. One society does not deal with another society as one individual does with another, on the basis of a simple decision, however laboriously it may have been arrived at. The actions of societies are usually resultants of numerous highly complex factors. Ultimately, those factors are theoretically traceable to interactions of individuals and decisions taken by particular persons. But seldom can they in any practical way be traced to such simple moral causes. And as a result, the correction of their abuses very often cannot be accomplished by individual enlightenment, repentance, and reform.

If a family behaves unjustly to those outside its circle, it may indeed be possible for its members by agreement, or for one member by recognized authority, to simply change bad ways to good ways. But in the case of larger societies, reform is seldom feasible on so personal and accessible a basis. For in large societies institutions are developed and policies are pursued on such a scale and often for such a duration of time, that their power and direction become to a great extent detached from any immediate personal control. Consequently, the cures for moral evils that are generated by such societies are usually as complex as the causes that bring them about. And this is especially true when societies are large and when their activities involve wide participation. Among the most lamentable consequences of this state of affairs is its capacity to divest members of societies of any sense of moral responsibility for society's actions and for reforming them when they are bad.

If a great nation has developed an oppressive empire by means of fraud and intimidation, and fashioned on that basis a whole way of cultural and economic life, there is no way that a sudden wave of ethical remorse, even if it should be universally shared, can suddenly put matters to rights. If a nation has launched a massive war, even the most conscientious second thoughts can neither instantly nor ever fully reverse the consequences. If commercial greed has built up a virtual monopoly of precious resources and reduced countless persons to economic dependence and cultural deprivation, no amount of philanthropic compunction can promptly restore equitable conditions. If one people has enslaved another and reduced them to generations of servility, an emancipation proclamation can only begin the complex and laborious process of restoring authentic freedom.

The immense complexity of social reform deters individuals from taking part in it, and the vast diffuseness of social responsibility deters individuals from acknowledging complicity in society's wrongdoings. Moreover, because the burdens of social reform cannot usually be distributed proportionately among the original perpetrators of social evil, individuals have an understandable sense of personal injustice in the very processes of reestablishing social justice. Very often the historical instigators of social wickedness have vanished from the scene long before a process of reform gets under way. As a result, children must indeed make reparation for their fathers' crimes. Persons who disapproved and even resisted the wicked ways of their societies are compelled to share in the making of painful amends. However much ethics of strictly individual responsibility for strictly individual actions may commend itself to modern ideologies, such ethics is simply inadequate to the realities of a social world. The supposition that no matter how much else in life is socialized and collectivized, moral responsibility remains a private individual matter, is either a gross error or a shabby pretense. Even that uncomfortable portion of the second Commandment which describes God as punishing the descendants for their ancestors' sins need not be so ethically primitive a conception as is often claimed, and the individualistic emphasis introduced by later prophets is a complementary, not an alternative insight.

BREADTH AND NARROWNESS OF SOCIAL VISION

Membership in nearly every society has a curious way of both expanding ethical perspectives and at the same time confining them. One who willingly participates in the common life of a society is almost compelled to become increasingly aware of responsibility for others. Such awareness often seems to originate in a kind of enlightened self-interest, based on the realization that mutual dependence is what makes societies worthwhile and in some cases indispensable, and that to profit from society one must also contribute to it. In most people that realization becomes the basis of an ethical conviction, even though some people habitually violate that conviction by trying to profit from society without contributing to it. From each according to his ability and to each according to his need had been a classical and a Christian idea long before it became a Marxist one. And as usually understood it expresses an underlying ethical conviction of members of all sorts of societies, from families to empires.

But at the same time that societies encourage their members to think less in terms of I and more in terms of we, they often have the further effect of encouraging a sense of opposition between us, the members of our society, and them, those who are not members of it. Thus one often finds that persons who are generously devoted to the interests of others in their own families, are neglectful or even contemptuous of the interests of others families. Variations of this phenomenon are observable in every sort of society, but perhaps nowhere more conspicuously than in political societies, which in our time are for the most part nations. It is depressing to observe how often and easily prevailing views of what constitutes ethical behavior within a society are directly contradicted by prevailing views of what is ethically acceptable between societies.

Thus nations that have to a great extent discredited the idea of ruthless competition as a tolerable way of life within their borders, readily adopt policies of ruthless competition across their borders. Persons who are genuinely horrified by domestic prospects of oppressors and oppressed, free and slave, affluent and indigent existing side by side, are often perfectly complacent that nations should exist side by side in similar relationship. Acts of coercion and intimidation regarded as criminal among fellow-citizens are not only tolerated but often glorified as national military exploits. And the most exploitative and fraudulent transactions are applauded as triumphs of international trade or diplomacy. Nationalism has, in short, become a colossal inducement to ethical insensitivity, while national civility goes hand in hand with international barbarity. And indeed, the national state has again and again been represented as the highest of all human goods, set equivalently in the place of God, as the sovereign arbiter of all values and disposer of all lives.

Nor is it only families and nations that manifest such ironically conflicting moral standards. Similar phenomena occur wherever the sense of who we are exists in sharp contrast with the sense of who they are, wherever one's position in the human world combines association with insiders and disassociation from outsiders. Social classes, economic factions, racial affiliations, and partisan groupings of all kinds generate the same tendency to develop a closed morality together with an open immorality. Most ironically, the same phenomenon has been painfully visible among explicitly Christian societies, including the churches themselves, ever since the time when an originally persecuted Christianity, having gained its legitimacy, became almost immediately in many respects a persecuting Christianity. Moreover, Christian churches have again and again given such uncritical allegiance to the nations they found hospitable, as to cooperate shamelessly in some of those nations' most immoral policies.

And yet Christian ethical tradition has never fully lost touch with the meaning of Jesus' parable about the Samaritan, and Paul's assertion that cultural and ethnic differences make no difference to the Gospel. Jesus scandalized his age by treating as merely relative and human values the ties both of kinship and of nationality. And in subsequent ages similar scandals have often attended the closest of his followers.

PROMOTING JUSTICE IN SOCIETY

Much of what has been traditionally discussed under the heading of social justice has had to do directly with distributive and legal justice. Clearly, one of the main ways that societies act more or less justly is in making available to their members those good things that society has at its disposal. Thus, there have been societies that restricted large and desirable tracts of land to the use of a single privileged class. There have been societies that limited public offices to adherents of a particular religion. There have been societies that treated as a criminal offense marriage between persons of different races. There have been societies that denied elementary privacy to certain political factions. And all sorts of public opportunities and public services have often been made unavailable by societies to certain of their members.

In such cases, which could be endlessly multiplied, societies are distributing among their members very unequally goods and services to which their members seem equally, or at least more equally, entitled. By their discriminatory distribution they are violating the basic understanding of justice as requiring similar treatment for similar cases. Societies may be similarly unjust in the demands they make of their members, such as requirements of taxation, military service, licensing, public disclosure, and countless other legal obligations. In such instances of legal injustice, as in the former ones of distributive injustice, the basic issues have mainly to do with unfair discrimination, with dissimilar treatment of cases that are similar in all relevant respects.

The types of social action represented by such examples can obviously be described as instances of social injustice, of societies' treating their members in ways that do not give them their due. One can therefore think of social justice simply as contrary types of social action, involving fair distribution of advantages by society and fair imposition of obligations to society. In this sense, social justice would be merely a more general heading, of which distributive and legal justice would be subdivisions. Often enough this is what the phrase social justice is understood to mean.

However, especially in a relatively recent phase of Catholic ethical tradition, social justice has taken on a different significance. Basically, it has come to refer to those actions whereby members of society try to influence society in such a way as to bring about a greater degree of distributive and legal justice. Social justice in this sense is expressed by what people do about their societies in order to get them to deal more justly with their members. The operation of social justice is the attempt to reform social structures, policies, and procedures in the interest of justice. It is based on the conviction that members of society have responsibility for what society does to and for its members.

The practical exercise of such responsibility depends, of course, on the situations of individuals within society. It may be exercised in one way by a voter or lobbyist, in another by a magistrate or legislator, and in still another way by a journalist or teacher. It may be exercised not only by individuals, but also by organizations within society, by various interest groups, parties, businesses, churches, schools, labor unions, professional associations, social fraternities, or special movements of protest and reform directed at specific problems. Merely to outline the scope of social justice and the variety of its agencies at a particular time and place would require a book larger than this one. But the basic idea, increasingly emphasized in Catholic ethical tradition, is that members of societies cannot in good conscience detach their thoughts and energies from the organized workings of society. Rather they must endeavor with the means at their disposal to bring about structural changes when such are prerequisite to the improvement of justice. And especially in quite recent times, there has been growing recognition that the task of social justice involves causing society to deal more justly not only with its own members, but with others as well.

In much of this growing emphasis upon social justice on a national scale, one may perceive a wholesome tendency to restore politics to a place it once occupied within the realm of ethics, and thereby make considerations of justice primary factors in the evaluation of political alternatives. Accordingly, in many places, Christian efforts in the name of social justice have involved strongly advocating particular theories of government. And it is, of course, perfectly possible that in some situations only by changing one's kind of government is there any realistic hope of obtaining a substantially more just regime.

But at the same time there is an obvious danger lest particular forms of government be given the status of ethical absolutes. It requires no extraordinary knowledge of existing and past societies to perceive that under different circumstances quite different forms of government may best serve the interests of justice. With political systems as with so many other human arrangements, one man's drink is often another man's poison. There is general awareness that considerable social harm was done in the past by the readiness of Christians to canonize certain theories and systems of government. Such awareness should engender caution about the unqualified approval some modern Christians tend to bestow on particular political systems.

SOCIETIES OTHER THAN NATIONS

The enormous social power of nations in the modern world makes political ethics a matter of intense importance. But that fact should not be allowed to exclude concern for social justice from other than national and political societies. Social justice means assuming proper responsibility for justice in any society of which one is a member or over which one has legitimate influence. Businesses, schools, churches, clubs, families and countless other institutions or associations are no less capable than nations of performing unjust actions and of perpetuating arrangements that encourage unjust actions.

In our own time, it is especially notable that certain non-political societies have achieved a degree of social power that rivals even that of nations. There are not a few nations, and not all of them new or under-developed, whose wealth is considerably exceeded by that of some multi-national business corporations. And although wealth is no adequate index of social power, it is obviously one of its major factors. When power of such magnitude is exercised with little regard for justice the results can be, and have been, horrendous. And when such power belongs not to a political society but to a competitive commercial enterprise organized solely for the profit of its owners, the chances of its disregarding justice are ominously great. The ethical irresponsibility of international trade has become notorious, and the need to control it is of the utmost urgency. Since hope of effective control depends very largely on political influence by the nations among which such business is transacted, social justice must already be a significant force within those nations before there is much likelihood of its greatly influencing international commerce.

One area in which social justice has special application for Christians is within the churches themselves. For, whatever else it may be, a Christian church is a society and it has humanly contrived structures and policies. In that respect, a church is a potential agent of distributive and legal justice or injustice. And on that account, a church is a proper field for the exercise of social justice by its members. Most churches have benefited from reform movements, and some of those movements have had social justice as a major component. Catholic tradition has always acknowledged the importance of developing just ecclesiastical structures and has accordingly given much attention to the development of ecclesiastical law. In its structural development, the Catholic Church relied heavily on lessons that could be learned from the political experience of imperial Rome, and church law borrowed extensively from Roman law. Valuable as the Roman analogy undoubtedly was, the Church has clung to it rather inflexibly, and been reluctant to alter the social structures based upon it. As a result, social justice has tended to be effective in the Church only to the extent that it proves compatible with traditional structures. In recent times there has been increasing recognition of the fact that changing some of these structures themselves may be among the most imperative demands of social justice in ecclesiastical society. It seems fairly clear that a distorted kind of respect for the Church has sometimes been a major obstacle to ecclesiastical social justice. Thus the Church is often paid by its members a dubious compliment of social irresponsibility, fostered by a confusion of the Church's divine foundation with its thoroughly human and ethically quite imperfect social organization. It would be ironic indeed if the Church's teachings concerning social justice should be least vigorously applied within the Church's own society.

STUDY QUESTIONS

1. What is the basic idea of social justice as distinct from other kinds of justice?

2. What problem results from considering social justice with reference only to one's own society?

3. What is the practical difficulty of likening justice between societies to justice between individual persons?

4. Why is social reform more complicated than individual moral reform?

5. How can ethics of individual responsibility conflict with efforts to establish social justice?

6. In what way does membership in a society tend to broaden ethical perspective?

7. In what way does membership in a society tend to limit ethical perspective?

8. How do national morals tend to diverge from international morals?

9. How does Christian church membership sometimes interfere with social justice?

10. In what sense is social justice reducible to legal and distributive justice?

11. How can individuals or groups within a society practice social justice?

12. How were ethics and politics traditionally supposed to be related?

13. How can the pursuit of social justice lead to advocacy of certain forms of government?

14. What difficulties can arise from advocating certain forms of government in the interest of social justice?

15. What other societies may have an influence on social justice comparable to that of nations?

16. To what extent should social justice be an internal concern of Christian churches?

17. What factors have particularly influenced social justice in the Catholic Church?

18. What frustrations are involved in attempting to reform injustices on a societal level? Illustrate this with a specific example from our own society.

Chapter Twenty

LAW AND ETHICS

LAW AND REASON

A great deal of modern thinking about law recalls an ancient classical tag preserved in the literature of Roman jurisprudence: What pleases the prince has the force of law. In other words, what constitutes a law is simply the decision of a legislator—whether technically a prince or anyone similarly empowered under another title. Given a lawmaker, all that is needed to have a law is the lawmaker's deciding to make one. And whether the decision is wise or foolish, helpful or hurtful, admirable or despicable, has really nothing to do with the question of whether or not it is a law.

Catholic tradition has adopted a position firmly opposed to this way of understanding law. The point of view characteristic of this position is formed by theology as well as philosophy. This can be seen clearly in the way that Thomas Aquinas, who has been very influential in this regard, organizes his fundamental ideas about law. On the highest or most comprehensive level is what he calls the eternal law, meaning the entire divine management of the universe according to an all-encompassing plan. Distinct from this is divine law, referring in a more particular sense to the directing of human beings towards their ultimate goal of union with God. This is further distinguished from natural law, which we have already discussed as the guidance of human beings, under conditions of ordinary human experience, towards achieving their proper well-being. And finally there is human law, designed by human beings to govern members of human communities in the interest of their common well-being.

In all this classification, one very important feature is conspicuous. That is, in every case, law is understood as a means to an end, and the end is understood as the inherent purpose of the subject of the law. Laws, in other words, are thought of as implementing plans. The plans are for keeping the world and its inhabitants headed in the direction that is proper for them. And what makes it proper for them is the fact that it leads to the fulfillment of their inherent purposes. That such purposes exist, and that they are real even for those who may be unaware of them, follows from the Christian belief in a providentially benevolent God on whom everything else depends. Christians' disbelief in purposeless creatures is simply an aspect of their belief in a purposeful Creator.

In this idea of law as giving purposeful direction another very important idea is implicit. That is, law is not simply an act of someone's will, but a determination of reason. Law is based on knowledge and understanding: knowledge of ends, and understanding of the means for attaining them. Hence this whole concept of law departs widely from the idea that what pleases the prince has the force of law. What makes a law is not simply a decision, but an intelligent decision, and what makes legal decisions intelligent is practical awareness of the purpose of those for whom the law is made, and practical discovery of means for achieving that purpose.

Insofar as God makes law, there can be no question about its intelligence, because there can be no ignorance on God's part of either ends or means. But when fallible human beings set about making laws, there is wide scope for the distortions of error, folly, and malice. Nevertheless, in consistency with the view that reasonableness is simply inseparable from law, irrational enactments are denied the very name of law. Out of this background emerges the traditional Catholic definition of law as an ordinance of reason, for the common good, promulgated by one who has care of the community.

HUMAN LAW

In this definition we find the purpose of human law referred to as the common good, that is, the purpose shared by all the law's subjects, in virtue of which they cohere as a community. We find in the same definition the characteristic insistence that it is reason, not mere will, from which law proceeds as an ordinance, that is, an ordering or directing principle. We find also the idea that law must issue from a legitimate source, identified as the caretaker of the community. And since law can be effectual only insofar as it is communicated from the mind of its maker to the minds of its subjects, it has to be promulgated, or publicized.

From this same definition it can be seen that there are many possible reasons why what are claimed to be laws might be judged not to be laws at all. Such would be the case with all arbitrary, unreasonable enactments. It would be the case also if the intended purposes were in the interest not of the community, but only of certain persons or groups within or outside the community. The same would hold if the so-called laws emanated from some unofficial or illegitimate source, or if they were not made public.

One of the peculiarities of this tradition is that, by defining law the way it does, it equivalently identifies all law with good law. This makes it simply illogical to talk about bad laws, and necessary to refer in some more roundabout way to would-be laws that lack some essential component of the definition of law. There is a famous and much-repeated saying of St. Augustine to the effect that whatever lacks justice cannot be law, and the definition we have been considering clearly means to include elements that are necessary for law to be just. Admittedly, there is something rather forced about defining law in such a way that one cannot speak meaningfully of bad law, and inconsistencies on this score are frequent even within the tradition.

Despite this difficulty of consistent usage, such a definition does provide a constant reminder of just what there is about law that makes it worthy of the name and of corresponding respect. Catholic tradition refuses to regard law as simply a fact of life, and insists upon regarding it as an achievement of morally motivated human reason. Legislation is a work of prudence in the interest of justice. Whatever is less than that has no claim on the obedience that is owed to proper law.

LIMITS TO OBEDIENCE AND TO DISOBEDIENCE

Laws which are in fact what laws are supposed to be command obedience on moral grounds, because such laws are, for members of legally constituted communities, necessary means to ends that love and justice are bound to respect. But if what is represented as law is something less than law, the question of whether or not to obey must be answered by prudence. In many communities legislators produce demands that are certainly unworthy of the name of law, whether as results of deliberate tyranny or of indeliberate stupidity. If such demands call for behavior that is itself plainly immoral, they cannot make right what is otherwise wrong, and they ought to be disobeyed. The enforcement of such demands is sheer coercion, which, if threatening enough, might reduce or eliminate the subjective guilt of persons who succumbed to such intimidation.

It is otherwise when legislators require conduct that, although not unequivocally immoral, is nevertheless unwarranted by the legitimate purposes of law. In such cases, circumstances may be such that disobedience is likely to have far more damaging consequences than obedience, in which case disobedience would be wrong, not because of its illegality, but because of its imprudence. To recognize the falsity of claims made in the name of law is to recognize that one does not have one kind of obligation. It is not to recognize that one does not have any kind of obligation, or that one has an automatic obligation to disobey. Good morals, and clear moral judgment, are never more necessary than in the context of bad law. In dealing with unjust laws, as in dealing with outlaws, discretion is the better part of valor. But discretion is not a substitute for valor or a justification for cowardice, nor is it synonymous with conformity. Discretion means weighing the possibilities for doing good, and calculating the risks. Discretion means looking before one leaps. It does not mean adopting a policy of never leaping.

A situation that has drawn much attention in recent times is that of evil laws which unjustly require actions that are not in themselves evil. For example, laws restricting members of a particular race to segregated areas of public transportation are obviously immoral. For the victims of such laws to occupy the segregated areas assigned to them is obviously not in itself immoral. To that extent, although there is no moral obligation to obey such travesties of law, neither is there a moral obligation for their victims to disobey them. And when such unjust laws are powerfully enforced and popularly supported, prudence might well counsel obedience on the ground that disobedience could make nothing better and would make many things worse. However, prudence might also counsel that only through disobedience was there any hope of arousing conscientious resistance to tyrannical bigotry. There is no easy general formula for such determinations of prudence, and in such cases prudence may need the assistance of more than ordinary courage. Nevertheless, the annals of history bear ample witness that circumstances do occur in which civil disobedience becomes inseparable from Christian virtue. There are times when one must refuse to do what the law requires, not because what the law requires is evil, but because the law that requires it is so very evil.

We speak of civil disobedience when such conscientious resistance is directed towards particular unjust laws of a government that is in most respects reasonably just. But it is possible, of course, for governments and their laws to become extensively and habitually unjust. In such cases resistance has the same kind of justification, but to be effective it must be organized much more thoroughly. At this point, the ethics of civil disobedience give way to the ethics of revolution, an issue of such complexity and enormity that both prudence and courage, discretion and valor, must be exercised to their very limits. Those who easily glorify revolution as a reliable instrument of justice should pause to study the history of revolutions, which have so often originated in pursuing justice only to end in multiplying injustice. To assert that revolution can have no good moral place in human life would be plainly rash. But to deny that revolution has a very bad moral record in human history would be plainly ignorant.

LEGISLATING MORALITY

It is commonly observed that human law and morality are two different things. So indeed they are. But they are very closely related things, and frequently have a great deal of influence on one another. We have already considered the very practical possibility that human laws may enjoin behavior which is morally bad, and of the moral obligation to disobey such laws and try to have them done away with. We have also considered the possibility of human laws enjoining behavior which, even if not morally bad, is simply none of the law's business. In cases of this kind, only prudence can determine in the particular circumstances whether obedience or disobedience is the wiser course to follow.

The notion of some behavior's being none of the law's business can be especially important in cases where laws

prohibit, or might prohibit kinds of behavior that are genuinely immoral but which nevertheless are not appropriately dealt
with by human laws. There are, for example, acts which, no
matter how morally indefensible they may be, are of so private a nature that their elimination is not sufficiently a part
of the common good to justify legal intervention. If two people
choose to insult one another in private, and in ways that have
no significantly public consequences, it is hardly a matter for
either the legislature or the police. If, however, they were to
shout abusively at one another in circumstances that constituted a public nuisance, it could be a different matter. And
indeed it would be much the same matter whether they were
disturbing the peace with shouts of abuse or of congratulation.

It is also the case that if some kinds of immoral behavior
were prohibited by law, there would be no practical and otherwise acceptable way of enforcing the law. In such circumstances, laws would not only serve no constructive purpose,
but, because they were unenforceable, they would contribute
to a disrespect for law that could have socially deleterious
effects. A law that cannot, at least usually, be enforced is a
bad law, and scarcely a contribution to the common good.

Special problems arise in cases where certain types of
behavior are regarded by many members of society as seriously immoral, but considered perfectly innocent by many others.
In very democratic societies, laws are not likely to be enacted
against such behavior. But even in such societies it does happen sometimes, as with prohibition in our own country, and it
may very easily happen that laws were enacted in the past
prohibiting behavior which was then generally considered
immoral, but remain in effect at a later time when a great
many people no longer consider the prohibited behavior immoral. Under such conditions, even if the laws do oppose what
is genuinely immoral and truly harmful to the common good,
the laws have a poor chance of achieving beneficial effects.
Without a reasonable degree of unanimity about their value to
society, laws usually work badly and often work perversely. In

such circumstances, a reform of public opinion is usually
necessary to ensure the effectiveness of law. And although it is
not impossible that a defense of existing laws or an appeal for
new laws may provide a means of influencing public opinion
in a morally constructive way, often quite the opposite is the
case.

No doubt the most important laws to try to preserve if one
has them, or to obtain if one has not, even in the face of
extensive public disapproval, are laws that provide vital kinds
of protection for which there is no generally available substitute. Such may have been the case with anti-slavery laws,
when many people did not yet have strong moral objections to
slavery. Such may be the case with anti-abortion laws, now
that many people no longer have strong moral objections to
abortion.

EQUITY

In classical ethics, and Christian ethics where it shows
strong classical influence, reference is frequently made to the
relationship between justice and something that in English is
usually called equity. Aristotle brought out with special clarity the practical significance of equity by describing it as the
way a balance of justice should be restored when that balance
is thrown off precisely by the law. He is not referring here to
what would normally be meant by bad law. Rather, he perceives that law, even at its best, suffers from an inherent
limitation that can result in genuine injustice, and therefore
needs a corrective. For whereas law, by its very nature, is
compelled to make general regulations based on general assumptions, those generalizations cannot do full justice to the
vast and unforeseeable complexity of the concrete realities
law must deal with. Law has to be fairly simple if it is to be of
any use at all, but it is bound to be over-simple with respect to
some situations that develop within its subject matter. No
matter how discreetly human laws are drawn up, circumstances can always arise in which their literal enforcement

would plainly be wrong. Even the soundest laws cannot safely be regarded as unexceptionable, and the exceptions cannot be specified in advance. The wisest of legislators must be prepared for eventual surprises, for unanticipated conditions in which even the best legislation simply does not serve the interests of justice.

In medieval literature one encounters an odd but eloquent word, half Latin and half Greek, for which there is no conventional English equivalent. It would be literally translated as bitterly-just. What it refers to is a perversion of justice that is often brought about in the name of justice itself. It is a characteristic failing of those who equate justice with a fanatical adherence to general regulations that are normally good, even in circumstances which make adhering to them obviously bad. Such bitter-justice is the vice to which equity is the opposing virtue. It is a vice that thrives most vigorously in an atmosphere of legalism, and in a personality that favors cut-and-dried answers and rigid guidelines. The effort to encompass justice so perfectly with law that justice is infallibly guaranteed by inflexible conformity to law, is an effort doomed to failure. It is doomed both by the limitations of human foresight and by the further limitations of human language. Hence the flexibility of virtue, as a living reality, must be relied upon at times to compensate for the lifeless rigidity of law.

STUDY QUESTIONS

1. What is the significance of the saying that what pleases the prince has the force of law?

2. How has Catholic tradition tended to respond to the ideas implicit in that saying?

3. Explain how Thomas Aquinas distinguishes eternal law, divine law, natural law, and human law.

4. What is common to the way law is understood in all these senses?

5. What practical difference does it make whether law is attributed to the will alone or also to reason?

6. What definition of law has been generally favored in Catholic tradition and what do its terms mean?

7. What difficulty does this definition present for discussing bad or unjust laws?

8. What general reason is there for supposing there is moral responsibility to obey laws?

9. When, if ever, ought bad laws to be disobeyed, and when, if ever, ought they to be obeyed?

10. How are civil disobedience and revolution similar and how are they different?

11. Is there any good reason why any behavior that is considered immoral should not be made illegal?

12. Is it ever justifiable to try to illegalize behavior considered immoral by some but moral by others?

13. What is the classic understanding of the idea referred to as equity?

14. Does an appeal to equity suppose that one is dealing with bad laws?

15. What is there about laws in general that makes equity indispensable?

16. What is the nature of the vice to which equity is considered the opposing virtue?

17. Can morality be legislated? What are the limits of law in relation to moral behavior?

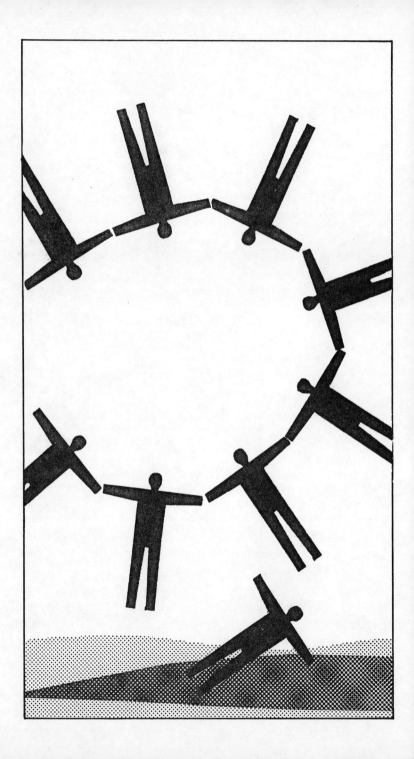

Chapter Twenty-One

GOOD SOCIETIES AND BAD
BEHAVIOR

THE WHOLE AND ITS PARTS

Something has already been said about the kind of ethical thinking that likens societies to individual persons, and on that basis attributes to societies some of the moral characteristics of persons: virtues and vices, good and wicked deeds. As we have seen, especially in connection with ideas of social justice, and of the just society, this way of thinking, though useful and perhaps indispensable, is also inexact and potentially misleading. The present topic may be appropriately introduced by considering under another aspect the moral analogy between societies and persons.

When we predicate virtue of a person we predicate it of the whole person. A person may be called just if he or she habitually behaves justly. This does not mean the person always behaves with perfect justice; occasional lapses do not nullify virtue. But it does mean the whole person ordinarily behaves justly, and it is hard to see how it could be thought to mean anything else. One cannot be just merely from the waist up, nor can one have a just mind in an unjust body or vice versa. The unity of a human person implies the unity (though not, of course, the perpetuity) of his or her moral acts and habits.

But with societies it is obviously different. Societies are made of individuals, and the moral unity of each individual is preserved in society and therefore implies a certain moral multiplicity in the society itself. And yet the ethics of a society and the morality of a society has no other source than the ethics and morality of its individual members operating in some kind of combination. Therefore, although it is absurd to attribute moral acts or attitudes differentially to different components of an individual person, it is quite otherwise with societies.

It is not absurd (although it is over-simplified) to say of a society comprising 100 members that 75 of them are just and 25 unjust—somewhat as in Abraham's famous debate with God. And at the same time it is not usual to mean by a just society one in which every single member is a just person. If one were told of two societies, in each of which 90% of the members were just and 10% unjust persons, it would not follow that they were equally just societies. And in fact, even the knowledge that one society has a considerably larger proportion of unjust members than another would not settle conclusively the question of which should be called the more just society.

Suppose, for example, that in a given society there were very few unjust persons, but, by luck or skill, those persons constituted a powerful oligarchy which ruled tyrannically and was solely responsible for public policies both foreign and domestic. Compare this with another society in which a much larger proportion of unjust persons existed but as subjects of a just governing body and wisely formulated, well-enforced laws that kept their relative affluence and influence within moderate limits. One might plausibly maintain that the society with fewer just members was in fact the more just society.

Three basic ideas may be suggested by these farfetched and artificial examples. The first is that to be a just or good society does not require an exclusively just or good membership. The second is that to be a just or good society does require some just or good members. And the third is that the relative justice or goodness of a society depends to a great extent on how its organization affects the practical relationships of its just or good members at any given time to its unjust or bad members. It is because of such considerations that social justice tends to be more concerned with the development of good social structures than with a kind of door-to-door moralizing. It is on the basis of such considerations that, in particular cases, some political systems may, on ethical grounds, seem preferable to others. And it is on the basis of such considerations that systems of law are expected to encourage just doings of just persons, and discourage unjust undertakings of unjust persons.

Every social organization must reckon with the likelihood of including members who, either occasionally or habitually, behave or try to behave unjustly. And where this is not done, whether in a family, a school, an association, a church, or a sovereign state, a tragic mess inevitably ensues. The goodness of any society depends in part on efficient arrangements which make it relatively easy to behave justly and pleasant to have done so, and relatively difficult to behave unjustly and painful to have done so. Hence, an important part of social justice consists in trying to introduce such arrangements and constantly improve them.

In political society, the principal arrangements of this kind are laws. And if laws are considered, as in Catholic tradition, rational ordinances for the sake of the common good, every good law should contribute in some way to fostering justice and minimizing injustice. But in addition to laws that provide ordinary regulations for a wholesome social existence, a special class of laws is obviously needed to cope with violators of those regulations. These are penal laws, laws that inflict punishment for punishable violations, called crimes.

It is sometimes complained, not without reason, that elementary psychology reminds us of two basic ways to reinforce desired kinds of behavior: punishment, and also reward. And it may seem perverse that the laws of nations should abound in punishments while including very little in the way of specific rewards. But without denying this has some practical point, it should be recalled that a rewarding element should be inherent in the ordinary rules of society. If they do, in fact, give reasonable directions for achieving the common good, then obeying them ought to be, at least in the long run and for most people, rewarding. But by the same token, when laws are violated very frequently and by a great many persons, there is reason to suspect that the laws themselves are either widely misunderstood or genuinely defective. When laws are very commonly broken, it may well be that the laws are more at fault than the violators. Merely to intensify punishment for the breaking of bad laws can only make matters worse. The prevalence of crime shows that there is something seriously wrong in society, but it may require considerable wisdom and knowledge to determine what is wrong and, on that basis, what ought to be done about it.

PUNISHMENT AND DEFENSE

Catholic tradition has never taken the position that punishment, the infliction of pain on offenders, is always a bad thing or likely to become a dispensable thing in this world. It has never endorsed utopian beliefs in the possibility of humanly constructing a paradise upon earth, devoid of sinners whose social abuses ought to be controlled by human penalties. It has never entertained a general presumption that refraining from all punishment will, even in the long run, make a morally better world than employing punishment judiciously. Nor has it ever admitted that even the primacy of love, and more particularly of forgiveness, is incompatible with the justification of punishment. From the first, Catholic tradition believed in a God who punished, developed in a Church that punished, supported a government that punished, and took it for granted that punishment has its place also in societies of more modest scope. Like parents and teachers of untold generations, Catholic tradition has supposed that love and justice sometimes demand punishment precisely of those to whom one is chiefly trying to be loving and just.

Punishment is seen as a morally corrective measure, a way, and sometimes the best way of reducing wrongness and expanding rightness in both individuals and societies. Thus punishment has been accepted as a way of limiting both moral and physical evil, preventing people from doing evil deeds and protecting people from suffering their consequences. Thus Catholic tradition considers punishment to be in principle morally sound enough for the classical virtue called vindication to be regularly included in Christian catalogues of virtue. This is not of course to deny that in practice many punishments may be morally unsound: imprudent, unjust, intemperate, unloving. Nor is to deny that at various times in history punishments have been employed under Catholic auspices in morally atrocious ways.

There is in this tradition no consistent pattern of categorically approving and disapproving specific kinds of punishments. Since, however, it is repeatedly declared that punishments should be of usual kinds, and that the virtue of vindication is radically opposed to the vice of cruelty, the tradition anticipates by many centuries our own constitutional rejection of cruel and unusual punishments. It likewise insists that punishment is not the business of private initiative, but only of recognized authorities within their proper spheres. Beyond these general restrictions, the decision of whether or not to punish, and of how to punish is to be determined by justice, prudence, and love. Punishment of the innocent is categorically forbidden, even at the cost of failing to punish the guilty, and the innocent include those who offend out of blameless ignorance. The selection of punishments is based upon their purpose, which is to reform the guilty and protect the innocent. This idea appears clearly in traditional discussions of capital punishment, where it is emphasized that the use of this extreme penalty is based not on the degree of sinfulness of an offense, but on the danger to others of treating it in any other way. And it is constantly insisted in the strongest terms that to inflict punishment out of hatred represents the transformation of a potential virtue into an actual vice that merits unqualified condemnation.

One recurrent theme of this tradition seems to be surprisingly little noted, but it sheds considerable light on how punishment is included within a Christian ethics that sets the highest value on unselfish love. No traditional theologian treating this topic could fail to perceive an apparent tension between accepting vindication as a human virtue and cultivating the attitudes exemplified by Jesus and crystallized in the Sermon on the Mount. But in very early writings and repeatedly thereafter, a very sharp distinction is made between refusing to retaliate against injuries done to oneself, and leaving unimpeded and unpunished acts that injure the neighbor or dishonor God. The former may well be counselled by a Christlike love of the offender. The latter is hard to reconcile with Christlike love of the offended. An indiscriminate rejection of any use of punitive force against malefactors, regardless of whom they threaten and how they threaten, is hardly a policy derivable from the norm of loving one's neighbor as oneself, and it is as absent from Catholic tradition as it is from the New Testament itself.

From what has been said it should be clear that there is a close relationship between punishment and defense. In practice the two often overlap, but they do not do so invariably. Punishment may be, but is not always defensive, and defense may not be, but is not always punitive. Punishment may be administered simply for the correction of a moral fault that poses no obvious major threat to others. Often, punishment combines with this morally curative intention the additional purpose of preventing or curtailing injuries. And sometimes, as outstandingly in the case of capital punishment, the protection of others is, practically speaking, the sole objective. Defense is simply a matter of warding off attackers, of whatever kind. It may be accomplished by punishment or threat of punishment, but often it can obviously be done much better in other ways. Catholic tradition has always recognized the moral acceptability of sometimes hurting and even killing defensively, provided defense does not become a mask for malevolence, and that the means employed are neither more hurtful than they have to be nor disproportionate to the danger they oppose. With regard to hurting or killing in self-defense, it may be recalled from our earlier discussion that this is not a right in the strict sense, but a privilege or liberty of acting in a way one is normally obliged not to act. Still less is it in itself an obligation. However, it is easy to imagine circumstances that could make it an obligation, as when a life that is threatened is one on which other lives critically depend. Self-love is not the only conceivable motive for even lethal self-defense, and the very highest Christian motives may at times support it.

WAR

The closely related topics of punishment and defense both have much in common with the topic of war. An important theory of jurisprudence has developed the idea that warfare has a function in international relations comparable to that of legal penalties in national affairs. And it is well known that defense against aggression has been the most generally respected basis for justifying warfare on moral grounds.

Christian tradition concerning the ethics of war has been complicated by evidence to the effect that during the first centuries after Christ, Christians were notorious for their refusal of military service. What is not so clear is the motivation of their refusal. There is good reason to believe that their major consideration was rather the elements of idolatry, especially emperor-worship, unavoidable in Roman military life, than moral revulsion from war itself. The Jews, at first commonly confused with Christians, had previously refused Roman military service because it entailed Sabbath violations, and finally secured legal exemption on that basis. In any case, once Rome became a Christian empire, Christian rulers made wars and Christian subjects fought, killed, and died in them, unimpeded by anything that could be considered a general moral objection to war as such. And at least from the time of Augustine, theories of just war have been considered applicable in practice. Such theories are attempts to specify the conditions under which war can be justly waged. The very existence of such theories implies, of course, that war can be unjustly waged.

Just war theory has two basic aspects. The first has to do with what justifies waging war at all. The second has to do with what is justifiable in the course of waging a war. In other words, there is first the question of when warring is justified, and second the question of what kinds of warring are justified. For the most part, questions such as these have been regarded as addressed to those who are officially responsible for embarking on wars, namely rulers or governments. But in recent times a great deal more attention than previously has been given to the further issue of the individual's responsibility to decide whether or not to take part in wars officially waged by his political leader. This latter development has been fostered by more democratic conceptions of citizenship and by the development of public communication to a point that makes causes and motives of war much more perceptible than they used to be.

Catholic tradition has generated a recognized approach to questions of the justifiability of war that concentrates on certain basic considerations. A primary consideration is rightness of intention, usually understood as meaning that what war is striving to achieve is the common good, or wholesome peace. Closely related to this is the justice of the cause, generally limited to responding to injuries, and often more particularly limited to defense against aggression. A relevant legal consideration is whether or not war is initiated by legitimate authority, normally conceived as requiring a declaration of war. A basic prudential consideration is that the good which war is expected to achieve should be proportionate to the harm it is likely to do. And a final consideration is whether or not alternative possible means have been exhausted before war is undertaken as a last resort.

Within these guidelines, two considerations are especially important under conditions of modern warfare. The first is a consequence of the immense and indiscriminate destructiveness inherent in modern arms and favored by modern strategies. Once recourse is had to weapons and techniques that inflict enormous devastation and make little distinction between combatants and non-combatants, it becomes barely conceivable that any hoped for good could outweigh such evil. And it is difficult to see how any anticipated consequences could justify the direct slaughter of non-combatants.

A second special consideration emerges from growing appreciation of the effectiveness, at least in certain circumstances, of non-violent modes of resistance to aggression. In the light of current events, it is clear that the means and methods of war have largely outgrown even the most liberal interpretations of just war theory. It has become a grave question whether the very building of nuclear arsenals for defensive purposes can be morally justified. For the intention of using such weapons entails the moral, if not the physical evil of actually using them. And to claim a merely pretended intention of using them strains the limits of even naive credulity. Moreover, an honest reading of history turns up depressingly few examples of warring that have any claim to be thought just, even in ages of less horrendous weaponry. Under the circumstances there can be no question that the initial Christian attitude towards advocacy of war must be one of extreme scepticism, or that certain courageous resisters of national war efforts take their place among the principal moral heroes of modern Christianity.

STUDY QUESTIONS

1. Do we attribute moral goodness or badness to societies in the same way as to individual persons?

2. Might one society be considered more just than another which had proportionately more just members?

3. To what extent is the goodness of a society dependent on the goodness of its members?

4. How can the organization of a society affect its moral goodness or badness?

5. What are penal laws and what is the reason for having such laws?

6. Is it unreasonable that laws tend to give great attention to punishments but not to rewards?

7. What alternative explanations should suggest themselves when laws are extensively violated?

8. How has Catholic tradition generally regarded the ordinary uses of punishment?

9. Does Catholic tradition discriminate between different kinds of punishment?

10. Is punishment reconcilable with Gospel appeals for non-retaliation?

11. How are punishment and defense related and how are they distinguished?

12. Can hurting and killing ever be obligatory in defense, including self-defense?

13. How are punishment and defense related to the waging of war?

14. How has Christian tradition generally viewed the morality of war?

15. What issues are raised by early Christian attitudes toward military service?

16. What two main aspects are considered in formulating theories of just warfare?

17. In Catholic tradition what factors are thought to contribute to the justification of warfare?

18. What special issues are raised by distinctively modern developments in warfare and defense?

19. Make a case for or against either capital punishment or war. Support your argument with your knowledge of the Catholic tradition.

Chapter Twenty-Two

REASONABLE MODERATION

THE BROADER SCOPE OF TEMPERANCE

As already indicated in a general account of temperance, it is a virtue which, in its most general significance, has very broad application. It is related to the classical ideal of living a well-rounded life, one that is neither unduly deprived of certain enriching experiences, nor unduly taken up with others. Hence the vices opposed to temperance are described in terms of living in a way that is in some respects defective and in other respects excessive. In this sense, temperance is applicable to a great many human interests and undertakings. Thus, in economic matters it would be intemperate to be either miserly or wasteful. It is no less intemperate to be compulsively gregarious than it is to be morbidly solitary. It is equally intemperate to work without resting and to rest without working. And so on, in countless areas of life. We are all aware of elements of lopsidedness in our own patterns of behavior and in those of others, and of how often this results in impoverishment of life and stultification of development.

Nevertheless, it is by no means obvious that matters of this kind can be regulated by anything like hard and fast rules. It would be absurd to suppose the ideal of human living is to be a sort of dabbler in as many as possible of the fields of experience our environment affords. And it would be equally absurd to deny that the unmistakable moral greatness of some human lives is inseparable from the fact that they have largely dispensed with whole areas of experience, while concerning themselves intensely with others. We deplore narrow-minded fanaticism, but we admire single-minded dedication. And it would be no easy matter to distinguish between the two simply on the basis of a kind of temperance conceived as consistently pursuing the golden mean in all things. What is moderation in one set of circumstances is not in another, and one person's moderation may be another person's excess. What is due moderation cannot be established statistically. It must be discovered by prudence, that is, by practical reason directed by moral principles and enlightened by an appreciation of relevant facts and objectives.

Because due moderation has to be determined by reason in the light of facts, it follows that when relevant facts change greatly, correct ideas of moderation must change with them. The present age abounds in important applications of this idea. Consider, for example, in how many ways rapid growth of the world's population leads to the conclusion that what was moderate yesterday would be immoderate today. Phrases like family-planning and planned parenthood remind us of the increasing likelihood that sheer procreative spontaneity will have results that, by rational ethical standards, are excessive and irresponsible. Uses of natural resources that were moderate enough in a less crowded world have become inexcusably wasteful. What was a moderate appropriation of land for private enjoyment becomes cruelly selfish as the wide-open spaces disappear forever. In these and many other respects it is clear how specific ideas about moderation are obliged to change as factual transformations give rise to new ethical perspectives.

Considerations of this kind should make us aware that temperance, the virtue of due moderation, is not a virtue simply of individual persons. It is a social virtue, and an indispensable attribute of good societies. If the indulgence of gourmet predilections in one society inflicts malnutrition on another, the former society must be considered in a general way to be wickedly gluttonous. If a fancy for big cars in a rich nation leads to major depletion of the world's fuel and major pollution of the world's atmosphere, such luxury becomes vicious self-indulgence. To eat five pieces of bread is hardly in itself definable as gluttony. But it is obscenely gluttonous to do so when only six pieces are served at a common table. Temperance must be perceived as a social virtue in order not to be conceived as a trivial virtue. The rich man in Jesus' parable who feasted sumptuously every day was demonstrably intemperate. But what demonstrated his intemperance was not obesity or indigestion. It was the wretched beggar lying at his gate.

THE NARROWER SCOPE OF TEMPERANCE

One reason for placing special emphasis on the social aspect of temperance is because until fairly recently Catholic tradition tended to display an opposite emphasis, on its strictly individual aspects. Thus, as was mentioned earlier, specific considerations of temperance generally concentrated on individual habits of eating, drinking, and sexual conduct. In all three areas, the basic approach was a typical application of natural law. That is, these activities were seen, in ordinary observation of common experience, to be spontaneously oriented towards definite purposes that are not simply invented by human beings, namely nourishment and reproduction. Wholesome behavior in these areas was understood to mean reasonable behavior, and therefore behavior that, on the one hand, was guided by sound reason and, on the other hand, did not itself interfere with the soundness of reason or its effectiveness.

The reason why eating, drinking, and sex were singled out

for special consideration in this respect is because in all three there is or can be an attendant pleasure that may be so attractive as to be sought as an end in itself. Such pleasure was regarded as serving naturally to stimulate activities necessary for the life and health of individuals or of the species. But such pleasure can be sought and indulged in in such a way or to such a degree that its natural purpose is neglected or even frustrated. Such conduct was deemed irrational and therefore unworthy of a human being. Moreover, not only can these pleasures be cultivated in disregard of reason, but they and the desire for them can reach an intensity that overpowers reason itself, and thereby fosters irrationality of other kinds. This latter consideration was thought to be especially relevant to the drinking of intoxicants and to sexual indulgence. The comparable effects of consuming various other chemicals, such as narcotics, to those of drinking intoxicants, led to their being treated in the same general category. The basic norm traditionally applied to all these is a negative one, regarding as immoral whatever kind or amount of consumption or indulgence impairs rationality and thereby strikes at the very root of all morality. For indeed, no one reaches maturity without gaining some awareness of how much of the world's misery and guilt derive from uncontrolled appetites for drink and sex. And if one considers the realm of economic injustice, especially between nations, uncontrolled appetite for food will not seem more innocent than those others.

CHASTITY

The term chastity is used in sexual ethics less frequently than it used to be. There is, of course, nothing sacred about the term, and it has become confusingly ambiguous, mainly because it is often used among Catholics as a near synonym for celibacy. Nevertheless, no other word seems to have replaced chastity as representing virtuous sexuality, and a consequence of its loss is that ethical thinking about sexuality tends to concentrate on isolated actions, paying little attention to traits of character. According to the traditional system of thought, chastity is understood as the form taken by the virtue of temperance in sexual life. Temperance implies a due moderation established by reason. And as already discussed, the way that reason goes about identifying this due moderation is by discovering through reflection on ordinary observation what appear to be natural purposes and the natural means for achieving them.

From this point of view, there was developed a basic understanding of sexuality that underlies a great deal of traditional ethical teaching. What are observed initially are the existence of male and female human beings and the occurrence, at a certain level of maturation, of sexual arousal entailing their mutual attraction. This arousal and attraction finds spontaneous expression in kinds of behavior we associate with courtship, involving more or less intense and more or less ingenious efforts by which one who is sexually attracted to another tries to evoke reciprocal interest. The outcome that courtship regularly envisages and occasionally achieves is the kind of behavior designated as mating, of which the culminating event is sexual intercourse and the climactic experience is sexual orgasm. This, in the normal course of things, leads to conception, gestation, and childbirth. Thus, mating behavior is typically followed by parental behavior, concerned with providing for the wholesome development of offspring up to a point when their own maturity makes it possible for them to enter upon a similar process of biological and interpersonal development.

Needless to say, this coldly schematic account prescinds from all the individual variations that make human sexual experience remarkable, and capable of exhibiting some of the best and some of the worst capabilities of human character. At every point of the process here outlined, there are extraordinary subtleties and intensities of personal feeling, understanding, and decision, offering boundless possibilities for joy and sorrow, wisdom and folly, nobility and depravity.

Whether or not Catholic ethical tradition has been insufficiently sensitive to these richer and more personal aspects, its basic approach to sexual ethics is neither unclear nor unintelligible. Given the point of view associated with natural law, it seemed evident that sexuality might be expected to function rightly if it was guided by respectful appreciation of its God-given purpose. That purpose was to be inferred from observing spontaneous human tendencies and their ordinary outcomes. Such observation revealed the typical sequence of events we have just reviewed. And it displayed the events of that sequence as purposefully leading up to a point which gave full significance to all that preceded it. This outcome is essentially the nuclear family, comprising a man and woman whose sexual love has made them parents, given them children, and thereby introduced them to new dimensions of love, with new opportunities and new responsibilities.

In Catholic tradition, basic sexual ethics is invariably conceived with reference to the process just described. This process is regarded as natural and good, and ordinary sexual morality consists in participating in it prudently, justly, and lovingly. Accordingly, the continuity of the process itself takes on a normative character, and attempting to isolate or displace elements of it is regarded as interference with a God-given design. Consequently, most of the traditionally specified offenses against chastity involve the taking of certain steps in that process without assuming responsibility for its further steps, and especially for the final step which involves conjugal and parental commitment, the institutional form of which is marriage. On this basis it is easy to understand traditional denunciations of such practices as masturbation, homosexual activity, rape, fornication, adultery, and contraception. For each of these practices represents an attempt to enjoy some part of a natural process while rejecting its place in a natural sequence. Basically, therefore, traditional sexual ethics takes an all-or-none position: either embark responsibly on the whole normal course of sexual living, or abstain from it altogether, either temporarily or permanently. Hence chastity is considered realizable in the long run in either of two ways of life, called marriage and celibacy. It is not considered realizable in a way of life that is neither the one nor the other.

COMPLICATIONS IN SEXUAL ETHICS

The apparently natural sequence of sexual events described in the preceding section has provided a basic frame of reference for Catholic tradition in sexual ethics. As already noted, there is in this tradition a general presumption that behavior which departs notably from this natural order is ethically wrong. And it is regularly observed that behavior which is criticized on that basis tends to manifest its wrongness in other ways as well, especially as conflicting with the demands of justice and love. Seduction is deceitful. Rape is violent. Adultery is treacherous. Fornication has a well documented reputation for leading from deception and self-deception to frustration and indignity, and all too frequently to cruel negligence and homicidal abortion. The amount of physical and moral tragedy that is traceable, in life as in literature, to such irresponsible pursuits of sexual gratification, is truly prodigious, and goes far to commend the basic validity of the traditional natural law conception of chastity.

Despite the value of considering the typical course of sexual events as a standard, indicating what is natural, reasonable, and good in sexual conduct, there is manifold danger of applying this general scheme over-rigidly as an ethical norm. Such over-rigidity results when insufficient attention is paid to differences and changes of relevant circumstances. For example, it would be plainly naive to condemn as unnatural every sexual relationship that deliberately stopped short of child-bearing, regardless of family resources and population growth. To denounce as unnatural and therefore immoral a couple who choose to adopt homeless orphans instead of having children of their own is plainly absurd. In fact, Catholic tradition has long conceded that there can be morally admirable reasons for a childless marriage, and has more recently conceded that limiting the number of one's children may well be a moral duty.

There is a danger of too easily assuming that what seem

to be unnatural departures from the typical sequence of sexual events must be otherwise harmful. Thus whole lists of supposedly dire effects of masturbation have been found unsupported by any serious evidence.

There is a danger of adopting too simple a view of the sexual characteristics of human beings. Thus, many evaluations of homosexual behavior have failed to appreciate the profound differences of psychological makeup between homosexual and heterosexual persons. As a result, homosexual behavior has often been morally evaluated as though it were merely the perverse conduct of typical heterosexuals. A different sort of over-simplification has too easily regarded as the definitive natural roles of males and females what are only conventional roles enforced by changeable and changing social conditions.

And there is a danger of failing to appreciate that the distinctively human capacity to alter certain natural processes is itself an attribute of human nature, and a divine gift which has its own proper uses. Paradoxical as it may seem, for human beings it is to a great extent natural to be artificial, for human beings are by nature artists and technicians. There is no reason to assume that human inventiveness is less capable of functioning constructively in sexuality than in other areas of life, or that unmodified biological spontaneity represents in all cases a moral ideal. Accordingly, such practices as artificial contraception, artificial insemination, and even artificial fertilization cannot be dismissed as self-evidently wicked. Such human contrivances must be evaluated in respect of the service and disservice they are capable of rendering to basic ethical values realizable in human sexuality. Evaluation of this kind is strongly characteristic of the current phase of Catholic tradition in sexual ethics. It is an undertaking in which basic ethical convictions need to be applied with great care to increasingly complex factual information. And an end of this process is no more foreseeable than an end of newly discovered relevant facts.

STUDY QUESTIONS

1. What classical ideal of a good human life is closely related to the understanding of temperance?

2. In general, what kinds of behavior are considered incompatible with temperance?

3. How can the notion of temperance be made impractical by an over-strict interpretation?

4. How can factual, historical developments affect the valid realization of temperance?

5. How can temperance be conceived as a social as well as an individual virtue?

6. In Catholic tradition, what kinds of behavior have been generally treated in connection with temperance?

7. How is natural law involved in the application of temperance to these kinds of behavior?

8. Why were these particular kinds of behavior singled out as especially relevant to temperance?

9. What special ambiguity has developed around Catholic use of the term "chastity"?

10. What was the basic traditional understanding of chastity as a virtue?

11. What conception of the natural course of sexual behavior has been generally operative in Catholic tradition?

12. How does Catholic tradition most typically distinguish between right and wrong sexual behavior?

13. What two ways of life correspond to alternative ways of living chastely?

14. Can behavior traditionally regarded as being unchaste be criticized on other grounds as well?

15. How can over-rigid application of natural law argument lead to doubtful moral judgments of sexual behavior?

16. How can over-simplified ideas of human sexual characteristics be ethically misleading?

17. How can the contrast between the natural and the artificial be used misleadingly in ethics?

18. How ought artificial or technical modifications of sexual behavior to be evaluated ethically?

19. Do you agree with the statement that "for human

beings it is to a greater extent natural to be artificial, for human beings are by nature artists and technicians"? How does your answer affect your view of human sexuality?

Chapter Twenty-Three

WAYS OF LIFE

DOING WITHOUT MARRIAGE

Although Catholic tradition regards the sexual tendencies and activities of human nature as finding their proper fulfillment in marriage, it has always regarded marriage as optional and celibacy as a highly respectable alternative. Positive views of celibacy are expressed in several New Testament writings and attributed to Jesus himself, who is also reasonably assumed, for total lack of any evidence to the contrary, to have led an unmarried life himself. Paul refers to his own deliberate abstinence from marriage, but also indicates that this was exceptional among the apostles. The New Testament nowhere asserts that there is anything morally or religiously wrong with marriage or its proper sexual activities, but rather adopts the Old Testament understanding of marriage as a divine institution and a great blessing.

It is their understanding of the Gospel itself that chiefly accounts for the early Christians' approval of celibacy. There are many indications of their conviction that, in view of the coming Kingdom of God, human social arrangements of this world take on a provisional character that makes them recede greatly in relative importance. The apparently widespread belief among early Christians that human history was soon to end would have made marriage, and many other matters of comparable seriousness, easy to take lightly. Marital arrangements, like commercial and governmental arrangements, simply are not constituents of the longed-for Kingdom of God, however much they may influence human preparations for that Kingdom. We have already noticed in the Gospel portrayal of Jesus, not only his sexual uninvolvement, but his significant failure to share contemporary enthusiasms of an economic or political nature. He is frequently represented as dissuading his followers from being too much concerned with worldly arrangements and their attendant hopes and fears. For human habits of treating such matters as though they were of ultimate importance can be the gravest of obstacles to faith in a Gospel that conceives ultimate importance very differently.

In the circumstances, it is easy to understand how Christian teaching might foster detachment from even the most estimable worldly preoccupations, in the very process of strengthening attachment to the hope of a divine realm that would make all such preoccupations forever irrelevant. Thus St. Paul remarks in concrete terms how concern about pleasing one's spouse can diminish a married person's devotion to God. It is clear that Paul saw the same sort of distraction as a potential obstacle to his own kind of ministry. But it should be clearly noted in all of this that there is nothing like a puritanical anti-sex campaign or the casting of aspersions on normal features of bodily, sensual life. Most unfortunately, such elements did appear later, along with new philosophical perspectives that sharply contrasted bodily and spiritual modes of existence. Subsequent Catholic tradition has seldom been unaffected by resulting tendencies to extol the spiritual at the expense of the bodily. But at the same time, Catholic tradition has consistently opposed the more fanatical manifestations of a tendency so hard to reconcile with as central a Christian belief as the incarnation itself.

Detachment from worldly preoccupation out of zeal for the Kingdom of God is one thing. Despising the human body out of admiration for the human spirit is quite a different thing. The former has deep roots in the central message of Jesus Christ. The latter has not, but is a heritage of pre-Christian pagan philosophies that can be of service to faith only if they are not made objects of faith. Human life evidently does present aspects significantly distinguishable as human body and human spirit. But both aspects can participate no less in human malice than in human goodness. And to identify the contrast of human body and human spirit with the contrast of good and evil is to depart radically from the perspective of the Gospel. The only spirit Christianity venerates is the Spirit of God, whereby human beings are sanctified in body and spirit alike. Celibacy, when adopted on Christian grounds, does not bear witness to the preeminence of the spiritual over the bodily. It bears witness to the preeminence of the Kingdom of God which the Gospel promises, over these human kingdoms in which the Gospel struggles to be heard.

MARRYING AS CHRISTIANS

What was said of marriage in the preceding chapters was only as much as is involved in the natural law understanding of human sexuality that has prevailed in Catholic tradition. That understanding is a product of reflection on observations of ordinary human behavior. Its ethical implications rest upon that basis. They have religious significance inasmuch as natural law is thought to reflect divine intention. They are not based on any more distinctly Christian convictions. But there are convictions about marriage that derive more directly and explicitly from Christian belief, and as a result Christian marital ethics goes beyond, though not against, implications of the natural law argument. This is especially evident, and especially important, in two respects: opposition to divorce, and understanding of a sacramental symbolism in marriage.

Mention has already been made of divorce as one of the few specific ethical issues Jesus is said to have dealt with. St. Paul, writing before the Gospels, already refers to Jesus' condemnation of divorce as to a thing well known among Christians. And the Gospels in several places describe Jesus denouncing divorce as morally equivalent to adultery. Jesus' strong teaching on this point is more notable for exceeding in strictness even the most conservative Jewish teachings of his time. And it is even more notable that in taking this stand Jesus sets aside even Mosaic tradition, in favor of his own interpretation of what God intended in creating the sexes to be two in one flesh. Jesus thus represents marriage as the fulfillment of a basic divine plan, and on that basis condemns divorce as the violation of a basic divine plan. It is significant that in doing so he departs entirely from the prevailing assumption that divorce is a male prerogative that women must simply endure. Since in the Gentile world divorce was possible for wives as well as husbands, the New Testament applies Jesus' teaching by condemning the disruption of marriage by either spouse.

St. Paul, dealing in one of his Gentile churches with the new phenomenon of marriages between Christians and pagans, encountered the problem of Christians whose marriages were repudiated by pagan husbands or wives. His response to such dilemmas is twofold. First, in fidelity to the Lord's teaching, every effort should be made to preserve a marriage or bring about a reconciliation. If, however, the obstinacy of a pagan spouse makes that impossible, the Christian spouse whose marriage has been irreparably destroyed is considered to be free. Thus St. Paul, confronted with new complications in Christian marital ethics, both reasserts Christian belief that to divorce is wrong, and attempts to cope reasonably with Christian experience that to be divorced is sometimes inevitable. Paul's conduct here provides a fundamental model for efforts to deal with factors that jeopardize or destroy the stability of Christian marriage. The basic obligation is clear, but violations of it are unavoidable and innocent victims of such violations must be sympathetically provided for. Nor is there any suggestion that the violations themselves are not, like all other sins, forgivable if repented of.

St. Paul is also the source of an understanding of marriage that both gives it a distinctive Christian significance, and indicates fundamental aspects of how a Christian married life ought to be led. Like Jesus, Paul refers to the creation account for his basic appreciation of marriage. But for Paul the union of husband and wife as two in one flesh is not only a fact but also a symbol. What it symbolizes is the union of Jesus Christ with his Church. The main aspects of this symbolism are taken up in his concluding appeal for husbands to love their wives and for wives to respect their husbands. Paul, like all his contemporaries, takes it for granted that wives are their husbands' subordinates. Correlative with this idea is his description of the husband as the head of his wife. This metaphorical sense of headship recalls Christ's position as the head of his Body the Church. In this way Paul is led to the application of Christ's kind of headship as a model for husbands. Christ's manner of exercising headship is based not on self-assertion but on self-giving, not on domineering use but on sanctifying devotion. This Pauline teaching has greatly influenced a Christian view of the personal relationship between spouses. For while, on the one hand, it does not relinquish the idea of wifely submissiveness to husbandly authority, it conceives that authority not as despotic control but as loving service. This understanding of a Christlike attitude between one spouse and another remains a constant factor in the tradition, even as social conventions change with respect to the distribution of authority between the sexes.

It is the same Pauline teaching that has provided a basis in Catholic tradition for considering marriage to be, in the technical liturgical sense, a sacrament. The development of this sacramental understanding of marriage has a long and complex history, with extensive implications in the realm of ecclesiastical law. Among these, the one that has most influenced and most complicated the ethics of marriage is the conviction that Christian spouses are not only morally obliged not to divorce, but legally incapable of doing so. On this understanding, even a perfectly innocent victim of a supposed divorce is unable to contract another marriage during the previous spouse's lifetime. Various attempts continue to be made by the formulators and administrators of Church law to mitigate the suffering inflicted by such circumstances, within limits imposed by the sacramental doctrine. One means to that end is by seeking any available evidence that the original marriage may have lacked certain conditions necessary for its validity, in which case divorce would not be made possible, but would be made unnecessary. Although this procedure has been a source of some relief, it is clearly a legal makeshift, open to serious abuses, and basic problems in this area remain difficult and urgent.

Catholic tradition's main contribution to dealing with the prospect of broken marriages and the miseries they occasion is not curative; it is preventive. The likelihood of divorce is not great when both spouses live their married lives even approximately as that tradition counsels. That is, on the basis of a familial commitment in which both conjugal and parental love achieve a harmony that only generosity makes possible. Despite all other advantages, selfish marriages regularly sicken and sadden, and very often die. And despite all other disadvantages, marriages founded on Christlike love have demonstrated again and again, in the plainest ways, a strength and joy unmatched in any other human social experience.

RELIGIOUS AND SECULAR CHRISTIANITY

Both celibacy and marriage are esteemed in Catholic tradition. Moreover, both are esteemed above all as being mean-

ingfully Christian, as expressing central Christian beliefs by
responding to them through a whole way of life. Christian
celibacy is not simply the bare fact of being a Christian without a spouse, nor is Christian marriage the bare fact of being
Christian with a spouse. For the point of view that makes
celibacy Christian is a point of view that must, if personal
integrity is to be preserved, extend also into other areas of life.
And so must the point of view that makes marriage Christian.

Celibacy, as we have seen, finds its Christian significance
in the witness it bears to the impermanence and undecisive-
ness of human culture and human history, and the contrasting ultimacy of the Kingdom of God. It is the adoption of a way
of life that deliberately emphasizes what is ultimate, and
deliberately deemphasizes what is not. But it would be humanly incongruous for so fundamental an emphasis to be realized
merely in one compartment of life and discarded in others.
Accordingly, celibacy, as a Christian way of life, has been
traditionally associated with a whole pattern of living that
consistently expresses the same emphasis. It has done so by
systematically minimizing the great preoccupations that
dominate most human enterprise and shape the course of
worldly history, and by systematically cultivating a
realization of the ultimate and eternal. Much of what is thus
minimized falls within the broad and closely related
categories of wealth and power, acquiring of property and
controlling of persons, the fundamental motives of economics
and politics. On this foundation of detachment from intense
economic, sexual, and political involvement, Christianity built
and Catholicism preserved the institution of monasticism and
a host of derivative variations called collectively the religious
life. The defining traits of this way of life have been celibacy,
closely associated with a systematic detachment from wealth
and power, represented in a somewhat technical sense by the
terms poverty and obedience.

Marriage obviously expresses a quite different point of
view and leads in a quite different direction. Christian mar-

riage achieves its Christian symbolism by reflecting the love shown by Jesus Christ in living and dying for his people. It is concentrated on the historical reality of Christ conceived as the immersion of incarnate divinity in a mortal, human world. To marry, whether as a Christian or otherwise, is inevitably to assume the ordinary preoccupations of a present though impermanent world. Sexual detachment, economic detachment, and political detachment, in any thoroughgoing sense, are incompatible with the way of life to which marriage naturally and normally leads. For what it leads to is a family and responsibility for a family. And a family is preeminently a sexual, economic, and political reality, which originates sexually, survives economically, and matures politically. Relations between spouses and between parents and children are a microcosm to their worldly environment, with its ceaseless dependence on material possession and distribution and on social direction and control. Nor is the family an isolated microcosm; it must collaborate with its neighbors and contend with them, and develop organized ways of doing both. This kind of life, to which marriage leads, is secular life, a life whose practical focus is upon this present world. If it is Christian secular life, its intimate dealings with this world must reflect Christ's dealings with it, serving its needs with love and resisting its evils with courage. For secular Christianity, the alternatives to poverty, celibacy, and obedience are not avarice, lust, and despotism. Its sexual involvement must express fidelity. Its economic involvement must achieve generosity. Its political involvement must serve truth and justice.

It takes little reflection to conclude that neither religious nor secular Christianity can exist in an absolutely pure form. A purely religious life is irreconcilable with historical existence. A purely secular life is irreconcilable with Christian faith. They are better described as ways of life than as states of life, for what distinguish them are their different directions or tendencies of thought and behavior. For individual lives to be human and Christian lives, both tendencies must be present, either one may predominate, and the predominance may be more or less extreme. Nevertheless, certain practical decisions expressing one emphasis or the other have implications that tend to intensify that emphasis and extend it. Of this, the outstanding instance is undoubtedly the option between Christian celibacy and Christian marriage. Needless to say, a Christian may, and often does, marry or not marry for reasons that have nothing to do with Christian convictions. In which case, neither religious nor secular Christianity results, but only sheer secularity.

THE WORLD'S WORK AND THE CHRISTIAN WORKER

Not only matrimonial decisions, but occupational ones as well, can profoundly affect the relative religious or secular orientation of one's Christianity. An intensely religious way of life naturally favors types of work that make modest demands on worldly preoccupation, and that foster a focussing of attention beyond the domain of merely human arrangements and temporal accomplishments. This is well illustrated by monasticism's traditional combination of simple and stable forms of industry to provide a basic independent security with generous opportunities for prayer and specifically religious modes of learning and art. Only a secular way of life can accommodate complex undertakings, broad collaboration, long-range projects, and enterprises that depend heavily on material wealth and social power. A Christian secular way of life can accommodate such activities only to the extent that it brings them into line with essential Christian values, making them works of love for God and neighbor, and evaluating them by that criterion alone.

Christianity inherited from the Old Testament a belief that good human work is divine service, and that the capacity to render such service is part of what it means to be created in God's image and likeness. The same tradition also teaches that when human work expresses not divine service but human pride it becomes blasphemous arrogance, ultimately destructive of those who engage in it. And the Old Testament as a whole is highly respectful of ordinary manual work, as well as of learned pursuits, and the former is never perceived as inherently disgraceful. A highly important New Testament supplement to these Old Testament ideas is a consistent and unequivocal insistence that there is not only nothing dishonorable about poverty, but nothing specifically honorable about wealth.

All these biblical ideas sharply conflict with elements of classical culture that extol basing human works on human pride, regard labor as fit only for the slaves it makes necessary, and consider poverty incompatible with human dignity. Christian history reveals at every point the tenacity of these pagan values with respect to human occupation. But it does also reveal an adherence to opposite values which goes well beyond lip-service.

In the lives of individual Christians, these radically conflicting values usually have their most critical encounters on occasions when major occupational choices are to be made. This is especially true in modern times, when occupations are seldom simply inherited as most of them once were. On such occasions, a Christian must be deeply concerned over how his or her chosen occupation responds to the law of love, over what good and what harm it is likely to do, and in what proportion and to whom it is likely to do them. And a Christian must prevent that concern from being suppressed or distorted by antithetical values. For a great many people, their choice of occupation has greater implications for social justice than any other single act they can perform. The occupation one chooses takes up a great deal of one's life and directs a great deal of one's energy. In terms of Christian morality, choosing an occupation simply for the money is no more respectable than choosing one's husband or wife simply for the money. Nor is there much likelihood that an occupation chosen out of pagan motives will be exercised out of Christian ones.

STUDY QUESTIONS

1. How has Catholic moral tradition typically regarded the possibility of abstaining from marriage?

2. What distinctive belief among early Christians contributed to the approval of celibacy?

3. How did the adoption of new philosophical ideas alter the Christian basis for approving of celibacy?

4. How is the distinction between the bodily and the spiritual related to the distinction of right and wrong?

5. Does Christian evaluation of marriage entail other factors than those related to natural law ethics?

6. How do the Gospels represent Jesus' attitude toward divorce?

7. What special problem did St. Paul have to deal with in connection with divorce?

8. How does St. Paul's teaching on divorce relate to the material in the Gospels?

9. What symbolism does St. Paul attribute to the marriage relationship?

10. What does St. Paul mean, practically speaking, by the headship of husbands?

11. What moral conclusion does St. Paul derive from his understanding of the symbolism of husbands' headship?

12. What is the biblical basis for Catholic understanding of marriage as a sacrament?

13. How has the sacramental understanding of marriage complicated the Catholic treatment of divorce?

14. To what attitudes and convictions does Christian celibacy properly bear witness?

15. How does emphasis on these attitudes and convictions tend to shape a way of life?

16. What attitudes and convictions correspond more closely with Christian marriage?

17. How do these attitudes and convictions tend to form a different way of life?

18. Why can neither religious nor secular Christianity exist in an unqualifiedly pure state?

19. How do occupational differences correspond to religious and secular orientations of Christian life?

20. How do biblical and classical traditions conflict in

their typical assessments of human occupations?

21. Why is occupational choice especially important for Christian social justice?

22. What relationship do you see between your life's work and the values you profess as a Christian?

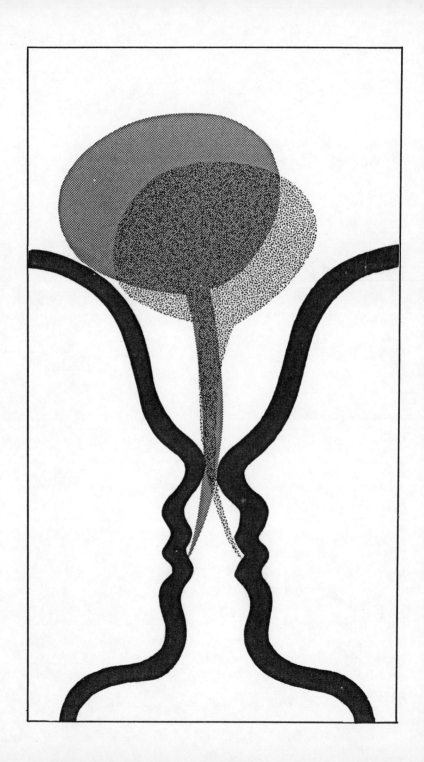

Chapter Twenty-Four

TRUE WORDS AND GOOD WORDS

HUMAN NATURE AND HUMAN SPEECH
Classically, human beings were distinguished from the rest of animal life mainly by their rationality. More recently, interpersonal or intersubjective relations have been much emphasized as signalizing the human. From either point of view, there is one kind of overt behavior in which humanness is vividly manifested and ordinarily perceived. That is verbal behavior, in the broadest sense of that phrase. For it is especially through words that human rationality is expressed, and it is especially through words that interpersonal relations are fashioned. It is not surprising, therefore, that the realm of morality penetrates very deeply into the realm of speech.

We have already remarked, in connection with the biblical prohibition of false witness, how essential to even a minimally satisfactory social existence is the belief that, in general, people tell the truth and, at least to that extent, can be trusted. And we have noted in the same connection how in certain circumstances, such as those of judicial testimony, the assurance of truthfulness becomes a vital public concern. To approach in this way the ethics of telling the truth can be regarded as a kind of natural law approach. That is, given the social nature of human beings which underlies so many of their efforts and tendencies, behavior that threatens the very coherence of society is unnatural, unreasonable, and therefore wrong. That lying is, on the whole, disruptive of human society, there can be no serious doubt.

This kind of natural law approach is quite different from another kind, which has often been used in Catholic tradition. Frequently one finds the wrongness of lying inferred from the nature not of human beings, but of speech itself. Thus it is argued that speech is by its very nature a sign of what is in the speaker's mind. If, therefore, speech is used to signify something different from what is in the speaker's mind, in the sense that it is different from what the speaker thinks to be true, such behavior is contrary to the nature of speech and therefore wrong. It is not altogether easy to see, however, how one is supposed to determine the nature of speech in itself. For speech does not exist in itself. It exists as a function of human beings, who do exist in themselves. The only way one can discover the nature of anything is by observing its actions as manifesting its basic tendencies. But speech does not have any actions; it is an action, and an action of human beings, which may have something to tell us about their nature.

It is of considerable importance not to confuse these two quite different natural law approaches, and to consider that one may have a great deal more plausibility than the other. One approach argues on the basis of human nature, understanding by that a distinctive inherent purposefulness, inferred from regularly recurring patterns of human behavior. The other approach refers not directly to human nature, but to the nature of certain functions, aspects, or parts of human beings. The mixing of these two kinds of arguments in Catholic tradition has often impeded understanding, and each should be evaluated on its own merits. To draw ethical implications from fairly definite and generally shared ideas of human nature is one thing. To do the same with set ideas about the nature of some human component is quite a different thing. Thus, criticizing certain uses of speech as contrary to human nature is a different way of thinking from criticizing them as contrary to the nature of speech itself. The difference may be brought out by considering two habits, both of them obviously bad, which can be developed in the use of speech.

Of some people it is remarked that they never seem to have anything good to say. These are, in various degrees, chronic complainers, or denouncers, or lamenters. Their social impact is plain enough, and plainly it is bad. Part of the bad effect is their own relative social isolation from that great majority of human beings who find a concentration of such talk tiresome and reprehensible, and who therefore limit their contact with those who compulsively indulge in it. Another social effect is demoralization of those who pay much attention to such talk, which has a souring and depressing effect that weakens social solidarity by depriving social life of much of the pleasure that normally reinforces it. It is, of course, quite possible for such people to be perfectly sincere, in the sense that the dreary things they say accurately reflect the dreary things they think. Consequently, one could not call their speech unnatural on the ground that the nature of speech is to signify what is in the speaker's mind. And yet, what they habitually choose to say is so contrary to basic human sociability that one might fairly call it unnatural on the ground that it frustrates in an important respect part of what human life seems to be all about.

The habitual liar may evidently be accused of unnatural behavior in the same sense as the habitual griper. Both habits are inimical to general human purposes as implied by ordinary human behavior. If, in this sense, human nature is evidently social, then habits of speech whose effects are intensely anti-social may be called unnatural. But the standard here is human nature, not the nature of something in or of human beings, such as the faculty of speech.

VARIETY IN VOCAL MORALITY

One unfortunate consequence of concentrating on the nature of speech instead of on human nature in assessing the morality of verbal behavior is that it can lead dangerously close to sophistry. This can be seen in a long history of forced and devious ways adopted to justify cases in which it is perfectly obvious that saying what one thinks would be a bad thing to do, and saying what one does not think would be a good thing to do. Everyone can think of plenty of examples of ethically commendable deception, of which only the most notorious is that of responding to a murderous assailant who inquires which way his intended victim went. Redefining the lie to exclude such cases is an unhelpful and potentially endless process. Even more unhelpful is the absurdity of recommending mental reservations or tricky turns of phrase as ways to secure the advantages of a lie without literally stating the opposite of what one thinks. Words contrived and intended to deceive, even though literally they are in some sense truthful, may win prizes for ingenuity, but one can hardly claim them for morality.

But perhaps the most serious consequence of concentrating on the nature of speech as a guide to the ethics of speech is that it tends, as usually understood, to narrow our attention to simple lying, and distract it from other ways in which speech can be ethically good or bad. For many of these ways depend on other factors than the mere correspondence of speech to what is in the speaker's mind.

Much of this broader field of verbal or vocal morality comes into view if we conceive speech in a somewhat different and more accurate way than simply as a sign of what is in the speaker's mind. And indeed it might be noted that even a blatant lie does not really fail to signify what is in the speaker's mind. For one does have to think up a lie before one can tell it. An untruth must be conceived, though not of course believed by a speaker, before it can be uttered. In this broader sense, speech is a sign of what is in the speaker's mind no matter what kind of speech it happens to be, and no matter how bad it happens to be.

One gets nearer to a useful ethical standard if one goes a step farther and inquires why what is in a speaker's mind gets outwardly signified in speech. And, apart from peripheral matters of talking to oneself, the reason is clearly because the speaker wants to get something into someone else's mind. Ordinarily, speech is a message to someone; speaking is communication with someone. It is social behavior, and its variations serve a vast range of social purposes and produce a vast range of social effects. To a great extent, it is those purposes and effects that determine the morality of speech.

The moral goodness of speech largely depends on those two virtues which largely account for moral goodness in all social conduct, namely justice and love. Speech ought to be used, as everything ought to be used socially, in ways that do not harm others but benefit them, and benefit them justly. But of course speech constantly is being used harmfully and unjustly. The harm and injustice done by lies is notorious, especially because virtually all lies have a potentially erosive effect on the quality of trust without which social life becomes unendurable. This destruction of trust is most extreme when lies deal with matters of public importance and when liars occupy positions of public trust. But commonplace and private lies may do great damage to the trust of individuals subjected to them, and if they are frequent or come from sources that are especially relied upon, their effect can be devastating.

But obviously it is not only lying speech that can be unjust and unkind. The fact that a statement is true does not make it any less wicked if it violates a secret, damages a reputation, delivers an insult, or bestows an unfair advantage. Nor is truth alone a sufficient justification for using speech in shocking, disgusting, depressing, aggravating, or even needlessly boring ways. In dealing with others verbally, as in dealing with them by other means, the standard remains that of loving one's neighbor as oneself while accepting all as one's neighbors. And that means speaking to them as one would wish to be spoken to, in a way that communicates something of value in a manner that respects human dignity and individual circumstances.

Nor is it only in our statements, whether true of false, that human communication must reckon with justice and love. We are responsible for many of our silences. There are things that should be said, as well as things that should not. The withholding of needed information can be bitterly unkind. The concealment of judgments, either in praise of what is right or in blame of what is wrong, can be profoundly unjust. Examples of wicked silence are innumerable. One rather specialized example that has become increasingly important in modern times has to do with the matter of informed consent. Ours is an age when more people than ever before are passively subjected to the complex technical procedures of various kinds of experts, engaged in operations as diverse as transplanting organs, dispensing pharmaceuticals, designing curricula, drafting contracts, and overhauling engines. No person knows much about many of these things, and most persons know little about any of them. But all persons have a right to know, insofar as they are capable of knowing, what is being done to them, and to determine within what limits they wish to entrust themselves, or their dependents, or their property, to others. Professional and expert activities that do not make reasonable efforts to honor that right are acts, not of service, but of violence. And we have reached a point in modern society where such violence is perpetrated not only frequently, but self-righteously and as a matter of course.

NEW MEDIA AND OLD ETHICS

The references in this chapter to speech must, of course, be understood in a very broad sense if they are to do justice to the realities of human development. The basic idea of speech as a delivering of messages to others is obviously applicable to a great deal more than simply oral expression. In addition to spoken messages humankind has developed long before the dawn of history many other ways of communicating, and during the course of history this development has gone on continually. Basically the same ethical approach is applicable to all of them, no matter how complex and innovative. The standards of love and justice remain normative.

These basic standards are likewise applicable to certain special variations of the communication process which, because of their importance and potential complexity, it may be useful to mention more specifically. One of these has to do with messages that are issued more or less indiscriminately, messages that are, so to speak, strewn about, to be received by whomever they happen to reach. This strewing about is the original meaning of what later became a more technical term, broadcasting. In a general sense, however, broadcasting is by no means limited to electronic devices or to the civilizations that make use of such devices. Pamphleteering and journalism represent older ways of delivering messages fairly indiscriminately (although the requisite literacy can be a very important discriminant). Notices and posters in public places represent a still older technique. And even the most primitive societies have always contrived their own ways of broadcasting, some of them remarkably ingenious.

The ethics of communication does take on special complexity in the case of all types of broadcasting. The effects of a broadcast message are to a great extent beyond prediction and control, because the recipients of the message and the circumstances in which they receive it can be foreseen only vaguely and uncertainly. Some broadcast messages do a great deal of good and some do a great deal of harm. There are many that harm only a very few people, but harm them terribly, while the good they do, although widespread, is trivial by comparison. A report or photograph that millions of people find mildly interesting, a few people may find bitterly humiliating. A type of message that has little effect in a single instance may have drastic effects when it continues to reappear in a thousand variations, as in political propaganda and commercial advertising. A bit of news that is merely informative in tranquil circumstances may be intensely provocative when public temper runs high. There is no simple formula for the social regulation of broadcasting. The extremes both of free expression and of censorship have such pernicious consequences that neither is tolerable in a wholesome society. But apart from institutional policies in this regard, it remains true that the personal regulation of broadcasting remains a matter of personal ethical responsibility regardless of one's social role.

A much more dubious ethical status must be assigned to what for lack of a better label may be called clandestine communication. By this is meant both the surreptitious reception of messages by those to whom they are not addressed, and the surreptitious delivery, of messages to those who do not welcome and may not even perceive them as messages. The former category ranges from commonplace snooping to elaborate espionage. The latter one ranges from snide insinuation to systematic brainwashing. Both are, in all their forms, more or less violent behavior, assailing elementary rights of privacy. As with certain other violent acts, extraordinary circumstances, such as those requiring self-defense, may justify them. As with other rights of privacy, extraordinary circumstances may entail a privilege of invading them. But under ordinary circumstances, ethical presumptions remain heavily in their disfavor. And the society which tolerates them without demanding and enforcing stringent conditions for their justification, is conspiring in its own deterioration.

STUDY QUESTIONS

1. In what respects is verbal behavior thought of as distinctively human?

2. How can the social effects of lying be related to a natural law obligation of truthfulness?

3. What quite different kind of natural law approach has often been adopted in Catholic tradition?

4. What objection can be raised to this latter kind of natural law approach?

5. In what sense can speech be considered unnatural regardless of whether or not it is untruthful?

6. Why is it unreasonable to regard all deceptive speech as immoral?

7. On what does the moral goodness of speech chiefly depend?

8. How can silence, no less than speech, deserve moral criticism?

9. What circumstances prevalent in modern life give rise to moral issues concerning informed consent?

10. What in general is meant by broadcasting, and why does it entail special moral problems?

11. What types of behavior can be classified as examples of clandestine communication?

12. What moral issues are raised by the main types of clandestine communication?

13. In what ways can speech be viewed as violent? What are the characteristics of speech that is just and loving?

Chapter Twenty-Five

CARING FOR HUMAN LIFE

AGAINST KILLING PEOPLE

In an earlier discussion of the biblical prohibition of killing, it was observed that this is a prohibition whose original understanding was more influenced by concern for public order than for individual life. For in ancient times in the Near East, more impressive even than particular cases of homicide were the all too frequent experiences of wholesale slaughter unleashed to avenge homicide. The very fact that revenge took so drastic a form no doubt testifies to the intensity of moral indignation caused by homicide. Nevertheless, such indignation was typically reserved for the killing of a member of one's own group, and not evoked by killing in general. With the establishment of more stable and consolidated societies, with better peace-keeping institutions, the moral condemnation of homicide seems to have been gradually broadened towards including all killing of the innocent, and thus towards supposing a basic human right not to be deprived of life. And with this negative right, not to be killed, there was increasingly associated a positive right to receive at least emergency assistance when one's life was imperilled, from anyone who could render such aid without grave personal risk. Thus Christianity inherited and greatly intensified a basic moral conviction of the inviolability of human life and of a general duty to support its preservation. Moreover, this duty was understood to entail more even than aiding human beings in their efforts to live, for it was opposed also to suicide. Thus Christian tradition asserts considerably more than a bare negative right to live, entailing a duty not to kill. It asserts more also than a positive right to live, entailing a duty to assist life. For it equivalently asserts a duty to live, in the sense of prohibiting the deliberate taking of one's own life.

The prohibition of suicide is probably the feature of this area of Christian ethics that most clearly suggests that here we are not dealing exclusively with social or interpersonal ethics. The norm of loving one's neighbor as one loves oneself and the norm of giving everyone his or her due are not fully adequate to the traditional Christian ethics of caring for human life. For this is in part a strictly religious ethics, constituting an immediate response to belief concerning divine reality. The relevant point of view is foreshadowed in a recurrent motif of biblical thought, where life is regarded as a divine gift that remains very intimately associated with its divine giver. Life is therefore in a special sense holy, and not to be profaned. From the point of view of religious ethics, God's gift of life must be seen as the foundation of everything else God gives to and asks of his human creatures. It is the essential condition of everything God intends for human beings, including, of course, the death God intends for them. Accordingly, self-destruction implies a rejection of God's will that is immensely more fundamental than any single act or limited pattern of disobedience; it is rejection of the very possibility of freely serving God; it is the most unqualified repudiation of a covenant relationship with a God who rules and saves.

None of this, of course, denies what seems fairly obvious, that suicide is often the result not of moral but of psychological deterioration, or that states of mind occur that so gravely impair understanding and freedom that under their influence suicide is scarcely if at all a morally significant human act. The conditions of liberty and knowledge that are requisite for moral responsibility in any behavior pertain equally to suicide.

Neither does any of this deny that risking one's life can be morally blameless and even highly commendable. The Christian ethics pertaining to suicide in no way imply that it is either obligatory or admirable to strive at all costs to stay alive as long as one can. Such a point of view could scarcely claim the sponsorship of one who died as Jesus Christ died, nor could it thrive within a Church whose principal heroes are its martyrs. Caring for life does not mean clinging to life. It means living life, and living it as well as one can, even when life's circumstances are such that the best way to live happens also to be the surest way to die. From a Christian moral point of view, to sacrifice one's life and to discard one's life are about as opposite as any two kinds of behavior can be.

The idea that living life well, rather than clutching life tenaciously, is a Christian's proper standard, has applicability outside the realm of heroism and altruism. Under conditions created by modern medical technology, there occurs more and more frequently a realistic option of living one kind of life for a shorter time, or living for a longer time an extremely different kind of life. There is no simple rule for such choices, which may be influenced by a variety of circumstances beyond anyone's capacity to predict. But the values that should dominate such choices are the same values that should dominate all choices, and there is no Christian value that implies that the best way to live is always, or even usually, the surest way to live longest.

Needless to say, decisions about how one is going to live, especially when they greatly affect how long one is likely to live, are decisions that individual persons are to make for themselves insofar as they are competent to do so. Yet there are, of course, occasions when such decisions have to be made and yet cannot be made by those whom they chiefly affect. Such is the case with young children, with the mentally disabled, or the unconscious. In such cases the decisions have to be made by someone else who legitimately holds the responsibility of a custodian. And they are to be made in what seem, on the most careful consideration, to be the best interests of the other. Since many such cases are of a clinical nature, it may be well to add that the making of such decisions does not properly belong to the professional capacity of a physician, whose definite role it is to do all that is medically indicated for the preservation and, if possible, the improvement of bodily life. The fact that a patient might justifiably refuse medically indicated treatment in no way implies that a physician might justifiably withhold such treatment. A professional's responsibility is to do, with the client's consent, what that profession exists to do, in the way that profession has best learned to do it, and for doctors, that means, exclusively, sound treatment in the interest of life and health.

BODILY INTEGRITY

Closely related in ethical tradition to the prohibition of killing is the prohibition of inflicting bodily injury. Underlying both is a conviction of the value of bodily life and therefore of the disvalue of either extinguishing or diminishing it. As with killing, so also with bodily injury, traditional ethical restrictions concern both what one does to others and what one does to oneself.

In this matter also, it is important to bear in mind that just as the prohibition of killing is not equivalent to an obligation of living as long as possible, neither is the prohibition of bodily injury equivalent to an obligation of staying as healthy as possible. If it can be good for certain reasons to risk one's life, it can also be good to risk one's health. If it can be praiseworthy for certain reasons to live in a way that abbreviates one's life, it can also be good to live in a way that diminishes one's health. In both regards, the ethical norm is not to live as long or as heartily as one can, but to live as morally good a life as one can.

Much attention has been given in the past to formulating ethical norms for cases of deliberate bodily mutilation. Apart from the question of punitive mutilation inflicted on criminals, most of this discussion has dealt with the justifiability of mutilating one's own body, or consenting to its mutilation. For such cases, the dominant principle is one that is in fairly evident agreement with common sense and common practice. Called the principle of totality, its basic assumption is that the body's living parts are naturally subordinated to its living totality. From this it is inferred that if some part should be in such a state that the body as a whole would be better off organically without it, the part might be sacrificed to the totality. This is, of course, what is taken for granted in having medical recourse to surgery. And in this context there is no reason to distinguish between surgery in the ordinary sense and other kinds of treatment, such as those employing chemical or radiological means, that entail damage to cells and tissues. Matters do become somewhat more complicated in cases where surgery is recommended not for what is normally meant by bodily health, but for the improvement of seemingly pathological behavior, as in various types of psychosurgery. Although a modification of the principle of totality is applicable in such cases, its application calls for great discretion. For it is all too easy in practice to interpret improved behavior as behavior that is better, not from the patient's point of view, but from that of others who have to deal with the patient.

What the principle of totality does not adequately cope with is the case of one who submits to the permanent damaging of his or her own body without intending or expecting thereby to improve the condition of the body as a whole. Such cases, formerly rather extraordinary, have become increasingly important with expanding possibilities for transplanting living organs or tissues from one living person to another. There are instances in which this appears to be the only way of giving effective medical treatment. Obviously, the living donor of a healthy organ is not, in most cases, organically benefiting by the loss. But there is no reason why the principle of totality should not be replaced in such cases by other ethical standards. If it should happen that the only way a blind person could be enabled to see was by transplantation of an eye from a living donor, such a donation could not be justified by the principle of totality. But in certain circumstances it might well be justified by unselfish benevolence, supposing, of course, that the beneficial effect could not be achieved by less drastic means.

There is a misapplication of the principle of totality which has appeared often enough, and with sufficiently grave consequences, to require specific mention. It is based on the analogy, which has already been remarked in another connection, between the individual living human body, composed of organically interconnected parts, and a human society, composed of persons having interdependent functions. On the basis of this analogy it has been periodically suggested that the principle of totality is applicable on a social scale. That is, just as part of a person's body may be sacrificed for the whole body, so too, it is suggested, the good of a whole society may justify the sacrifice of some of its component individuals. Sometimes in Catholic tradition this position has been invoked to justify punishing by death an individual who seriously endangers society as a whole. Nevertheless, that tradition has increasingly recognized that this kind of argumentation is invalid and unsafe. The individual is not subordinate to society in the way that an organ is subordinated to an organism. The social whole exists for its members, and not the other way around. To suppose that human persons can be disposed of as mere parts of a social totality supposedly of greater value than persons implies a totalitarianism that is deeply incompatible with Catholic ethical tradition.

KILLING THE UNBORN

Moral denunciation of abortion is about as early and as continuous a specific ethical condemnation as can be found in the records of Christian tradition. Throughout most of the history of that tradition it was not even treated as a subject requiring lengthy discussion. It was perceived as an especially plain case of something that was plainly wrong, the killing of innocent human beings. It was also perceived as an especially hideous kind of homicide on account of the unborn child's total dependence on its mother, and the highly sensitive response of normal mothers to their unique responsibility and to their dignity as the recipient of the holiest of all natural blessings. The characteristically tender protectiveness of a pregnant woman towards her unborn child is so proverbial that literature abounds in passages using it to exemplify the most unquestionably genuine and spontaneous natural human love. Indeed, among life's ordinary natural occasions there is perhaps none that bears a closer resemblance to the kind of love Christians attribute to God himself and to the human lives most influenced by his Spirit.

Naturally, moral condemnation of abortion generally took it for granted that what a pregnant woman bears within her body is a human being, that she is, as common language expressed it, "with child." There did take place at various times, in places influenced by Aristotelean psychology, academic speculation about when in the course of fetal development a spiritual soul was introduced. Answers to such questions had, from the nature of the case, to be highly conjectural, nor was it ever supposed that such conjectures were sufficiently reliable to form the basis of ethical decision.

With the development of an increasingly thorough science of human embryology, every major advance in knowledge has served to emphasize the extraordinary continuity of fetal development, and offered no support whatever to the supposition that at some point after conception and before birth the fetus suddenly becomes a radically different kind of being. And the concomitant development of genetic science has steadily accumulated evidence of the continuity of basic unique determinants of life from the moment of fertilization to the moment of death. There has never been less reason than there is in our present state of knowledge for doubting that a single individual human life is coextensive with the whole course of fetal and post-natal development. If abortion is to be defended at present, it is hardly persuasive to base the defense on doubts that are less plausible now than they have been at any point in human history. It defies the limits of credulity to suppose that any informed person wants, gets, or performs an abortion on the basis of an objective, reasoned conviction that a fetus of some specified age is not a human being. That defenders of abortion should wish to doubt that the fetus is a human being is understandable in the same sense as it is understandable why slaveholders wished to doubt that blacks were human beings in the same sense as their masters. That such rationalizations are natural and intelligible is not to say that they are rational or intelligent.

Where such wishful thinking manages to prevail, it is not the thinking but the wish that has to be coped with. If abortions were not intensely desired, such naive rationalizations could scarcely exist. But as long as the desire is strong and frequent they are sure to exist, and to reinforce one another to the point of constituting a social myth in support of a social practice whose traditional moral repulsiveness needs to be offset if it is to endure.

A great many factors have undoubtedly contributed to intensified demand for abortion and for social approval of it. Among them is the sobering fact of tremendous population growth, with the present inconveniences that entails and the much graver ones it foreshadows. In addition, conditions of extreme economic inequality make the prospect of parenthood for many people extremely intimidating, with little realistic hope of avoiding even more painful circumstances for themselves and for those who depend upon them. Moreover, modern medical techniques have increased the possibility of anticipating with at least very high probability that certain pregnancies can issue in the birth only of tragically handicapped offspring.

Real and serious as these objective considerations are, however, they can account for a greatly increased demand for abortion only if they are combined with subjective and moral factors. For it is obvious enough that a goal of limiting the number of births, either in general or in particular circumstances, is achievable without recourse to abortion. Babies do not get born (or aborted) if they are not conceived. And even the most generous allowance for both sexual ignorance and sexual violence can account for only a tiny proportion of those pregnancies that are sufficiently regretted to raise the prospect of abortion. One does not have to be cynical or insensitive to conclude that in the vast majority of cases, pregnancies that are not wanted, but are not precluded by either abstinence or contraception, are the result of what is technically and meaningfully described as lust. And however unfashionable may be the classical and Christian view that lust clouds the mind, it is a view hard to repudiate when millions of women have recourse to the malice, peril, and indignity of abortion because of their neglect of even readily available contraception. Only in a culture that has systematically persuaded itself that lust is both lovely and irresistible could such a situation be unsurprising. Abortion, as a widespread and almost casual practice in a modern civilized society, is a climactic triumph of lust, and a climactic defeat of chastity and the familial virtues it exists to serve.

The traditional moral condemnation of abortion is essentially a particular application of the broader condemnation of killing innocent human beings. It does not therefore entail a categorical prohibition of ever doing anything that is likely or even certain to result in the death of a fetus. Accordingly, the principle of double effect, discussed in an earlier chapter, has been commonly applied to abortion as to other cases in which killing is an incidental consequence of a morally good action that seems to be the only feasible way of accomplishing a proportionately good purpose. Thus, in cases where surgery necessary to preserve the life or health of a mother is not directly abortive but does have abortive consequences, such medical intervention has been commonly regarded as justifiable. It might be additionally argued that even direct abortion can be justified in order to save a mother's life if otherwise neither mother nor fetus had any prospect of survival. Highly controversial at present is the further question of whether or not fetal life could be justifiably sacrificed to safeguard any other value than the mother's actual life, as, for example, when a continued pregnancy promises to be gravely damaging to physical or mental health. Questions that arise in this connection have many significant similarities to questions concerning killing in self-defense, which has often been approved for the protection not only of life, but also of health and even of property. One should not, however, rule out the possibility that a comparison of these cases indicates not that abortion is too strictly forbidden, but that killing in self-defense is too easily permitted.

PREVENTING HUMAN LIFE

Referring to human life-prevention strikes an unpleasantly chilling note among all but the most coldblooded hearers. Presumably the reason is because the phrase life-prevention suggests such analogous phrases as fire-prevention, flood-prevention, accident-prevention, and disease-prevention. And since in all these familiar phrases the object of prevention is something evidently bad, the phrase life-prevention may seem to connote an assessment of human life itself as bad. And one might understandably react by declaring a personal conviction that human life is good. Such a reaction is exemplified by the recent popularity of the phrase pro-life, mainly stimulated by the increasingly widespread approval of abortion in our society. Nevertheless, emotional reaction to phrases and emotional construction of phrases is seldom helpful to ethical discourse. Pro-life does not express an idea definite enough to assist ethical thinking. All such a phrase could signify is a general opposition to those who might be oppositely labeled. And one would look far to find anyone willing or seriously eligible to be generally described as anti-life. The description of someone merely as being pro-life simply is not useful information for practical purposes.

The most that pro-life could possibly mean (once the topic is restricted to human life—as it would not be in certain non-Christian religions), is something hardly anyone in our society is likely to mean by it. That is, that every human life ought to be preserved, at all costs, by all possible means, and that every potential human life ought at all costs to be actualized. Our previous discussion has already indicated that Christian tradition has always recognized, in very explicit and affirmative ways, that there can be morally excellent reasons for not employing certain means, even means quite innocent in themselves, for preserving certain human lives, including one's own, in certain circumstances. And it is even more obvious that Christian tradition has consistently opposed the idea that there is anything desirable about indiscriminately multiplying human lives.

Indeed, birth-control is an essential ingredient of the traditional Christian understanding of marriage itself. The reason most often given for prohibiting sexual intercourse outside of marriage was precisely to prevent human beings from being born in circumstances unlikely to provide a wholesome environment for new lives. As already noted, Catholic tradition has habitually striven to direct sexual activity towards family responsibility. And of course a major part of the underlying assumption is that a family provides, generally speaking, a uniquely good setting in which to be born and raised. It is important to remember this practical motivation of traditional opposition to producing children if one is not married. For the kind of thinking involved makes it absurd to imagine that once one is married, children might be produced at whim, without prudent reflection. For if the concrete circumstances of a particular family were ill-suited to provide a wholesome environment, either for any children or for more children, to go on having children anyway would be to ignore the very purpose of restricting reproduction to marriage. What Christian sexual ethics traditionally supposed is that typically, and under ordinary circumstances, marriage provides a good environment for children. It does not suppose any miraculous guarantee that every marriage will do so automatically and for any number of children.

Christian tradition has also always acknowledged the importance of sexual gratification, and recognized the satisfaction of human sexual drives as among the purposes and advantages of marrying. Unfortunately, the same tradition was early infected by some grotesquely negative evaluations of sexual pleasure and by a contrastingly fanatical ideal of virtually disembodied spiritual rationality. Although Christian tradition was neither the originator nor the sole victim of such ideas, it was deeply influenced by them. One example of this influence was a recurrent suggestion that sexual gratification, though acknowledged to be a purpose, benefit, and preservative of marriage, required nevertheless to be excused, even within marriage, on the basis of procreative intentions. Among consequences of this delusion has been a widespread tendency to suppose that renouncing sexual gratification was, as it were, the price one had to pay for birth-control.

Still another difficulty about practicing birth-control without renouncing sexual gratification arises from a quite different idea. It is very similar to the idea discussed at the beginning of the previous chapter, of human speech as by its very nature a sign of what is in the speaker's mind, so that speech which does not reveal the speaker's mind is wrong because it is unnatural. Similarly, it has been argued, sexual intercourse is by its very nature procreative, so that to engage in it while directly interfering with its procreative potentiality is wrong because it is unnatural. Here again, it is misleading to pass from generalizations about human nature to generalizing about the nature of functions human beings exercise. Like human speech, human sexual intercourse does not have a nature of its own with moral implications of its own, independently of the human beings who express basic tendencies by the actions they perform. Ethical rightness and wrongness may be assessed partly on the basis of purposes attributable to human beings, but not to bodily organs and organic functions.

This line of thought is in evident harmony with an increasing tendency to base moral judgments concerning contraception rather on its human motives than on its technical means. From this point of view it is particularly difficult to see why the deliberate restriction of sexual intercourse to times of infertility should be morally a greatly different situation from the deliberate use of artificial contraceptive devices, if both procedures are adopted for the identical purpose of having sexual intercourse while avoiding procreation. Especially since a contrary view has been officially expressed in modern papal teaching, it is significant that this issue remains a notoriously controversial one among Catholics.

STUDY QUESTIONS

1. How does the original understanding of the biblical prohibition of killing differ from affirming a right to life?

2. What is implied practically in a positive, as distinct from a negative, right to life?

3. How does the Christian prohibition of suicide involve more than social or interpersonal ethics?

4. Why is suicide, although forbidden, often assumed to be morally blameless?

5. To what extent does the prohibition of suicide prohibit risking or shortening one's life?

6. Why does modern medicine create new dilemmas concerning the preservation of life?

7. What has to be done for patients who cannot make personal decisions affecting the preservation of their lives?

8. Why is it improper for physicians in their professional capacity to decide against the use of measures to preserve life?

9. What general obligations affect the preservation of bodily integrity and health?

10. Why do procedures like psychosurgery call for more than usual moral discretion?

11. What is meant by the principle of totality as applied in medical ethics?

12. Why is the principle of totality usually inapplicable to living donors of healthy organs for transplantation?

13. Can any other ethical principle be used to justify such donation of living organs?

14. How long and how consistent is the Christian moral tradition of condemning abortion?

15. To what extent was the tradition affected by doubts about when a fetus acquires a spiritual soul?

16. To what extent has advanced embryological knowledge cast new doubt on the humanity of fetal life?

17. What factors have in modern times contributed to increased demand for abortion?

18. Why is widespread recourse to abortion hard to reconcile with responsible moral attitudes?

19. Does moral opposition to abortion imply that fetal lives are to be preserved at all costs?

20. In what respect can abortion and killing in self-defense be justified on similar grounds?

21. Why is pro-life an unhelpful designation for an ethical position?

22. In what sense has Catholic tradition been favorable to birth control?

23. What notions of sex have tended to distort Catholic perspectives on birth control?

24. What kind of natural law argument emphasizes a moral difference between periodic continence and artificial contraception?

25. How do you define the term "pro-life"? In what senses do you consider yourself pro-life?

Chapter Twenty-Six

ETHICS OF FAITH

BELIEF IN REVELATION

Christianity has always been identified as a religion that considers itself to be based on divine revelation. The derivation of the word revelation, which suggests an unveiling, implies its meaning as the making perceptible of what would not otherwise be perceived. As Christian theology conceives it, revelation is an unveiling by God, and likewise an unveiling of God. What God reveals is always, in the last analysis, God; what God makes perceptible is his own reality. In the Old Testament, this self-revelation by God is found above all in historical events of such a kind that, in experiencing or recalling them, human beings were led to perceive them as the doings of God, and as doings which made possible a deeper understanding of what God is like and of what he intended for them. Naturally, such events can be experienced and recalled without any such understanding. They can be thought of as meaningless, or as having only such meaning as can be established on a strictly naturalistic basis. The difference between an apprehension of events that entails some knowledge of God and one that does not is a basic aspect of what in Catholic tradition is referred to as faith. Such familiar metaphors as the eyes of faith convey the idea that faith involves a special kind of perception which discovers a special kind of meaning in certain experiences, a meaning whose significance entails awareness and partial understanding of God. The experiences that occasion such perception are immensely various. Some are highly intellectual and others extremely emotional, some are concentratedly vivid and others are subtly cumulative, some are intensely social and others profoundly solitary, some are delightful and others terrifying, some are humanly arranged and others seem completely fortuitous.

It is beyond the scope of this book to survey the variety of religious experience out of which arise those personal apprehensions of God and understandings of God that are the groundwork of faith. Religious experience is not faith. Faith is a response to religious experience that embraces as valid the awareness and understanding of God that the experience engenders. As Catholic tradition conceives it, faith involves both divine and human action. It is God who provides what is religiously experienced and who enables human beings to experience it religiously. It is God who makes it possible to find meaning in religious experience and to assent to that meaning as true. But the assent itself is an exercise of human freedom. It is an assent that can be initially withheld or subsequently withdrawn or practically ignored.

Christian faith is a kind of religious faith, just as Christian revelation is a kind of divine revelation. It exists wherever awareness and understanding of God is founded on the religious experience of Jesus Christ. As Christian records amply attest, there is great variety in the religious experience of Jesus Christ. But the essential act of specifically Christian faith is an assent to the discovery in Jesus Christ of divine meaning. Such discovery may be initially more or less extensive and more or less clear. And this faith may be said to grow as assent keeps pace with increasing understanding.

For the ordinary Christian believers, the experience of

Jesus Christ is, or at least initially appears to be, a kind of second-hand experience. It is the experience of a Jesus Christ about whom one is told by others. It is the experience of a Jesus Christ who is described or explained by others, or suggested by the behavior of others. Hence Christianity is a religion based not only upon revelation, but upon revelation transmitted by human means, revelation conveyed by tradition. And here again, with respect to Christian tradition, variety defies summation. The ways in which human beings are led to the threshold of Christian faith by what other human beings say, or do, or are, are unimaginably diverse. And of course they include not only direct encounters with Christians who give some expression to their faith, but also indirect encounters, which may be no less intense, through various media. Of the latter, the written Bible is the outstanding and normative example, but by no means the only one.

What the Christian by faith assents to in virtue of his or her experience of Jesus Christ is called the Gospel—not one of the documents bearing that word as a title, but what such documents exist to convey. That is the good news (which is what the word gospel literally signifies) that in Jesus Christ God is revealed as invincibly loving, and as rescuing human beings from every kind of evil that they do or suffer, in order to lead them into perfect union with a goodness that is absolute and eternal. To be drawn towards Christianity is to suspect that this is true. To begin to be a Christian is to believe this is the most important of all truths. And to live as a Christian is to make the supreme importance of this truth the ultimate standard of human freedom.

From the first, Christianity has recognized with respect to faith a kind of duty that often seems incomprehensible to those who are little acquainted with faith or who have thought little about it. That is the duty of preserving one's faith. Christians have always considered that there are dangers to faith, different for different individuals, in the sense that certain lines of thought and certain lines of conduct make it much harder to believe, and much easier to disbelieve or disregard what faith assents to. Serious Christians have always urged that irresponsible exposure to such danger be kept to a minimum. To many people, this sort of religious prudence seems rather a vice than a virtue. For it is generally thought that for mature human beings deliberately to avoid challenges to their beliefs is to offend against their very rationality. Openness of mind is an admired characteristic, and to credit someone with a closed mind is seldom a statement of praise. Thus a Christian's interest in preserving faith may very easily appear, and may sometimes be a sub-rational kind of behavior, clinging to some naive credulousness by closing one's eyes to all conflicting evidence. Since such behavior is typical of highly prejudiced people, Christian efforts to preserve faith are easily interpreted as merely the unfortunate symptoms of a kind of bigotry that seems to take root easily in religious soil.

In order to deal correctly with this issue, it must be recognized that Catholic tradition has never endorsed any kind of faith that plainly contradicts what reason plainly establishes. It must also be recognized that according to that tradition, the human act of faith expresses a genuine conviction of truth, and not a mere fondness for certain notions however implausible. The Christian believer is not one who merely finds the Gospel attractive, but one who judges it to be true. That judgment of truth is based on evidence, which may be of a very personal, very extraordinary, or very complicated kind, and therefore very difficult to communicate to others with logical neatness. But as evidence, nevertheless, it is experienced. Indeed, the annals of Christian conversion are replete with examples of persons who found that what such evidence led them to believe was by no means the sort of thing that would have satisfied their wishful thinking.

It is, of course, perfectly true that Catholic tradition, while affirming the reasonableness of faith, has never supposed that faith was or could be a conclusion based simply upon reason, or that an airtight argument could be constructed from which only stupidity or dishonesty could fail to infer the truth of the Gospel. The special action of God is acknowledged to influence both the evidence of religious experience and the mind's capacity to affirm its truth. And the religious experience itself, as already observed, has great individual diversity and complexity.

Nevertheless, Christian believers are not unreasonably impatient with a great many of those who appear to disdain their faith in the name of reason. Often such disdain is expressed more or less as a challenge to prove that which is believed, and very often the sort of proof that is looked for is of the sort most people understand as scientific proof. Indeed, it would be absurd to suggest that one can demonstrate that the volume of a gas increases with its temperature or that the diameters of a circle intersect at its center. But the ironic thing about this sort of argument is that the standards of evidence required for Christian belief are not the standards required for life's ordinary and highly-esteemed beliefs. A chemist does not withhold belief that his dinner is non-toxic until he has tested it in the laboratory. The investigator does not consider his wife's fidelity an open question until she has been placed under round-the-clock surveillance. The traveler does not wonder where his airplane is going until he has mastered the techniques and scrutinized the data of his navigator. In these and a thousand more important matters, daily life proceeds by a faith the rejection of which is considered nothing short of insanity. Such faith is founded on evidence. But the evidence on which it is founded would be very difficult to summarize, and impossible to express in a terse, indubitable argument. The faith of a Christian is likewise founded on evidence, which the Christian, in the light of his or her experience, can hardly be expected to repudiate merely because someone else who has not had that experience does not share that belief. The fact that it is not tidy, simple, flagrantly public evidence merely puts it into the same class with most of the evidence on the strength of which normal people lead normal lives.

Moreover, efforts by Christians to preserve their faith are not greatly different in principle from more ordinary efforts to preserve more secular faiths. One who ignores defamatory statements about a trusted friend is not a paragon of prejudice. And one who clings to scepticism despite a convergence of plausible assurances is not an exemplar of reasonableness. The jealous lover, the cagey friend, the wary colleague, the tester of every untried step and doubter of every reported fact are among the saddest and maddest of human specimens. And Christians, once persuaded both of their truth and of its supreme importance, are not incomprehensibly concerned to keep a mental and moral hold on it, avoiding what detracts from its appreciation or distracts from its influence. One who has, out of genuine conviction, embraced a pure love does not display admirable breadth of mind by giving equal time to prostitutes. One who has, after serious deliberation, espoused a noble cause is not guilty of bigotry in turning a deaf ear to cynics.

In point of fact, what the conviction of Christian faith needs chiefly to be guarded against is not subsequent thoughts, but subsequent feelings. Well-grounded faith in God, like well-grounded faith in people, seldom falls victim to refutation, but often falls victim to conflicting and distracting moods. Keeping faith is the duty of a Christian believer in much the same way that it is the duty of a devoted wife or husband. And in the one case as in the other, this duty cannot be fulfilled without constant effort to refresh one's fundamental conviction and revive one's basic commitment, and to put forth this effort the more intensely, the less cooperative are one's current feelings and circumstances.

DISCIPLESHIP AND APOSTLESHIP

It is no mere coincidence that unfamiliar readers of the New Testament so often mix up the terms disciple and apostle. For although the words have, strictly speaking, quite different meanings, they have been mixed up in Christian tradition from the very start and, in a sense, they are supposed to be mixed up. Apart from more technical usage, a disciple means one who is learning from someone else, whereas an apostle means one who has been sent on a mission by someone else. For Christianity, these two ideas are inseparably related. The Christian disciple is one who learns from Jesus Christ. The Christian apostle is one sent on a mission by Jesus Christ. But as we are reminded by the concluding words of one of the Gospels, it is his disciples whom Jesus sends to be apostles, and what he thereby sends them to do is precisely to make disciples. Thus there is a basic cycle in Christianity whereby discipleship leads to apostleship and apostleship leads in turn to new discipleship.

The very life of historical Christianity is this unending sequence of discipleship and apostleship, of receiving the Gospel message and passing it on to other recipients who will pass it on in their turn. With the development of social structures in the Church, this essential process is assisted by definite arrangements to ensure that the basic message may be transmitted reliably and efficiently. Hence the importance in Catholic ecclesiastical doctrine of such notions as apostolic succession and hierarchical magisterium. Indeed, the central function of the Church as a social institution is to preserve the Gospel message and transmit it by every means that can enable it to be more widely known and more deeply appreciated. Missionary undertaking is not optional for the Church. It is essential to it, a condition of its authentic being.

Nevertheless, institutional means for transmitting the Gospel do not replace but rather reflect the apostolic role which belongs to every Christian. Whoever is called by Jesus Christ is also, within the limits of his or her circumstances, also sent by Jesus Christ. In Catholic tradition, the sacraments of Baptism and Confirmation have often been regarded as ritual symbols which respectively emphasize these two complementary aspects of Christian faith. Christian belief is never conceived as a kind of spiritual private property. It is a gift that cannot be hoarded but must be passed on. The parable about how one does not light a lamp only to hide it under a bushel container gives memorable expression to this idea. For familiar household practice would have suggested to hear-

ers of that parable that covering a lamp in such a way would
not merely conceal it; it would extinguish it. And Christianity
has always supposed that those who would keep their faith
hidden from others must for that very reason cause it to
dwindle and die.

Naturally, as applied to ordinary Christians, this does not
mean that all are expected to set up as amateur preachers or
teachers. What it does mean is that their faith must be allowed to show itself, and must be prepared to declare itself. A
great many Christians avoid doing things or saying things
that are obviously prompted by their faith precisely because
their religion might in this way be brought to the attention of
others, with possibly embarrassing results. Such an attitude is
even thought of often enough as a kind of courtesy to others.
Yet it is difficult to imagine how those who consider their
faith as assenting to the most important of all truths, could
consider it a kindness to keep that faith from others. One who
believes the Gospel is the kind of good news it claims to be can
scarcely suppose it would be better not to share such news. We
admire the heroic devotedness of people who, having made
great practical discoveries, have not recoiled from ordeals of
ridicule and opposition in order to persuade others of what
they know is greatly for their good. It would be a pitiful irony
to suppose that one who really believes the Gospel is what
Christians say it is should think it a kindness not to trouble
others with that belief. The principal heroes of Christianity
have always been the martyrs. The word martyr is a Greek
word for witness. And the greatness of martyrdom is in its
insistence on bearing witness to the Gospel's truth at no
matter how great a cost.

GOOD NEWS AND BAD TACTICS

If the ethics of faith requires that believers should bear
witness to what they believe, this requirement must not be
confused, as it often has been, with a quite different and
entirely reprehensible idea. To some Christians it has seemed
that since the purpose of witnessing to belief in the Gospel is

enabling others to share that belief, a clearer statement of Christian duty in this regard is to say that Christians are supposed to get non-Christians to become Christians, and also see to it that other Christians continue to be Christians. Perhaps this rather crude way of putting it could be given a defensible interpretation. But history has furnished much evidence of a quite different practical interpretation. Whenever the aim of witnessing to the Gospel is replaced by the aim of getting people to become and remain Christians, many ugly consequences tend to follow. The annals of Christianity are sadly replete with what might be called ruthless conversion. Non-Christian individuals and non-Christian peoples have been brought to baptism at the point of a sword. Christian societies have systematically made life miserable for the non-Christians in their midst. Missionaries have solicited converts by material inducements tantamount to bribery. Christian preachers have employed the shabbiest tricks of unscrupulous rhetoric, propaganda, and thought control. And Christians convicted of unorthodoxy have been intimidated, tormented, and even slain.

In all this hideous record of religious violence, much of it carried out with the sincerity of fanaticism, and some of it with shameful ulterior motives, one perceives a fundamental distortion of Christian witness and a fundamental misconception of Christian faith. The Christian apostle is one sent by Jesus Christ as Jesus was sent by God his Father, to make known God's love and the salvation that love accomplishes. It is a declaration of gracious love, to be received with loving gratitude. But loving gratitude is a response of human freedom, which cannot be extorted, or inveigled, or compelled. A response of faith cannot be a response to force. Nor can a show of force be a declaration of love. Good news cannot be imparted by trickery or terror, and where good news is not imparted the Gospel is not proclaimed. Slyness and intimidation can no more be equated with Christian evangelism than seduction and rape can be equated with marital courtship. And in both cases, the reasons are the same.

STUDY QUESTIONS

1. What is the basic idea of revelation as Catholic tradition understands it?

2. How is revelation generally represented in the Old Testament?

3. What is the relationship of religious experience to faith?

4. What is the role of freedom in the exercise of faith?

5. What is the essential aspect of faith that makes it specifically Christian?

6. How is Christian revelation typically conveyed to potential believers?

7. What is the basic content of the Gospel to which Christians assent in faith?

8. What does living by Christian faith basically mean?

9. What do Christians understand as constituting a duty to preserve their faith?

10. What do unbelievers typically find to criticize about Christian efforts to preserve faith?

11. What relation has Christian faith to the use of reason and evidence?

12. Why are Christians unimpressed by the criticism that what they believe is not scientifically proved?

13. Against what are efforts to preserve one's faith mainly directed?

14. What is the difference of literal meaning between discipleship and apostleship?

15. In Christian living, what is the normal relationship between discipleship and apostleship?

16. How are institutional structures in the Church related functionally to discipleship and apostleship?

17. What is the place of missionary activity in the Christian Church?

18. What does the apostolic aspect of Christianity enjoin on the individual Christian?

19. What is the significance of martyrdom in the context of faith and apostleship?

20. What are some of the ways in which the function of apostleship is distorted and abused?

21. Keeping in mind the distinction between apostleship and discipleship, in what ways do you see yourself as a disciple? As an apostle?

Chapter Twenty-Seven

ETHICS OF HOPE

HIGH HOPES AND LOW HOPES

The fact that hope is a strong word in the vocabulary of Christian ethics is obscured by the fact that in secular usage it is very often a weak word. What are commonly referred to as hopes are mere wishes, as when we hope someone may be feeling better, or hope it will not rain, or hope we did not forget to turn off the headlights. Popular usage sometimes tries to convey a less feeble notion of hope by using such phrases as high hopes. Perhaps on that basis a distinction can be made, consistent with usage, between high hopes and low hopes, the latter being the mere ineffectual wishes referred to previously. High hopes, on the contrary, suggest strong expectations, strong both in the sense that they are entertained with firm confidence, and in the sense that they exert strong influence on the attitudes and actions of those who do entertain them. And for hope to have so strong an influence is only possible when that which is hoped for is regarded as something of great importance.

In terms of these distinctions, what Christians mean by hope is high, never low hope. Christian hope is not mere wishfulness, but solid confidence. It is not a mere mood of anticipation, but a powerful well-spring of disposition and behavior. And it is directed not to some minor gratification, but to the very greatest of values. It is because Christian hope is of this kind that it can be regarded as a virtue, an habitual source of right action.

It may seem paradoxical that metaphors applied to hope seem to be of opposite kinds. On the one hand, hope is represented as something that holds one firm. On the other hand, it is also represented as something that draws one forward. In fact, both ideas belong together in an authentic account of hope, for it is at once a stabilizing factor and a motive force. Moreover, it is precisely as a motive force that it confers stability. One of the outstanding New Testament passages dealing with hope refers to it, in two immediately successive verses, as something set before us which we are encouraged to seize, and also as a firm and trustworthy anchor. These are, of course, very mixed metaphors, but the mixture is a significant one. On the one hand, hope is the sort of thing a life-preserver would be to a person floundering about in mid-ocean. It is something the prospect of which gives activity a confident purpose and a definite direction. On the other hand, hope is also the sort of thing a substantial anchor would be to a ship tossed by wind and waves. It is something that makes it possible to withstand the random pressures of a chaotic environment. The hope represented by an anchor is something one already has, a present possession. The hope represented by an object we are encouraged to seize is something one does not have, a future anticipation. And both of these aspects belong to the Christian understanding of hope.

Christian hope, like everything else that is distinctively Christian, is rooted in the Gospel and in that acceptance of the Gospel's truth which we call faith. The Gospel is the good news of salvation by God through Jesus Christ. And salvation means rescue from evil, from both the doing of evil and the suffering of evil. For one who believes that good news to be true, hope is a present, stabilizing reality. It is an anchor, in the sense that it abolishes the sense of hopelessness engendered by experiencing a world that is full of the ebb and flow of innumerable currents and cross-currents which, taken collectively, seem merely chaotic. Hope establishes the confidence that this impression of chaos is not the final account of things. Christianity does not, like some other religions, suppose that the disorder and instability we experience is an illusion, a kind of bad dream which can be dispelled by better managing our thoughts. On the contrary, Christianity precisely reckons with a world full of frustration and conflict, precarious to live in and perplexing to think about. But Christianity supposes that, although this is a correct analysis, it is not the last analysis, and that in the last analysis frustration is overcome and perplexity is resolved. Christianity affirms that the world, although accurately portrayed by comedians and tragedians, is nevertheless a world of which God is the maker and master. And it proclaims that in Jesus Christ God assures us that our chaos and strife are ultimately subordinate to his peace and love. To believe that is to possess hope as an anchor. It is to be enabled to ride out the storm.

HOPE AS A MORAL STIMULUS

Nevertheless, the image of hope as an anchor conveys an idea that can be misleading if it is taken alone. For the anchor which serves to stabilize serves also to immobilize. And it is possible to conceive Christian hope as a kind of spiritual stolidity, enduring or ignoring the buffets of a stormy world while waiting confidently for balmier days that shall come in God's own time. It is this sort of hope that has stimulated some notorious criticism of Christianity as a religion that fosters unwholesome indifference to present human predicaments. For if what hope entails is God's assurance that in the long run everything will be all right, one might infer that the best thing to do is simply hold out until everything does get to be all right.

It would be a mistake to reject this criticism so indiscriminately as to deny that its perception of Christianity has any point at all. There can be no serious doubt that Christianity does foster a kind of indifference to things about which a great many human beings are habitually very anxious. There is something rather shocking about the exhortation attributed to Jesus, not to be anxious over what we shall eat, or drink, or wear, but to trust a heavenly Father who provides for the birds of the air and the lilies of the field. Clearly such an exhortation is intended to be startling when uttered in a world where food, clothing, and shelter are what most people spend the better part of their time worrying about. But, even allowing for a kind of poetic exaggeration in such passages, it should not be overlooked that what Jesus is here opposing and telling his followers to avoid is anxiety, worry, fretful solicitude. It should be noticed also that the anxiety he denounces is expressed in questions about what we are to eat, drink, and wear—not about whether we are to be nourished or clothed at all. And the reference which follows to the beauty of the wild flowers that puts even Solomon's wardrobe to shame strongly suggests that the worry he has in mind pertains rather to the elegance of apparel than to its decent adequacy. Moreover, any idea that Jesus is saying there is no importance to proper nourishment and dress is clearly excluded by another, equally well-known passage in the same Gospel, where Jesus represents God's judgment of human lives as based on whether or not they bothered doing anything about other people's hunger, thirst, and nakedness.

These two passages, and the ideas they respectively represent, do not cancel one another out, and they do complement one another. Moreover, their complementarity has a practical aspect that is by no means altogether unworldly. For what is it, after all, that makes it possible for so many quite ordinary people totally to disregard the plight of the hungry, the thirsty, and the naked? Is it not above all their everlasting anxiety over what they themselves shall eat and drink and put on? Is it not some people's concern to have more than enough, and ever increasingly more than enough, that more than any other factor compels other people to have less than enough? And is not the practical ignoring of God implied in both the compulsiveness of providing for oneself and the ruthlessness of failing to provide for others? Both the insatiability and the pitilessness of human greed testify alike to a kind of practical atheism. For, practically speaking, there is very little difference between having no trust in God and having no God to trust. Jesus' exhortation not to be eternally worrying about ourselves is not a counsel of irresponsibility. Rather it is a prerequisite for broadening responsibility. The basis for heeding that exhortation is the practical love of God who is our Father. And a major consequence of heeding it is the practical love of the neighbor who is our sister or brother. In the context of hope, as in all Christian contexts, the twofold commandment of love retains its unity.

The way St. Paul concludes one of the most famous of all passages dealing with Christian hope is highly revealing. The passage declares that Christian hope effectively nullifies what has always been the greatest objection to every other kind of human hope, the terrifying inevitability and dreadful finality of death. And the passage ends with a practical conclusion, introduced by a therefore. Because of this hope, says Paul, Christians should be steadfast and immovable. But how far he is from understanding this as a kind of complacent inertia is made plain by the concluding phrase which immediately follows. His Corinthian readers are to be steadfast, immovable, and—abounding in the work of their Lord, knowing that in their Lord their toil is not in vain! As implied in the mixture of metaphors referred to previously, hope may indeed by likened partially to an anchor, but it is an anchor of a very peculiar sort, for it is also a force of propulsion. The immovable Christian is not an unmoving Christian, but rather an unswerving Christian, who cannot be moved out of a path the following of which is the following of the Lord. That path leads the Christian, as it led the Lord, to death. But the Christian's hope is a firm confidence that as for the Lord, so also for his followers, death is by no means the end of the line.

THE AUDACITY OF HOPE

From what has been said it may be possible to perceive that hope has a very considerable place in Christian ethics, and exercises a very major influence on Christian moral behavior. In its most obvious manifestation, this influence may appear to be an extraordinary kind of courage. And yet, one might argue that courage, as ordinarily understood, is not precisely the proper word for it, although it certainly is involved in it. Wherever Christian life has been lived wholeheartedly, it has certainly been characterized by a kind of audacity, a spontaneous defiance of those threats which ordinarily keep people from living up to their own ethical standards. In its earliest years, Christianity astonished pagan observers by an acceptance of death at the hands of enemies, without much sign of dread, rancor, or even sadness. Visitors to the catacombs are still greatly moved by the fact that the crude memorial inscriptions on those simple tombs are typically so different from what one expects to find in graveyards. For what they express is neither a proud remembrance of fallen heroes, nor a mournful record of painful bereavement. What characterizes them is above all a tone of downright cheerfulness, of unpretentious joy. More than anything else they resemble messages of congratulation, strikingly different from solemn accolades of deceased greatness. Good pagans of course knew how to die heroically, and were fully persuaded that there are things well worth dying for. That an honorable death is preferable to a shameful life was a commonplace among classical moralists, and there were many who braved death's terrors in brave obedience to that principle. But among Christians, although such an attitude may have its place, a distinctive principle is operative. For them it is not chiefly a matter of braving death's terror in fidelity to a lofty ideal. It is rather a matter of being convinced that objectively death holds no terror whatsoever, because Christ has conquered death and revealed it to be not an end but a beginning. Where Christian hope is possessed in its fullness, it produces a kind of behavior in the face of death that has much in common with courageous behavior. And yet its primary effect is not so much a calling forth of courage, as a replacing of courage with the conviction that there is nothing to fear.

Needless to say, so great a fullness of hope is seldom achieved by even the best of Christians, and courage in the face of death can seldom be wholly replaced by an absence of fear. Convictions, no matter how genuine, can rarely altogether extinguish contrary emotions, and nearly everyone experiences at one time or another a sense of fear despite thorough confidence that there is no real danger. Moreover, even if what Christians believe removes the fearfulness from death itself, it does not, of course, abolish all the fearfulness associated with death. One modern victim of religious persecution is reported to have said that his Christian faith freed him from the fear of being dead, but it did not free him from the fear of dying. The distinction is obviously a meaningful one, and no doubt there are many Christians who would acknowledge their need of courage to face not the fact of death, but the process of dying. The fact that one is serenely confident about the outcome of an operation does not exclude the possibility of fearing the operation itself, as everyone who has visited the dentist is well aware.

Catholic tradition has attached a distinctive kind of importance not only to death, but also to dying. Indeed, a substantial literature was built up during and after the middle ages devoted to what came to be called, in a phrase that sounds strangely to modern ears, the art of dying well. That phrase itself brings out an important feature of the tradition. For it implies that dying is not simply something that happens to one. It is conceived as something that one does, may do well or badly, and can even acquire a sort of technique for doing well. Clearly, such an idea of dying well is not to be confused with mere clinical objectives, however good in themselves, of making dying as painless as possible. Underlying the idea of dying well is the notion that dying is not merely a biological process, but a personal religious opportunity. For it requires no great imagination to perceive that the circumstances of dying can be for a Christian the best of all means for doing what other circumstances make it so hard to do: to surrender himself or herself unreservedly to God in faith, hope, and love. The undoubted proximity of death dissolves the specious arguments that support most human pride and motivate most human wickedness. It mocks all claims of self-sufficiency and all illusions of superiority, thereby transforming the whole order of usual human priorities. By making it easy to relinquish what had previously been passionately clung to, dying makes it more than ever possible to entrust oneself as a sinful creature to a creating and redeeming God. There is frequent reference in Catholic tradition to deathbed conversion. And often, even among Christians, the idea of deathbed conversion is the object of a certain scorn. For the deathbed convert certainly is not a hero, and certainly is an opportunist. And yet it is no part of Christian belief that salvation can be achieved from God by human heroism, whereas it is an essential part of Christian belief that salvation must be received from God in humble submissiveness. It is not without significance that the Bible likens faith to dying and Baptism to burial, or that the imagery of death figures so largely in mystical accounts of progressive union with God. Nor is it by chance that the Gospel narratives focus so long and intensely upon the account of Jesus' dying. For to Christians, it is in the Lord's Passion that the art of dying well exhibits its exemplary masterpiece.

ON EARTH AS IT IS IN HEAVEN

There is a way of representing the standards of Christian behavior that is often called utopian, both by those who admire it and by those who do not. Most often the Sermon on the Mount is mentioned as the outstanding illustration, although actually it is only certain elements of that section of the Gospel that tend to be cited in this connection. In particular, what these elements are judged to express is a quixotic combination of nobility and impracticality. They are passages which bring out extraordinary aspects of moral character. But they also bring to mind the presumably disastrous consequences of trying to display such beautiful moral characteristics in the circumstances of the real world.

Actually, those who represent the Sermon on the Mount as proclaiming a lovely but totally impractical manner of life tend to exaggerate the impracticality. Most of what is recommended there is not behavior of which human beings are totally incapable. Much of it is, to be sure, behavior which most human beings would find extrememly difficult, and which they could not make their own either immediately or perfectly. But most of it is behavior which, with God's grace, they can make their own gradually, partially, and increasingly. And there is nothing utopian about recommending behavior of which that is true. Indeed it is generally true of positive, as contrasted with negative, moral norms. If I merely urge someone to be kind, I am not generally thought to be commending a utopian fantasy. For although it is clear that no one can all of a sudden become perfectly kind, just about anyone can be kinder than he or she has been in the past and can, on the whole, become increasingly kind as time goes on. And one who does so is thought to respond quite satisfactorily to the appeal for kindness.

The same is true of most, if not all of the things Jesus tells his followers to do or be in passages like those of the Sermon on the Mount. One can simply refrain from murder and adultery, but one cannot quite so simply refrain from inwardly hating and lusting. And yet one certainly can manage one's thoughts and feelings in such a way that one becomes increasingly patient and benevolent, respectful and chaste. And in the same way, one can become increasingly detached from material acquisitiveness, increasingly restrained in reacting to injuries, and increasingly generous to demands upon one's resources.

The word utopia means no place. And to describe ethical norms as utopian means that there is really no place where such norms are or can be abided by. The Christian response to those who call the Sermon on the Mount utopian is not total disagreement. But it is not total agreement either. For the Christian view, at least in Catholic tradition, is that the kind of behavior there described has as its place the Kingdom of God. It is also part of the same view that the Kingdom of God is not yet fully accessible to us, but already is partly accessible to us. And to do the best one can towards shaping one's life by the Sermon on the Mount is to achieve, in the moral realm, such access to the Kingdom of God as is now possible. It is to live, as far as one can, as children of the heavenly Father, in the conviction that ultimately we shall live completely as children of the heavenly Father. And that conviction is the essence of Christian hope.

In the best known of all Christian prayers, that hope is expressed as a plea that God's Kingdom should come. And the prayer proceeds at once to a further plea that God's will should be done on earth as it is in heaven. Both pleas refer to the same thing. The coming of God's Kingdom precisely means the coming about of a state of affairs in which God's will is done on earth as it is in heaven. Christian hope is a confident expectation of and an eager longing for that state of affairs. The ethics of Christian hope is a way of life consistent with that expectation and longing. If one genuinely wants God's Kingdom to come, then one must want God's will to be done on earth as it is in heaven. But one could not sincerely want that without wanting and trying to do what one can towards bringing it about. And passages like the Sermon on the Mount are the Christian's reminders of what he or she can, in fact, do about it, however slowly, uncomfortably, and inadequately. The Sermon on the Mount's final bidding, to be perfect as our heavenly Father is perfect, refers primarily to the destiny at which we are ultimately to arrive. But by the same token it does also refer to the direction in which we are supposed already to be moving.

STUDY QUESTIONS

1. Why does hope, as ordinarily understood, inadequately represent the Christian virtue?

2. How do different biblical metaphors for hope bring out contrasting aspects of it?

3. How is hope related to Gospel faith?

4. How is the Christian view of the world's wickedness and confusion related to Christian hope?

5. How can hope be so conceived as to lead to a disregard of serious human problems?

6. Is there any sense in which Christianity properly fosters indifference to normal human concerns?

7. How should one understand Jesus' instruction not to be anxious over food, drink, or clothing?

8. In what sense might such freedom from anxiety be a help to social compassion and service?

9. What is the chief obstacle to hope in general which Christian hope is supposed to overcome?

10. How is Christian hope related to courage?

11. How does a Christian attitude toward death differ from one of brave resignation?

12. Is fear irreconcilable with a Christian attitude toward death?

13. In what sense have Christians conceived dying as a positive value and religious opportunity?

14. What validity has the claim that distinctively Christian moral goals are essentially utopian?

15. Why should Christian moral life in this world reflect Christian ideas of the kingdom of God?

16. How does the paradox that the kingdom of God is already present but not yet fully present affect Christian life?

Chapter Twenty-Eight

WRONGDOING, GUILT, AND SIN

VARIETIES OF GUILT

Most mature people are aware that the terms guilt and guilty are commonly used in very different, though not altogether unrelated ways. Actually, these terms are applied to quite a number of distinguishable realities, but two classes of references are especially important, and need to be readily distinguished. In one of these classes, guilt is a moral or legal concept. In the other, guilt is a psychological concept. Moral or legal guilt is attributed to one who has freely and knowingly violated a moral or legal norm. It may be attributed by anyone who is convinced both that a valid norm exists, and that a free and knowing violation of it has occurred. It may be attributed by the violator to himself or herself, as in the case of someone who pleads guilty in a courtroom or admits guilt in a confessional. It may also be attributed to the violator by someone else, as when a judge or jury finds a defendant guilty despite his or her plea to the contrary.

Psychological guilt is attributed to one who experiences certain characteristic, strongly emotional attitudes. The kinds of feelings involved in psychological guilt are those which are normally considered appropriate to one who is sensitively conscious of his or her moral guilt. Thus guilt feelings typically entail a sense of disappointment with oneself, of self-reproach, of unfitness for wholesome social relationships, and of deserving to be blamed and punished. Nevertheless, it is well known that feelings of this kind sometimes occur in persons whom no one, including themselves, can reasonably judge to be correspondingly guilty of any proportionate moral violation. And it is equally well known that objectively grave moral violations, even when they are frankly acknowledged by the violator, often are not accompanied by feelings of this kind. Apparently, then, one can be guilty without feeling guilty, and feel guilty without being guilty, even though feeling guilty is understood as feeling in a way that is suited to being guilty.

More detailed consideration of guilt feelings and of legal guilt belong respectively to the study of psychology and of law. But some further discussion of moral guilt is appropriate to our present context and must at certain points touch again on the psychological and legal realms.

FREEDOM

It has already been noted that ordinary thinking about moral guilt tends immediately to introduce three basically relevant ideas, the ideas of a moral norm, of relevant knowledge, and of the freedom to abide by the norm.

To begin with the last of these ideas, it was remarked in an earlier chapter that human freedom is generally recognized as a prerequisite of human morality. Actions that are performed without freedom may be considered welcome or unwelcome, pleasant or unpleasant, desirable or undesirable. But they are not, or should not be, on that account alone accorded moral praise or moral blame. And by the same token, actions are more or less eligible for moral praise or blame accordingly as they are more or less free. For this reason, moral and legal writers have often proposed catalogues of factors that limit freedom for the guidance of those who wish to assess moral or legal guilt. But since factors of this kind are enormously various, with new ones always turning up, such catalogues can only be illustrative, and never exhaustive. Moreover, ordinary human experience and imagination seldom have much trouble discovering for themselves the factors included in such lists.

There are, however, elementary cautions that need to be kept in mind when one is inquiring about the freedom, or relative freedom, of human actions. Perhaps the most important of those cautions is a warning against short-sightedness. For it often happens that an action's freedom is greatly reduced by certain factors that are operative only because of some previous abuse of freedom. One who commits assault in a state of intoxication may not have acted freely as an assailant, but may have acted quite freely in getting intoxicated. One who causes a highway collision because of defective brakes may not have freely collided, but may have freely neglected the responsibility to keep a vehicle in safe mechanical repair. One who participates in violence or injustice under threatening pressure from a group to which he or she belongs may not be acting freely under the intimidating circumstances, but may have acted freely in becoming and remaining a member of a group notorious for such behavior.

And on the reverse side of the same picture, one may with unreflective spontaneity perform highly admirable and beneficial actions, and at the same time owe that unreflective, spontaneous goodness to a hard, deliberate process, undertaken long before, of self-discipline in the cultivation of virtue. To form any reliable estimate of the moral value of human behavior on the basis of freedom, one may have to be acquainted not only with immediate circumstances, but with relevant aspects of a long and complex personal and social history.

Together with freedom, knowledge is a commonly recognized prerequisite for human morality. Indeed, knowledge is a condition of freedom itself, inasmuch as, practically speaking, one is not free to choose unless one knows the options. One who is invited to choose between a real one dollar bill and a skillfully forged five dollar bill can hardly be said to freely choose the latter. Even the famous story of the tragedy of Oedipus, who unknowingly married his own mother, has nothing to do with what, in an ethical sense, is meant by guilt. In general, it is taken for granted that unless one knows both that an obligation exists, and that one's action is a violation of it, one cannot be considered morally guilty of the violation.

Nevertheless, qualifications must immediately be introduced here, similar to those previously brought in with regard to freedom. For it is obvious that ignorance which is alleged to exclude moral guilt may be, and often is, itself a result of moral guilt. A physician who injures a patient by using inappropriate treatment may be thoroughly guilty if the ignorance involved is a consequence of indolence or negligence. And one who refuses to think seriously about the moral implications of certain actions can hardly be free of guilt if those actions are plainly wrong.

Very frequently, the ignorance that accounts for wrongdoing finds its explanation in certain kinds of social relationships. In particular, these are relationships of dependence or reliance on certain kinds of authority. Scarcely anyone in the modern world is unaware of the extraordinary moral atrocities that have been perpetrated by some people solely on the assurance of other people, whom they regarded as authoritative, that it was commendable or permissible and desirable to do so. In some cases, such authorities have considerable force at their disposal, enabling them to reduce human freedom as well as to restrict the influence of human knowledge. But very often, such is not the case, and a great deal of immorality finds its explanation in the readiness of people to let other people do their ethical thinking for them.

There can be no doubt, of course, that at ethical thinking, just as at other kinds of thinking, some people are much better than others. Neither can there be any doubt that some moral decisions depend on kinds of factual information that to most people are largely unintelligible or otherwise unavailable. Hence our ethical judgments, like our other kinds of judgments, cannot simply dispense with knowledge and advice provided by others. Nevertheless, the fact that one cannot personally ascertain everything relevant to all one's moral decisions does not constitute an excuse from finding out as much as one reasonably can, or from requiring explanations and justifications that can reasonably be given. A morally sound human life cannot dispense with faith in the assurances of others. But neither can it afford to make trustful docility a pretext for irresponsible laziness of mind. Praise is often given to those who possess, as we say, the courage of their convictions. What that phrase usually means is the courage to act consistently with one's convictions. But what is too often forgotten is that an even more basic courage is often required to form real personal convictions in the first place.

Granted that all of us must at times rely on the moral advice of others, that very fact makes it especially important to choose such advisers carefully and hear them critically. To choose a moral adviser because he or she offers the kind of advice one wishes to hear is to seek not an adviser but an accomplice. And to justify one's conduct by appealing to the authority of one's chosen accomplice is either self-deception or hypocrisy. Moreover, of all moral advisers there is none except the Catholic Church that makes any kind of claim to infallibility. But since that Church itself has never claimed that any of its ethical teachings were in fact given infallibly, even the most faithful Catholic cannot in good conscience replace respectful docility with mindless conformity. Pagan religions claimed to have oracles, always unerring, but coldly indifferent and cruelly obscure in their pronouncements. Christian religion claims only to have teachers, humanly imperfect, but schooled in a tradition derived from and preserved by a wise and loving God.

KNOWING THE RULES

Reference has been made repeatedly to the common assumption that there can be moral guilt only if someone has freely and knowingly violated a moral norm. And knowingly to violate a moral norm is possible only if one knows the moral norm itself. And yet it is notorious that among students of ethics in general, and of Christian ethics in particular, a great deal of disagreement is expressed about what are valid moral norms, and even about whether or not there are any at all. Catholic tradition has, of course, always assumed or explicitly affirmed that there are valid moral norms and that they are quite knowable. Nevertheless, it would be difficult to draw up any definitive list of such norms that would currently win wide acceptance even among Catholics.

Recent times have witnessed considerable popularization, not least among Christians, of the idea that the concrete situations in which moral decisions have to be made are, in fact, unique, and that these situations themselves, rather than any abstract general norms, are the proper determinants of moral choice. Stated thus simply, such a position seems neither to reflect the way people go about making moral choices, nor to offer them any meaningful alternative. For someone who is realistically trying to decide the morally right thing to do, being advised to consult the situation is not very helpful. To recall a theme of an earlier chapter, what are usually referred to as situations belong to the factual realm, the realm of is—simply the existing circumstances in which a moral decision is to be made. But the moral decision itself depends on answering not only is questions, but ought questions as well. And people do not generally find that answers to ought questions are directly provided by concrete, factual situations. It may, of course, be argued that concrete factual situations are what we experience, and that unless our moral convictions are derived from experience they must be something our minds simply make up or that are somehow implanted in our minds.

But although difficult philosophical and psychological questions are here involved, it is not necessary to solve them before acknowledging that scarcely anybody seriously supposes that moral convictions are, or should be, formed afresh from each new experience as it occurs. Even if moral convictions derive originally from the experience of concrete situations, it is commonly assumed that once they have been so derived they can be re-used, so to speak, in any similar situations that occur subsequently. Thus, once one has acquired moral conviction that it is wrong to be cruel, or deceitful, or treacherous, situations that offer opportunities for cruelty, deceit, or treachery no longer constitute strictly novel experiences. One may not have had precisely these experiences before, but one has considered such experiences before, and has on that basis formed a general policy for dealing with them.

Considered in this way, the acceptance of general moral norms seems to be so much a matter of elementary common sense that it may seem absurd that there should be any controversy about the matter. Nevertheless, those who warn us not to rely on general moral norms, but to attend instead to concrete situations, have an important lesson even for those who adhere to quite traditional ethical approaches. For although it is true that general moral norms are applicable over a wide range of similar situations, it is also true that each situation is ultimately unique, that no similarities are perfect, that close similarities in one respect may coexist with wide dissimilarities in other respects, and that some situations are far more notable for their novelty than for any resemblance they may bear to other situations. Consequently, moral norms are always more or less rough generalizations, which can fit different situations only in the way that ready-made clothes can fit different people—approximately. In certain situations such norms may have to be supplemented, revised, or refined. Moral generalizations, like other practical generalizations, are always imperfect rules for coping with a world whose complexity our minds can never fully master and whose novelty they can never fully anticipate. And even if such rules were to come to us directly from God himself, the fact that they should have to be conceived in human thoughts and expressed in human words would leave us always with humanly imperfect ethics.

To try to do without general moral principles in our personal lives is a more extreme form of the same kind of folly as trying to do without general legal principles in our political lives. But we have no more right to claim perfection for our humanly formulated ethics than we have for our humanly formulated laws. Indeed, the fact that in Christian tradition ethics has been commonly thought of as closely analogous to law should serve to remind us of the imperfections they have in common. Just as even the best of laws, when applied with mechanical rigidity, tends ultimately to defeat the very purpose of law, so too does even the best of ethics. The very complexity of moral life which makes general ethical norms indispensable, also make them always more or less inadequate.

SIN, SINFULNESS, AND SINS

The analogy between morality and law, historically rooted both in the Bible and in certain classical moral philosophies, has been a conspicuous feature in Catholic tradition. Thus, secular ethics has been frequently translated into religious terms by identifying the comprehensive norm of all morality as the law of God. On that basis, it becomes possible to speak of any morally good conduct as obeying the law of God, and of any morally bad conduct as disobeying it. Mention has already been made of the development in Catholic tradition of a moral theology which recognizes different levels and categories of law, all ultimately traceable to God. Given such a system, all areas of ethics can be brought within the scope of both legal and religious thought.

It is on this basis that the idea of sin came to be expressed most typically in Catholic tradition as the violation of divine law. Thus, especially since the Protestant Reformation, Catholic catechetical instruction generally defined sin as any thought, word, deed, or omission contrary to the law of God. This way of thinking about sin was further reinforced by Catholic usage in the sacrament of Penance, where the penitent was required to list the number and kinds of his or her serious sins. Penitents were thus led to think of sins mainly as violations of specific rules, equivalent practically speaking to distinct divine laws.

There is a fairly obvious advantage to thinking about sin in this way, inasmuch as it encourages one to be quite definite about the acknowledgement of personal sinfulness, and such definiteness can be a considerable help to the genuineness and pointedness of repentance. Merely to profess oneself a wretched sinner, or even to declare that (like everyone else) one has sinned exceedingly, in thought, word, and deed, through one's own fault ... can easily become a routine recitation that stimulates very little realization of one's moral or religious condition. To state plainly that, during the past several weeks one has stolen a large sum of money and had sexual intercourse twice with someone else's spouse is likely to have a considerably more enlightening and deterrent impact on personal conscience.

Nevertheless, there are likewise obvious disadvantages to thinking and talking about sin mainly in terms of breaking divine laws.· For one thing, preoccupation with what are thought of as God's laws can very easily displace attention from God himself. In this way, religion may become the service not of a personal God but of an impersonal set of regulations. Salvation itself becomes a matter of scoring high on a sort of divinely standardized achievement test, and an achievement rather of human diligence than of divine grace. Another consequence of thinking about religious ethics largely in terms of divine laws is a tendency to emphasize negative norms and minimize positive ones. We have already noted that negative formulations have much to recommend them for purposes of human law. But once the will of God is habitually expressed in terms of prohibitions, sins of omission or of remissness become very easy to overlook.

Exaggeratedly legal conceptions of religious ethics foster a misleadingly impersonal view not only of God, but also of the human moral agent. The moral assessment of human beings tends to be assimilated to the surveying of a criminal dossier. Sins become comparable to black marks on a kind of celestial record, and forgiveness itself to the mere striking out of unfavorable notations. What are lost sight of are the historical continuity and general direction of a moral life, and the personal relationship to God which alone gives distinctive meaning to human sin and divine forgiveness.

Although not originally restricted to religious usage, sin has long been a distinctively religious term. As such it stands for the interpretation of moral evil which belongs uniquely to a religious understanding of the world. It thus represents the tragic absurdity of creatures' ignoring in practice their fundamental dependence upon God. It represents the ultimate futility of a life directed towards other goals than those for which it is created. It represents the deterioration of that personal relationship from which all other personal relationships derive. It represents the sickening and dying of the highest level of created life. For the Christian, who conceives that life as one of faith, hope, and love, sin represents the kind of faithless, hopeless, and loveless existence that finds expression in the horrifying imagery of hell. To the extent that sin is allowed to become nothing more than a word used in religious circles as a synonym for wrongdoing, the whole distinctive significance of religious ethics disintegrates, and a Christian Gospel whose basic proclamation is the salvation of sinners becomes largely unintelligible. Recurrent Christian protests against overemphasizing sin are understandable, and sometimes they are clearly commendable. For sin is not, of course, the ultimately important idea of Christian religion. And yet it is an idea without which the real importance of Christian religion can never be understood. There can be little incentive to hail the Light of the World for one who is insensitive to the depth of the world's darkness.

STUDY QUESTIONS

1. What are two significantly different meanings of guilt?

2. To what extent do moral or legal and psychological guilt coincide?

3. What is the relationship between guilt and freedom?

4. Can one be guilty of behavior that is performed with little or no freedom?

5. To what extent does the spontaneity of habitual virtue exclude the moral value attached to freedom?

6. In what sense can freedom be said to depend on knowledge?

7. Is it true that bad actions based on ignorance or error are always guiltless?

8. Does appeal to human authority have any proper place in ethical thinking?

9. Does following the guidance of others exempt one from guilt?

10. How should moral consideration influence the choice of a moral guide or authority?

11. Does Catholicism's claim of infallibility make a practical difference in this regard?

12. What does Catholic tradition assume about the validity and knowability of general moral norms?

13. What is the difficulty about limiting all moral judgments to particular situations?

14. How can general moral norms be derived from concrete particular experiences?

15. Is there any validity to warnings against reliance on general moral norms?

16. Why does the idea of sin tend in Catholic thinking to involve the idea of law?

17. What advantages and disadvantages are there to conceiving religious ethics in terms of divine law?

18. How can sin be described, in a general way, from a Christian point of view?

19. Why cannot the understanding of Christianity dispense with the idea of sin?

20. Why are general ethical norms always more or less inadequate? Can you give a specific example of this?

Chapter Twenty-Nine

DIVINE LOVE AND HUMAN ETHICS

THE CHRISTIAN KIND OF LOVE

No discussion of Christian ethics can go on very long without introducing the idea—or some ideas—of love. We have already referred to the predominance of love in Jesus' teachings and in those of the New Testament writers; we have given some account of relevant background in the covenant theology of Israel; and we have discussed the attempts of a number of Christian ethical teachers to establish love, in the form of a principle of beneficence, as the sole and sufficient standard of all ethical judgment. The purpose of this concluding chapter will be not to repeat these matters, but to indicate somewhat more systematically how love is understood in Christian theology, and what bearing this understanding has on the idea that love is the foundation of Christian ethics.

Most people who can recall even one biblical saying that seems to typify Christian ethics tend to think first of all of the double commandment to love God with all one's heart, mind, and strength, and to love one's neighbor as oneself. One of the most significant things about this statement, as a typically Christian saying, is the fact that its form is that of a commandment. Pre-Christian pagan literature has a great deal to say about love. But for the most part, the kinds of love in which it is chiefly interested could scarcely form the object of a commandment. The kinds of love that engaged the serious interest of pre-Christian Western philosophers are not such as could reasonably be enjoined as duties. The idea of being compelled to love was very familiar. But the idea of being obliged to love would have been quite unfamiliar and not readily intelligible.

The outstanding classical reflections on love dealt mainly with two kinds of love which were then, as they still are now, important aspects of nearly everyone's experience. One of these is what we normally refer to as friendship. The other, for which we have no popular term more specific than simply love, refers to the kind of passionate attraction and attachment of one person to another, heterosexual or homosexual, that we normally designate as erotic. Both the love of friendship and erotic love were generally thought of as experiences that people have more or less despite themselves. People can, of course, with some success, try to foster such experiences, or try to avoid or curtail them. But they cannot, generally speaking, simply make them happen. And for that reason they cannot treat them as matters of obligation. Friendship has been generally esteemed as a great social blessing, to be cherished and cultivated, and yet as depending ultimately on a certain amount of luck in finding the right sorts of persons in the right sorts of circumstances.

About erotic love, on the other hand, there have been extraordinarily varied estimates, ranging from those who consider it a kind of degrading psychological disease, to those who extol it as the most ennobling of ecstasies. But regardless of its evaluation, erotic love has generally been considered as something that happens to people, largely unpredictably, more or less uncontrollably, and often quite inconveniently. Perhaps the commonest ingredient in a long history of accounts of erotic love is their emphasis on its unreasonableness. For some, this has been one of its chief claims to glory, that it lifts human lives above the dull prosaic plane of prudent calculation into a realm of uninhibited rapture. For others, it has been a main ground of apprehension and disapproval, that it puts human lives at the mercy of moods, and destroys responsibility by releasing conduct from the supervision of reason.

Both the love of friendship and erotic love have been commonly perceived to have another feature in common. That is their particularity, or relative exclusiveness. Neither profound friendships nor intense love affairs can be numerous for any given person at any given time. Many people do, of course, have simultaneously a number of friends, but for most people the number is always rather small, and for no one is it ever extremely large. The conditions for friendship are in every case simply too special to be indiscriminate or universally satisfied. And the case of love affairs is notoriously even more restrictive. It is widely supposed that one can be seriously in love with only one person at a time, and the most characteristic behavior of lovers tends to reinforce an unwritten code of exclusiveness.

One other relevant observation about these familiar kinds of love has to do with what might be called their moral record. Do the love of friendship and erotic love produce results that incur the praise or the dispraise of morally conscientious people? Surely the only plausible answer is both. Friendships and love affairs are found to exist between all sorts of people, including some who are wonderfully good, some who are dreadfully bad, and most who rank somewhere in between these qualitative extremes. And both friendships and love affairs have often been deeply involved in the doing of both thoroughly admirable and thoroughly despicable things. Neither of these kinds of love is ever automatically a force for either good or evil. And whether in particular cases they contribute to moral goodness or moral wickedness depends largely on the virtues and vices of the parties involved.

These considerations, and others as well, make it quite clear that when Jesus, and the New Testament, and Christian tradition point emphatically to love as the supreme principle of the kind of life to which God calls us, they are not talking about either the love of friendship or erotic love. And in fact, the New Testament expresses hardly any interest, either positive or negative, in either of these kinds of love. Which is to say not that the writers, or Jesus himself, were unaware or unappreciative of friendship and erotic love, but simply that they did not perceive them to be significantly related to their message. Indeed, St. Paul does take note of the kind of love which belongs to friendship precisely in order to point out that it is not what he is calling for. Kinds of love that are largely spontaneous and upredictable cannot be enjoined as ethically normative. Kinds of love that are always more or less particular and exclusive cannot be envisaged by an appeal for universal love. And kinds of love that are of themselves morally indifferent cannot be extolled as expressing the Holy Spirit at work in human lives.

For understanding what the Christian kind of love is, after having determined at least in part what it is not, the New Testament furnishes two very basic indications. For we are not simply told to love, and then left to interpret that in accordance with whatever happen to be our own habitual ideas about loving. We are not only told to love, but we are also told how to love. And we are told that in two different ways. In the first place, we are told to love our neighbor as ourselves. And in the second place we are told to love as we are loved by God. These are not two conflicting sets of directions. But neither are they simply two ways of saying precisely the same thing. They are harmonious, but they are also complementary and progressive.

The instruction to love our neighbor as we love ourselves

provides us with a highly practical starting point, and its practicality has already been discussed in an earlier chapter. There it was noted that as soon as we reflect on how we love ourselves, what we perceive in normal human lives is a habitual tendency to watch out for our own interests, seeking whatever is or currently seems to be good for us, and avoiding, resisting, and heartily disapproving whatever impedes or threatens to impede that quest. This understanding of loving is evidently far removed from the realm of erotic love or personal friendship. And clearly it is a kind of loving one could meaningfully undertake to do irrespective of the state of one's feelings and of fortuitous circumstances. For we do go right on loving ourselves in this pragmatic fashion whether we are exhilarated or despondent, pleased with ourselves or disgusted with ourselves. In this sense, self-love is remarkably tolerant, maintaining its devotedness to the self's real or supposed welfare, no matter how boring or bad the self manages to become.

And that, of course, is precisely what we are asked to do with regard to our neighbor. We are to watch out for his or her interests with unrelenting practicality, whoever or however he or she may be, and regardless of how much or little our neighbor happens to please us. Jesus' parable of the Samaritan, in response to a question about who one's neighbor is, presents what is probably the Gospels' most forceful reminder of how indifferent to personal likes this love is required to be. Indeed, the conclusion of that parable virtually invalidates all questions about who one's neighbor is by recognizing as the only real issue whether or not one acts as a neighbor, that is, kindly and helpfully, to whoever happens, here and now, to need one's help and kindness. Christian love, therefore, is intended to be in one sense very undiscriminating and in another sense very discriminating. It is undiscriminating in the sense that it should make no difference to its exercise whether or not, or to what extent, one's neighbor is personally pleasing and satisfying to oneself. It is discriminating in the sense that it is sensitively alert to the needs of others, and to how those needs can be provided for.

GOD'S KIND OF LOVE

It is probably at this point that the idea of loving one's neighbor as we love ourselves is most understandably linked to the idea of loving one's neighbor as we are loved by God. For the whole basic message of the Gospel centers on the assurance that God loves us with that same combination of indiscriminacy and discriminacy. A fundamental presupposition of the Gospel is that its message is not addressed to hearers who are notably pleasing to God. Moreover, one of the most discomfiting currents of thought in the Gospel warns us that there can be no greater religious folly than to suppose that we are pleasing to God and, on that account, more or less entitled to his enthusiastic support. The parable of the Pharisee and the publican, with their marvellously contrasting prayers, is probably the most memorable indictment of that folly. And the whole pattern of Jesus' public life, so exasperatingly ostentatious in its persistent association with acknowledged sinners, reinforces the insistence that his ministrations have nothing to offer those who have, as he put it, no need of a physician. It is to a world morbid with sin and hostile to God that Jesus brings his assurance, expressed in both words and deeds, of divine forgiveness and salvation. What Christians perceive in that strangest of all religious symbols, the Cross of Jesus, is the fundamental tension between God and humanity as an encounter of sheer love with stark malice. And what Christians believe by the resurrection of Jesus is that in this encounter it is God's love that must finally triumph and our malice that must finally give way.

In Catholic tradition, this encounter and its outcome are believed to take place within the personal life of every believer. Each of us, by our self-idolatry, confronts God as God's enemy—only to discover, sooner or later, that there is not and cannot be any enmity in God. God's inextinguishable love proves to be the ultimate frustration of human malice. Human sin assails God like angry infantile flailings against the invincible patience of an inexhaustible parental love—pitifully, ludicrously, and futilely. Until at last that lesson begins to be learnt which is the whole meaning of the Gospel, that God is love and that nothing we can do will ever make God into anything else. Thus the essence of Christian faith is the conviction that God's love, like God himself, is ultimately omnipotent. The immediate implication of that faith is the further conviction that human sin is ultimately impotent. And the practical consequence is plain. A God who cannot be beaten can only be joined. Because God is God he cannot be avoided. And because God is love, love cannot be avoided. By God's love we exist as creatures. By God's love we are forgiven as sinners. And by God's love we live at last in his peace and joy. As confronted by a parent's inexorable love infant rage gives way to resentment, and resentment to weariness, and weariness to rest, so does human sin give way to the love of God until final surrender brings final peace and the newness of life.

This newness of life is the newness of eternal life, which is the only life that does not die. It is the life of which God is the Father, by which we become his children and brothers and sisters of his Son, and into which we are reborn by the giving of his Spirit which is love. It is the life by which alone one can live in the Kingdom of God, where God's will is done. It is the life by which God's will is done on earth, and by which God's Kingdom exists on earth. It is the life by which God's will is done on this same earth where God's will also is not done, and by which God's Kingdom struggles and strains against other kingdoms. It is the life by which faith works, and the life by which hope endures. It is the life of Christian worship and it is the life of Christian morality.

But although this divine love is the life of Christian morality, it is not a scheme or a program of Christian morality. Neither is it a substitute for such schemes and programs, or an excuse for despising or neglecting them. In other words, that love which is the life of Christian morality is not Christian ethics as it were in a nutshell, and it does not dispense us from the often tiresome and always imperfect tasks of Christian ethics. Although this might seem too obvious to mention, one does hear with significant frequency observations to the effect that a determination to act lovingly is the only ethical principle necessary or proper for one who is a real Christian.

To a certain extent, the foolishness of such a view comes to light as soon as one considers in a practical way the Gospel norm of loving one's neighbor as oneself. For one of the questions that must often arise for anyone who undertakes to apply this norm is, which neighbor? This is not the question, who is my neighbor? that Jesus disposed of so effectively in the parable of the Samaritan. It might be raised by another parable in which a good Samaritan found a number of sufferers and a variety of sufferings on the road from Jerusalem to Jericho, and had to decide on which of them to expend resources that could never provide for them all. Whoever sets out conscientiously to love the neighbor will meet a great many neighbors in very practical need of love, and painful choices have to be made. In such circumstances, considerations of prudence and justice, and often very subtle ones, are indispensable for the guidance of love. And the responsible exercise of prudence and justice often requires in addition a great deal of factual knowledge that is by no means always easy to acquire. To love one's neighbor in better than a randomly sentimental way requires not only a generous heart but a competent head, and part of the requisite competence belongs to the quite human and fallible discipline of ethics.

Reflections of a quite similar kind arise also when one seeks a standard for loving one's neighbor in the loving of oneself. As already remarked, we are so constituted that self-love comes to us as natural and spontaneous motivation. We do habitually consult our self-interest in determining the course of even our most trivial conduct. And yet, even though we tend in practice to love ourselves quite steadily, we often manage in practice to love ourselves extremely unwisely. How often does not self-love find expression in forms of self-indulgence that are in many ways self-destructive? Even the most consummate egoist requires prudence, and temperance, and courage merely to keep from becoming, in the familiar phrase, his or her own worst enemy. Just as self-love may be very intense, and yet very foolish, so also may the love of neighbor. To avoid folly, and the ills that attend on folly, the one requires no less than the other an organization both of habits and of thoughts that can only be achieved through serious discipline. And an indispensable part of the requisite discipline is, once again, human and fallible ethics. Catholic tradition has always typically insisted that the grace God gives does not annul the nature God gave, and that one cannot cease to be human as one begins to be Christian. And whereas it is indeed sub-Christian to think without loving, it is likewise sub-human to love without thinking.

LOVE AT THE TESTING POINT

There is one point, and an absolutely crucial one, at which divine love, as the life of Christian morality, implies an immediately practical ethical standard. It is a point which is called to our attention again and again in the New Testament, and in words recorded there as spoken by Jesus himself. For just as the divine love which Jesus reveals as the very heart of the Gospel is a love of forgiveness, so too the human love he most insistently requires is a love of forgiveness. God loves us despite the profound universal sinfulness that makes us his enemies. And by so loving us he enables us to make his love our own. But to make our own the love of a boundlessly forgiving God is only possible by making our own a boundlessly forgiving love.

As God's redeeming love is forgiveness of his enemies, so the transformation it works in redeemed lives is unmistakable only in their forgiveness of their enemies. Thus we are instructed, in Christianity's most fundamental prayer, to combine the plea for our Father's forgiveness with the assurance of our own forgiveness. "Forgive us ... as we forgive ... " For God's love can be a part of us only as forgiveness is a part of us, so that our very readiness to be forgiven is inseparable from our readiness to forgive. Thus we are told to forgive our enemies and pray for our persecutors, so that we may be children of our heavenly Father. Thus we are called to be perfect as a heavenly Father is perfect who makes his sun rise on the evil and the good and his rain fall on the just and unjust. Thus we are warned not to judge that we may not be judged, and to forgive seventy times seven times. And in a remarkable variety of ways, the same lesson reappears, plainly and emphatically. Here, if anywhere, Christian moral teaching becomes, at its very source, unmistakably specific. And here the meaning of Christian love becomes undisguisably definite. For forgiveness, the love of those who fail to love, is love at its testing point. It is love at the height of its freedom and in the fullness of its power. It is the purest moral semblance of divine love, and the surest moral sign of divine life. In human life and in human society it is the entering wedge of the newness of life.

STUDY QUESTIONS

1. What is usually considered the New Testament's classic summation of Christian ethics?

2. How does a commandment to love imply that certain meanings of love are not intended?

3. Did classical thought entertain the idea of being compelled to love?

4. What were the two kinds of love that classical thought chiefly dealt with?

5. Have both friendship and erotic love been uniformly esteemed as human values?

6. What has generally been considered the relationship of erotic love to reason?

7. Compare friendship and erotic love with reference to spontaneity and to exclusiveness.

8. What can be said in general about the moral influence of friendship and of erotic love?

9. Why cannot friendship and erotic love be what Jesus meant to enjoin on his followers?

10. To what extent does the New Testament deal with erotic love and with friendship?

11. To what extent does the New Testament indicate how we are to love?

12. What practical inference can be drawn from the instruction that we are to love our neighbor as ourself?

13. In what sense should Christian love be undiscriminating and in what sense should it be discriminating?

14. How should the idea of loving as God loves affect our love for the neighbor?

15. What does the Bible indicate is God's reason for loving human beings?

16. How does the account of Jesus' life imply an understanding of how God loves human beings?

17. What does the cross represent for a Christian understanding of love?

18. Why does forgiveness hold a special place in any account of Christian love?

19. Why is forgiveness regarded as that form of love that most closely resembles divine love? Do you argree with this assessment? Why or why not?

SUGGESTIONS FOR FURTHER READING

GENERAL REFERENCE

Ferm, V., ed. *Encyclopedia of Morals* (N.Y.: Greenwood, 1969)

Macquarrie, J., ed. *Dictionary of Christian Ethics* (Philadelphia: Westminister, 1967

HISTORY

Beach, W. and Niebuhr, H. R. *Christian Ethics: Sources of the Living Tradition* (N.Y.: Ronald, 1955)

Bourke, V. *History of Ethics* (N.Y.: Doubleday, 1968)

Flew, R. N. *The Idea of Perfection in Christian Theology* (London: Oxford, 1934)

Johnson, O. A., ed. *Ethics: Selections from Classical and Contemporary Writers* (N.Y.: Holt, Rinehart & Winston, 1958)

MacIntyre, A. *A Short History of Ethics* (N.Y.: Macmillan, 1966)

Maritain, J. *Moral Philosophy: An Historical and Critical Survey of the Great Systems* (N.Y.: Scribner's, 1964)

Osborn, E. *Ethical Patterns in Early Christian Thought* (Cambridge: Cambridge U., 1976)

Schweitzer, A. *The Philosophy of Civilization* (N.Y.: Macmillan, 1960)

Sidgwick, H. *Outlines of the History of Ethics* (London: Macmillan, 1910)

ETHICS IN GENERAL

Brandt, R. B. *Ethical Theory* (Englewood Cliffs, N.J.: Prentice-Hall, 1959)

Broad, C. D. *Five Types of Ethical Theory* (Paterson, N.J.: Littlefield, Adams, 1959)

De George, R., ed. *Ethics and Society* (N.Y.: Doubleday, 1966)

Fagothey, A. *Right and Reason* (St. Louis: Mosby, 1976)

Frankena, W. *Ethics* (Englewood Cliffs, N.J.: Prentice-Hall, 1973)

Frankena, W. and Granrose, J., eds. *Introductory Readings in Ethics* (Englewood Cliffs, N.J.: Prentice-Hall, 1974)

Hospers, J. *Human Conduct* (N.Y.: Harcourt, Brace, Jovanovich, 1972)

Kockelmans, J., ed. *Contemporary European Ethics* (N.Y.: Doubleday, 1972)

Maguire, D. C. *The Moral Choice* (N.Y.: Doubleday, 1978)

Melden, A.I., ed. *Ethical Theories: A Book of Readings* (Englewood Cliffs, N.J.: Prentice-Hall, 1955)

Sahakian, W. *Ethics: An Introduction to Theories and Problems* (N.Y.: Barnes & Noble, 1974)

Sidgwick, H. *The Methods of Ethics* (London: Macmillan, 1907)

Varga, A. *On Being Human* (N.Y.: Paulist, 1978)

ETHICS AND RELIGION

Danto, A. *Mysticism and Morality* (N.Y.: Basic Books, 1972)

Davis, C. *Temptations of Religion* (N.Y.: Harper & Row, 1973)

Ellul, J. *The New Demons* (N.Y.: Seabury, 1975)

Little, D. and Twiss, S. B. *Comparative Religious Ethics* (N.Y.: Harper & Row, 1958)

Outka, G. and Reeder, J. *Religion and Morality* (N.Y.: Doubleday, 1973)

Smurl, J. *Religious Ethics: A Systems Approach* (Englewood Cliffs, N.J.: Prentice-Hall, 1972)

Tillich, P. *Morality and Beyond* (N.Y.: Harper & Row, 1963)

ETHICS AND THE BIBLE

Birch, B. C., and Rasmussen, L. L. *Bible and Ethics in the Christian Life* (Minneapolis: Augsburg, 1976)

Davies, W. D. *The Sermon on the Mount* (N.Y.: Cambridge, 1966)

Dodd, C. H. *Gospel and Law* (N.Y.: Columbia, 1951)

Furnish, V. *The Love Command in the New Testament* (Nashville: Abingdon, 1972)

Furnish, V. *Theology and Ethics in Paul* (Nashville: Abingdon, 1968)

Haggerty, B. A. *Out of the House of Slavery* (N.Y.: Paulist, 1977)

Houlden, J. *Ethics and the New Testament* (Baltimore: Penguin, 1973)

Jeremias, J. *The Sermon on the Mount* (Philadelphia: Fortress, 1963)

Manson, T. W. *Ethics and the Gospel* (N.Y.: Scribner's, 1960)

Nielsen, E. *The Ten Commandments in New Perspective* (London: S.C.M., 1968)

Sanders, J. T. *Ethics in the New Testament* (Philadelphia: Fortress, 1975)

Schelkle, K. H. *Theology of the New Testament. Vol. 3: Morality* (Collegeville, Minn.: Liturgical Press, 1973)

Schnackenburg, R. *The Moral Teaching of the New Testament* (N.Y.: Seabury, 1973)

Sloyan G. *Is Christ the End of the Law?* (Philadelphia: Westminster, 1978)

Stamm, J. J. and Andrews, M. E. *The Ten Commandments in Recent Literature* (Naperville, Ill.: Allenson, 1967)

Yoder, J. H. *The Politics of Jesus* (Grand Rapids: Eerdmans, 1972)

Ziesler, J. *Christian Asceticism* (Grand Rapids: Eerdmans, 1973)

CHRISTIAN ETHICS IN GENERAL

Bonhoeffer, D. *The Cost of Discipleship* (London: S.C.M., 1959)

Bonhoeffer, D. *Ethics* (N.Y.: Macmillan, 1955)

Brunner, E. *The Divine Imperative* (Philadelphia: Westminster, 1947)

Curran, C. *Catholic Moral Theology in Dialogue* (Notre Dame, Ind.: Fides, 1972)

Curran, C. *Contemporary Problems in Moral Theology* (Notre Dame, Ind.: Fides, 1970)

Curran, C. *A New Look at Christian Morality* (Notre Dame, Ind.: Fides, 1970)

Curran, C. *New Perspectives in Moral Theology* (Notre Dame, Ind.: Fides, 1974)

Curran, C. *Ongoing Revision* (Notre Dame, Ind.: Fides, 1975)

Curran, C. *Politics, Medicine and Christian Ethics* (Philadelphia: Fortress, 1973)

Curran, C. *Themes in Fundamental Moral Theology* (Notre Dame, Ind.: Notre Dame U., 1977)

Delhaye, P. *The Christian Conscience* (N.Y.: Desclee, 1968)

Dyer, G., ed. *An American Catechism. Part 2: Moral* (Mundelein, Ill.: Chicago Studies, 1974)

Ellul, J. *The Ethics of Freedom* (Grand Rapids: Eerdmans, 1976)

Ferré, N. F. S. *Christianity and Society* (N.Y.: Harper & Row, 1950)

Ford, J. C. and Kelley, G. *Contemporary Moral Theology* (Westminister, Md.: Newman, 1958)

Forell, G. *Ethics of Decision* (Philadelphia: Fortress, 1955)

Fuchs, J. *Human Values and Christian Morality* (Dublin: Gill & Macmillan, 1970)

Gaffney, J. *Moral Questions* (N.Y.: Paulist, 1973)

Gilson, E. *Moral Values and the Moral Life* (St. Louis: Herder, 1931)

Gustafson, J. *Can Ethics Be Christian?* (Chicago: U. of Chicago, 1975)

Gustafson, J. *Christ and the Moral Life* (N.Y.: Harper & Row, 1968)

Gustafson, J. *Christian Ethics and the Community* (Philadelphia: United Church Press, 1971)

Gustafson, J. *Protestant and Roman Catholic Ethics* (Chicago: U. of Chicago, 1978)

Gustafson, J. *Theology and Christian Ethics* (Philadelphia: Pilgrim, 1974)

Häring, B. *The Law of Christ* (Westminster, Md.: Newman, 1963)

Hauerwas, S. *Vision and Virtue* (Notre Dame, Ind.: Fides, 1974)

Hildebrand, D. von. *Ethics* (Chicago: Franciscan Herald, 1953)

Hildebrand, D. von. *Transformation in Christ* (Baltimore: Helicon, 1948)

Jersild, P. and Johnson, D. *Moral Issues and Christian Response* (N.Y.: Holt, Rinehart & Winston, 1971)

LeClercq, J. *Christ and the Modern Conscience* (N.Y.: Sheed & Ward, 1962)

Lehmann, P. *Ethics in a Christian Context* (N.Y.: Harper & Row, 1963)

Lewis, C. S. *Mere Christianity* (N.Y.: Macmillan, 1943)

Long, E. L. *A Survey of Christian Ethics* (N.Y.: Oxford, 1967)

May, W. E. *Becoming Human* (Dayton, Ohio: Pflaum, 1975)

McDonagh, E. *Gift and Call* (St. Meinrad, Ind.: Abbey, 1975)

Mehl, R. *Catholic Ethics and Protestant Ethics* (Philadelphia: Westminster, 1970)

Milhaven, J. G. *Toward a New Catholic Morality* (N.Y.: Doubleday, 1970)

Niebuhr, H. R. *The Responsible Self* (N.Y.: Harper & Row, 1963)

Niebuhr, R. *An Interpretation of Christian Ethics* (N.Y.: Harper's, 1935)

Niebuhr, R. *The Nature and Destiny of Man* (N.Y.: Scribner's, 1943)

O'Connell, T. E. *Principles for a Catholic Morality* (N.Y.: Seabury, 1978)

Ramsey, P. *Basic Christian Ethics* (N.Y.: Scribner's, 1950)

Ramsey, P. *Deeds and Rules in Christian Ethics* (N.Y.: Scribner's, 1967)

Regan, G. M. *New Trends in Moral Theology* (N.Y.: Newman, 1971)

Robinson, N. H. G. *The Groundwork of Christian Ethics* (Grand Rapids: Eerdmans, 1971)

Sittler, J. *The Structure of Christian Ethics* (Baton Rouge, La.: Louisiana State U., 1958)

Thielicke, H. *Theological Ethics* (London: Adam & Charles Black, 1968)

Van der Marck, W. H. *Toward a Christian Ethic* (N.Y.: Newman, 1967)

Van der Poel, C. J. *The Search for Human Values* (N.Y.: Newman, 1971)

Wogaman, J. P. *A Christian Method of Moral Judgment* (Philadelphia: Westminster, 1976)

AUTHORITIES AND PRINCIPLES

Böckle, F. *Fundamental Concepts of Moral Theology* (N.Y.: Paulist, 1968)

Böckle, F. *Law and Conscience* (N.Y.: Sheed & Ward, 1966)

Curran, C. E., ed. *Absolutes in Moral Theology* (Washington: Corpus, 1968)

Fletcher, J. *Situation Ethics* (Philadelphia: Westminster, 1966)

Fuchs, J. *Natural Law* (N.Y.: Sheed & Ward, 1965)

Grisez, G. and Shaw, R. *Beyond the New Morality* (Notre Dame, Ind.: U. of Notre Dame, 1974)

Hughes, G. H. *Authority in Morals* (London: Heythrop Monographs, 1978)

McCormick, R. *Ambiguity in Moral Choice* (Milwaukee: Marquette U., 1973)

Nelson, C. E. *Conscience: Theological and Psychological Perspective* (N.Y.: Paulist, 1973)

Nelson, C. E. *Don't Let Your Conscience Be Your Guide* (N.Y.: Paulist, 1978)

Rommen, H. *The Natural Law* (St. Louis: Herder, 1948)

VIRTUES

Burnaby, J. *Amor Dei* (London: Hodder & Stoughton, 1934)

Cousins, E., ed. *Hope and the Future of Man* (Philadelphia: Fortress, 1972)

D'Arcy, M. *The Mind and Heart of Love* (N.Y.: Holt, 1947)

Ellul, J. *Hope in Time of Abandonment* (N.Y.: Seabury, 1972)

Ellul, J. *The Presence of the Kingdom* (N.Y.: Seabury, 1967)

Geach, P. *The Virtues* (London: Cambridge U., 1977)

Gilleman, G. *The Primacy of Charity in Moral Theology* (Westminster, Md.: Newman, 1959)

Hauerwas, S. *Character and the Christian Life* (San Antonio: Trinity U., 1975)

Haughey, J., ed. *The Faith That Does Justice* (N.Y.: Paulist, 1977)

Lewis, C. S. *The Four Loves* (N.Y.: Harcourt, Brace, Jovanovich, 1960)

Moltmann, J. *Theology of Hope* (London: S.C.M., 1967)

Nygren, A. *Agape and Eros* (N.Y.: Harper & Row, 1967)

Ogden, S. M. *Faith and Freedom: Toward a Theology of Liberation* (Nashville: Abingdon, 1979)

Outka, G. *Agape: An Ethical Analysis* (New Haven: Yale U., 1972)

SIN

Maly, E. *Sin: Biblical Perspectives* (Dayton, Ohio: Pflaum, 1973)

Menninger, K. *Whatever Became of Sin?* (N.Y.: Hawthorn; 1973)

Monden, L. *Sin, Liberty, and Law* (N.Y.: Sheed & Ward, 1965)

Pittenger, N. *Cosmic Love and Human Wrong* (N.Y.: Paulist, 1978)

Rondet, H. *Original Sin* (Staten Island, N.Y.: Alba House, 1972)

Schoonenberg, P. *Man and Sin* (Notre Dame, Ind.: U. of Notre Dame, 1956)

Shea, J. *What a Modern Catholic Believes About Sin* (Chicago: Thomas More, 1971)

Wakin, E. and McNulty, F. *Should You Ever Feel Guilty?* (N.Y.: Paulist, 1978)

Williams, N. P. *The Ideas of the Fall and of Original Sin* (London: Longmans, 1929)

POLITICAL AND ECONOMIC MORALITY

Abell, A., ed. *American Catholic Thought on Social Questions* (Indianapolis: Bobbs-Merrill, 1968)

Bennett, J. C. *Christian Ethics and Social Policy* (N.Y.: Scribner's, 1946)

Bennett, J. C. *The Radical Imperative* (Philadelphia: Westminster, 1975)

Callahan, D. *The Tyranny of Survival* (N.Y.: Macmillan, 1973)

Ellul, J. *False Presence of the Kingdom* (N.Y.: Seabury, 1972)

Gremillion, J. *The Gospel of Peace and Justice* (Maryknoll, N.Y.: Orbis, 1976)

Gutiérrez, G. *A Theology of Liberation* (Maryknoll, N.Y.: Orbis, 1973)

Jegen, M. E., ed. *The Earth Is the Lord's* (N.Y.: Paulist, 1977)

Maritain, J. *The Rights of Man and the Natural Law* (N.Y.: Gordian, 1971)

Messner, J. *Social Ethics* (St. Louis: Herder, 1949)

Mische, G. and P. *Toward a Human World Order* (N.Y.: Paulist, 1977)

Murray, J. C. *We Hold These Truths* (N.Y.: Sheed & Ward, 1960)

O'Brien, D. and Shannon, T., eds. *(Renewing the Earth: Catholic Documents on Peace, Justice, Liberation* (N.Y.: Doubleday, 1977)

Ramsey, P. *Christian Ethics and the Sit-In* (N.Y.: Association, 1961)

Ramsey, P. *War and the Christian Conscience* (Durham, N.C.: Duke U., 1961)

Temple, W. *Christianity and Social Order* (N.Y.: Seabury, 1977)

Troeltsch, E. *The Social Teaching of the Christian Churches* (London: George Allen & Unwin, 1931)

Vree, D. *On Synthesizing Marxism and Christianity* (N.Y.: Wiley, 1976)

Weber, M. *The Protestant Ethic and the Spirit of Capitalism* (N.Y. Scribner's, 1958)

Wogaman, J. P. *The Great Economic Debate* (Philadelphia: Westminster, 1977)

Yoder, J. H. *The Original Revolution: Essays on Christian Pacifism* (Scottdale, Pa.: Herald, 1971)

SEXUAL AND MARITAL MORALITY

Bassett, W. and Huizing, P. *Celibacy in the Church* (N.Y.: Herder, 1972)

Bertocci, P. *Sex, Love, and the Person* (N.Y.: Sheed & Ward, 1967)

Bird, J. and L. *The Freedom of Sexual Love* (N.Y.: Doubleday, 1970)

Curran, C. E. *Issues in Sexual and Medical Ethics* (Notre Dame, Ind.: Notre Dame U., 1978)

Dedek, J. *Contemporary Sexual Morality* (N.Y.: Sheed & Ward, 1971)

Doherty, D. *Divorce and Remarriage* (St. Meinrad, Ind.: Abbey, 1974)

Evely, L. *Lovers in Marriage* (N.Y.: Doubleday, 1975)

Häring, B. *Marriage in the Modern World* (Westminster, Md.: Newman, 1964)

Hildebrand, D. von. *Marriage* (N.Y.: Sheed & Ward, 1948)

Jewett, P. *Man as Male and Female* (Grand Rapids: Eerdmans, 1975)

Keane, P. *Sexual Morality: A Catholic Perspective* (N.Y.: Paulist, 1977)

Kosnik, A., Carroll, C., Cunningham, C., Modras, R., and Schulte, J. *Human Sexuality* (N.Y.: Paulist, 1977)

McNeill, J. *The Church and the Homosexual* (Kansas City: Sheed, Andrews & McMeel, 1976)

Noonan, J. *Contraception* (Cambridge, Mass.: Harvard U., 1956)

Rougemont, D. de. *Love in the Western World* (N.Y.: Harper & Row, 1956)

Schillebeeckx, E. *Marriage: Human Reality and Saving Mystery* (N.Y.: Sheed & Ward, 1965)

Scorer, C. G. *The Bible and Sex Ethics Today* (London: Tyndale, 1966)

Thielicke, H. *The Ethics of Sex* (London: James Clarke, 1964)

MEDICAL MORAL ISSUES
Behnke, J. and Bok, S. eds. *The Dilemmas of Euthanasia* (N.Y.: Doubleday, 1975)

Boyle, J. *The Sterilization Controversy* (N.Y.: Paulist, 1976)

Gustafson, J. *The Contributions of Theology to Medical Ethics* (Milwaukee: Marquette U., 1975)

Nicholson, S. *Abortion and the Roman Catholic Church* (Knoxville: Religious Ethics Inc., 1978)

Noonan, J., ed. *The Morality of Abortion: Legal and Historical Perspectives* (Cambridge, Mass.: Harvard U., 1970)

Ramsey, P. *Ethics at the Edges of Life* (New Haven: Yale U., 1978)

Ramsey, P. *The Ethics of Fetal Research* (New Haven: Yale U. 1975)

Ramsey, P. *Fabricated Man: The Ethics of Genetic Control* (New Haven: Yale U., 1970)

Ramsey, P. *The Patient as Person* (New Haven: Yale U., 1970)

Reiser, S., Dyke, A. and Curran, W. *Ethics in Medicine* (Cambridge, Mass.: MIT, 1977)

Shannon, T., ed. *Readings in Bioethics* (N.Y.: Paulist, 1976)

Weber, L. *Who Shall Live?* (N.Y.: Paulist, 1976)

AUDIO-VISUAL
BIBLIOGRAPHY

The following is a select bibliography of audio-visual material for use with this book. Teachers are advised to preview any material before using it with a class. Please consult the distributors' list at the end of the bibliography for information about ordering material.

Brown, James, *et al.* "Making a Decision." *The Spirit of the Lord,* Paulist Press (35mm filmstrip with cassette)

Gaffney, James. "Right to Life." *Family Parish Religious Education*, Paulist Press (35mm filmstrip with cassette)

Gaffney, James. "World Hunger." *Family Parish Religious Education,* Paulist Press (35mm filmstrip with cassette)

Giombi, Gary. "Beatitudes: Spiritual Values of Jesus." *Service Filmstrip Series,* Paulist Press (35mm filmstrip with record or cassette)

Haggerty, Brian. "Commandments: Alternatives for Community Life." *Service Filmstrip Series,* Paulist Press (35mm filmstrip with record or cassette)

"I've Made a Decision." Teleketics (35mm filmstrip with record)

McGinnis, James. "Bread, Justice and Global Interdependence." Paulist Press (35mm filmstrip with cassette)

McGinnis, James. "Bread, Justice and Multinational Corporations." Paulist Press (35mm filmstrip with cassette)

McGinnis, James. "Bread, Justice and Trade." Paulist Press (35mm filmstrip with cassette)

"A Note from Above" (2 min., color, 16mm film), available from Mass Media Ministries

O'Grady, John. "Commandments." *Family Parish Religious Education,* Paulist Press (35mm filmstrip with cassette)

"Sermon on the Mount, Now" (19 min., color, 16mm film), available from Mass Media Ministries

Stroik, Stefan, prod. "Justice in the World." Paulist Press (3 filmstrips/3 records plus handbook)

FILM DISTRIBUTORS

Some of the audio-visual material cited is available for rental;
some material is not. Where rentals are not obtainable
through publishers or distributors, teachers are advised to try
their diocesan religious education offices. Many dioceses pur-
chase AV materials and rent them to religious institutions
and schools at reasonable rates. Below are the locations of
publishers and distributors mentioned in the bibliography.
Their catalogues are available on request.

BREAD FOR THE WORLD
207 East 16 Street
New York, N.Y. 10003
212/260-7000

PAULIST PRESS
545 Island Road
Ramsey, N.J. 07446
201/825-7300

MASS MEDIA MINISTRIES
2116 N. Charles Street
Baltimore, Md. 21218
301/727-3270

TELEKETICS
1229 S. Santee
Los Angeles, Cal. 90015

MASS MEDIA MINISTRIES
1720 Chouteau Avenue
St. Louis, Mo. 63103
314/436-0418

DEMCO 38-297